ELI AND THE OCTOPUS

ELI AND THE OCTOPUS

The CEO Who Tried to Reform One of the
World's Most Notorious Corporations

MATT GARCIA

HARVARD UNIVERSITY PRESS

CAMBRIDGE, MASSACHUSETTS

LONDON, ENGLAND

2023

First printing

Publication of this book has been supported through the generous provisions of the Maurice and Lula Bradley Smith Memorial Fund.

LIBRARY OF CONGRESS CATALOGING-IN-PUBLICATION DATA

Names: García, Matt, author.
Title: Eli and the octopus : the CEO who tried to reform one of the
world's most notorious corporations / Matt Garcia.
Description: Cambridge, Massachusetts : Harvard University Press, 2023. |
Includes bibliographical references and index.
Identifiers: LCCN 2022038951 | ISBN 9780674980808 (cloth)
Subjects: LCSH: Black, Eli M., 1921–1975. | United Fruit Company. |
Jewish businesspeople—United States—Biography. |
Chief executive officers—United States—Biography. | Business ethics.
Classification: LCC HF3023.B53 G37 2023 |
DDC 658.4/2092 [B]—dc23/eng/20221026
LC record available at https://lccn.loc.gov/2022038951

For Edith

CONTENTS

PREFACE

Among the many things I have learned from veterans of the farm worker movement is that all enemies are not alike. In fact, some enemies are not enemies at all.

Marshall Ganz, a former organizer and executive board member of the United Farm Workers (UFW), conveyed this lesson most clearly to me in 2008 when I spoke to him at his home in Cambridge, Massachusetts. Recalling the fruit and vegetable growers who had been quickest to sign contracts with the UFW, Ganz noted that many of them were Jewish—and the most notable of these was Eli Black. A former rabbi turned chief executive of United Brands, Black had built a multinational conglomerate that counted among its holdings Inter Harvest, the largest lettuce producer in the state of California, its parent company United Fruit, the world's leading banana producer, and John Morrell and Company, the nation's fourth-largest meat producer. In 1970, after Cesar Chavez had signed the UFW's first contracts with grape growers in California, he assumed that the lettuce growers of Salinas, united in a trade group called the Grower-Shipper Vegetable Association of Central California, would prove a more formidable foe. To everyone's surprise, Eli Black decided it would be better to come to terms with Chavez than to suffer a protracted labor war and damaging boycotts of his lettuce and banana brands. Ganz, the son of a rabbi himself, told me he admired Eli's courage to break ranks with the other growers—and to take the "anti-Semitic shit" directed at him after his controversial decision. As it turned out, Salinas still erupted into a bitter labor war, but Chavez and Eli became friends and remained so while they both lived.[1]

Chavez's life would last many more years, but Eli's death would come sooner, and in a manner much more sensational and consequential to his legacy. On February 5, 1975, at the age of fifty-three, Eli Black knocked a hole through the quarter-inch-thick glass of his office window in a midtown Manhattan skyscraper and jumped. The reasons for his suicide were initially a mystery, although many had known Eli was under stress. Within months the newspapers revealed that United Fruit had bribed the president of Honduras to cut his country's export tax on bananas and also asked him to disrupt the workings of a banana cartel newly formed by several Latin American countries, which aimed to impose substantial customs duties. Eli achieved in death what he strove to avoid in life: he tarnished the public perception of his cherished company and its brands. Over the years he had done much to overcome United Fruit's history as an exploiter of resources and people in Latin America, making great strides by investing heavily in worker housing, boosting Honduran employment, and leading other reforms. In many ways, Eli Black chose to do business differently in the interests of doing good. The circumstances of his death reversed those gains.

I began in earnest researching the life of Eli Black by inquiring with his living relatives. Eli and his wife, Shirley, had raised two children, Judy and Leon. Shirley had passed away in 2014, and Judy in 2015. Leon, however, was alive and well. The cofounder and former CEO of the private equity firm Apollo Global Management, Leon Black is also known as an art connoisseur and patron. Besides Eli's chauffeur, Leon was likely the last person to speak to Eli. Although I anticipated a difficult conversation, I imagined that Leon might be interested to offer his unique perspective on his father's legacy.

While learning about Eli from the archives, I wrote Leon to request a meeting, and told him a little bit about my progress. Mutual friends had put us in touch via email. Leon did not respond. I then asked our mutual friends to reach out on my behalf. They assured Leon that I believed his father's life merited reconsideration, and that I was hoping to go much deeper than the scandalized press reporting of the time. Still, nothing.

This silence was discouraging, but research on other fronts continued to inspire my efforts. In many ways, Eli's life read like one of the great works of American immigrant fiction, reminiscent of Abraham Cahan's *The Rise of David Levinsky*.[2] Like the title character in that famous 1917 novel, Eli arrived in the United States from Eastern Europe, trained to become a rabbi like generations of men in his family before him, then abandoned that trajectory for a career in business. By the end of his fictional life, Levinsky expressed regret for that decision, and perhaps in real life, Eli did, too, in the most dramatic way possible.

When I joined the faculty of Dartmouth College, Leon's alma mater, I thought Leon might have a change of heart. He is among the most generous donors to the college, having contributed $48 million to build the Black Family Visual Arts Center and endowed two professorships, including the Eli Black Chair of Jewish Studies. My history department colleague Jim Wright took an interest in my project; as former Dartmouth president he had worked closely with Leon and considered him a friend. He offered to write to Leon on my behalf and include a forthcoming article I'd written in which I presented Eli as a sympathetic figure. Yet to Jim's surprise and for the first time in their relationship, Leon did not respond.[3]

Like most historians, I believe in the importance of speaking to those who lived the history I'm writing about; Leon's silence was frustrating. I wondered why he would not want to support a fresh exploration of his father's life. Understandably, suicide raises uncomfortable memories for loved ones. Yet Leon endowed professorships and

speaker series in his father's name and seemed invested in Eli's reputation. He also clearly understood the power of biography, having given
his support to a major book series committed to exploring "Jewish
Lives."[4] I was prompted to look at Leon's life and career for clues about
his silence. Did he not see the good his father attempted to achieve
through his leadership of United Brands? Did he personally believe
what his father had said about social responsibility as a cornerstone of
doing business in America? How much did the well-being of his
employees, investors, and the public factor into his own decisions as
a business owner?

Partial answers arrived in 2019. When federal agents in New York
City took Jeffrey Epstein, the infamous financier and convicted pedo-
phile, into custody on sex-trafficking charges, reporters put a spotlight
on Leon's relationship with Epstein. The two enjoyed a friendship that
had begun in the late 1990s and continued even after Epstein spent thirteen months in jail for soliciting sex from underage women in Florida
in 2008. Over that time, Epstein served as a director of the Debra and
Leon Black Family Foundation, joined Leon in investments in publicly-
traded companies, facilitated Leon's contributions to charitable and
university projects, and provided tax advice to his friend. Leon also visited Epstein at his Manhattan home—the now infamous mansion where
Epstein is known to have hosted extravagant parties that involved young
women being forced into unwanted sex acts. After Epstein's August 2019
suicide in a New York jail cell, unanswered questions prompted Leon to
publicly address the controversy with his investors. He also granted an
exclusive interview to *Bloomberg Businessweek,* a rarity for Leon. The
weekly painted him as a "ruthless" businessman who made his fortune
by "skating on the edge of other people's catastrophes," but did not
provide more substantial evidence of any complicity in Epstein's crim-
inal life.[5]

The news was worse in March 2021, when an investigation of the
relationship commissioned by Apollo revealed that Leon had paid
Epstein $158 million in the years 2012 through 2017, supposedly for

advice related to estate planning. The report prepared by Wall Street law firm Dechert raised suspicions about whether Epstein could have rendered such vast advisory service to Leon and triggered more skepticism among investors and journalists.[6] Within a week of the announcement, Leon agreed that, on his forthcoming seventieth birthday in July, he would retire as head of Apollo. His departure was accelerated when Guzel Ganieva, a Russian model, accused Leon of sexual harassment, abuse, and trafficking—alleging in part that he took her to Epstein's estate in Palm Beach, Florida, to provide sexual favors to both men. Leon denied these charges but the accusation alone was damaging. He left his post as chief executive officer of the private equity firm he built on March 22, 2021, to concentrate, he said, on his family and his health.[7]

In light of these developments, Leon's silence could be interpreted differently. Even his past philanthropy seems to have served multiple purposes, with donations in his father's name affecting not only Eli's image but his own. By reopening the case of Eli, perhaps my project threatened to invite in nuances and conflicting accounts that would threaten Leon's story about his family, and, by extension, about himself. Having already written a book that challenged the public memory of Chavez, I had some experience with the ways people fight to hold on to a treasured, sometimes idealized image. I knew I would have to overcome silences and voids in the record to get beyond abstractions and fractured narratives. In the case of Eli, who tried to live according to the strictures of the Talmud and who seemed to hold himself to a higher standard than his peers, withdrawing from the project because of Leon's avoidance of it would seem to betray a man who expected accountability for himself and his employees. It did not help that United Fruit executives failed to maintain a company archive for these later years. I have had to bring together shards of evidence to construct a coherent portrait of the man and his company.

The larger-than-life history of United Fruit provides essential details that close some of the gaps in Eli's personal story. Tales of treachery and deceit in Central and South America across more than three-quarters of a century have made the company's name synonymous with US corporate imperialism. The unchecked pursuit of wealth at the expense of Latin American sovereignty, worker efficacy, and environmental health by former leaders of United Fruit, from railroad builder Minor Cooper Keith to boardroom interloper Samuel Zemurray, have drawn the attention of historians interested in knowing the capitalists behind the company.[8] Eli's reign as "banana king" lasted far fewer years than his predecessors' but the influence he wielded compels us to consider what he did with it when he had it. As with Keith's and Zemurray's lives, Eli's provides insight into the place of United Fruit in American foreign policy, and the United States in Latin America. By telling Eli's story, we also come closer to understanding how United Fruit affected the lives of people who encountered the company in the final years of its existence.

"The book of Eli," as I came to think of this project, is written with the intent of learning from his failure. While I am inspired by heroic acts in human history, I think we learn much more from the stories of those who fell short of their dreams, or even betrayed themselves. As Eli rose in the business world, he fashioned a message of social justice from the art of cultivating and marketing fruits and vegetables, seeing in his success the possibility, even the responsibility, to improve the lives of those who worked for him or consumed his products. In an era when virtually all owners of business say they want to achieve these things, but most spend their money instead on accumulating greater wealth and leaving our planet behind (in some cases literally), Eli's reinvestments in his employees and the people he shared a faith with are refreshing—even if he didn't succeed. My hope is that, by exploring the ambitious but flawed plans of an immigrant entrepreneur to rehabilitate a predatory multinational corporation and to improve the world through business, we can gain a more profound understanding of the limits and possibilities of free enterprise to heal the suffering in our own times.

PROLOGUE

ON THE MORNING OF JANUARY 20, 1969, Eli Black stood in his office at 245 Park Avenue in Midtown Manhattan keeping an eye trained on the scrolling digits of the stock ticker while also taking in the inauguration of a new president, Richard Nixon, playing on the television in the background. The two men had traveled similar paths to reach this moment. Nixon, born in Yorba Linda, California, to a down-and-out lemon farmer and lapsed Quaker, had arrived at the highest political office in the land. Eli, born in Lublin, Poland, and raised on the Lower East Side as the son of a *shohet,* a kosher poultry slaughterer, was just about to receive official word that he was the new president of United Fruit, one of the country's largest food producers and parent company of the Chiquita brand. Although separated by geography and religion, the two shared a faith in food production as a vehicle for positive social transformation. The man who took the oath of office on the US Capitol's East Portico had worked in the citrus groves of his hometown and seen a community take shape around the cultivation of fruit. During his years as a state elected official, he watched California farms become the foundation of US "agribusiness" and the cornerstone of a postwar Western economy. He fought to bring America's agricultural products into global markets, so that his home state could generate a greater share of the world's food production. Eli, who watched his father earn a living through the kosher slaughter of poultry in his orthodox Jewish neighborhood, saw as a child the link between food production and family and community survival. What he saw on the stock ticker that morning drove home a lesson learned in childhood, writ large.

Not surprisingly, Nixon and Eli both saw the potential for expanding the United States' role in the world through an expansion of agriculture. They believed that increased profits for US food companies like United Fruit could lift the country out of a decade marred by war, social conflict, and sagging profits, but that success would depend on overcoming legacies of conflict and suspicion. Nixon was desperate to find a way to extract the nation from a bloody, dead-end conflict in Vietnam, one that confirmed the worst impressions of the United States as an imperialistic world power and nation hell-bent on eliminating communism wherever policymakers thought it existed. The company in which Eli had just taken a controlling interest, United Fruit, had contributed to that same dark impulse, earning the dubious nickname *el pulpo*—the octopus—for its long, acquisitive reach in seemingly every direction in Latin America. The company was notorious for buying up land, exploiting Central American labor, and soliciting US government intervention in countries that opposed its business interests. Somewhat diminished by a decade of competition with rival companies and antitrust lawsuits, United Fruit remained an enviable acquisition for Eli who saw possibilities for reforming its practices and reputation and growing a business dedicated to feeding the world. If United Fruit was to play a role in Nixon's new economy and serve as a beacon for change in Latin America, Eli would have to convince skeptics of his good intentions and host nations of the company's new ways.

To arrive at this day, Eli had to persuade the Brahmins of Boston to loosen their grip on United Fruit and accept a newcomer to the upper echelons of the business world. Sitting in an office decorated with abstract paintings by his wife, Shirley, and contemplating his broadening future, Eli had traveled much farther than most of his corporate peers.

As an immigrant, he had much more in common with the fabled huddled masses at Ellis Island than he did with the blue bloods running America's most elite companies. He attended synagogue every week and observed the Jewish sabbath in his private study at his country home in Westport, Connecticut, every Saturday, often with his friend Rabbi Jonathan Levine. Together, the two engaged in long discussions about the troubles confronting Israel, the challenges of running a business while honoring the lessons of the Talmud, and how Eli could model behavior that would honor his late parents and inspire his children, Judy and Leon, to live a life worthy of admiration. Known as a "serious man" even to his friends and family, Eli spent more time reading than playing catch with his son. He liked to quote Robert Browning's line, "Ah, but a man's reach should exceed his grasp," including to Leon as words to live by.[1] His family found comfort in his self-confidence and surehandedness. Anyone glancing at his diplomas on the wall, from Yeshiva College for his undergraduate studies and from Rabbi Isaac Elchanan Theological Seminary for his rabbinical degree, was reminded of the Jewish tenets and culture that guided his decisions in life. While he had broken the chain of ten generations of rabbis in his family, he strove to maintain a strong connection to his faith through his gifts of money, commitments of time, and most of all, his sense of purpose in all his business. Over the time he first entered a career in finance in 1945 to this momentous occasion in 1969, he had come to believe that the top job in a large company constituted a "public trust" that required an executive to serve more than its shareholders. Driven by a desire to do right by the thousands of people who made their living working for his companies, and the millions who benefited from the products he produced, Eli sought to extend his hand for the benefit of others.[2]

Only four years prior to his purchase of United Fruit stock, Eli had been a relative unknown, the CEO of an obscure bottle-cap manufacturer, AMK. During that period, he had pulled off an acquisition of a giant meat producer in a deal that many Wall Street insiders regarded as "one of the biggest financial coups of the year."[3] Observers noted Eli's extraordinary ability to uncover value in existing assets that others had failed to recognize. They also noted his tolerance for the apparent mismatch between his company associated with manufacturing food containers and one that disassembled animals.[4] The purchase of Morrell, a company twenty times the size of AMK, catapulted Eli into the limelight of financial news and gave him the means to mount a serious offer for United Fruit. When Eli bought more than 9.5 percent of available United Fruit stock on the open market, the purchase triggered a flight response from United Fruit executives who believed Eli lacked the track record to take over such a storied company. John M. Fox, the company's chairman, and H. C. Cornuelle, its president sent an open letter informing shareholders, "your company isn't for sale; it isn't on the auction block," while privately appealing to CEOs at other companies to step in and replace Eli and AMK. Eli calmly pressed forward, assuring Fox that all competitors would eventually fade away.[5]

Fox spent the fall of 1968 scrambling to find an alternative to AMK, despite Eli's assurances that no one would beat him. Fox's first inquiry went to Honolulu-based shipping and construction magnate Lowell Dillingham. Dillingham had risen to the rank of CEO of Dillingham Corporation, but neither he nor his company were Johnny-come-latelies to the corporate world. His grandfather had founded Oahu Railway & Land Co. in the 1880s, laying the foundation for Hawaii to become a tropical destination for agriculture and recreation well before it became a state in 1959. The family added shipping to its portfolio in 1955, expanding the potential for the movement of fruit between the island and the mainland. Dillingham's land investments and transportation networks mirrored those of United Fruit, which had built the first transcontinental railroad, Tela, on the Central American isthmus. Lowell Dillingham fancied United Fruit but his stockholders resisted adding bananas to its tropical fruit portfolio. Eli calmly watched as Dillingham's offer fell apart.

A cartoonist's depiction of the takeover of United Fruit, with AMK the victorious pirate. *Reproduced from Chris Welles, "The Battle for United Fruit,"* Investment Banking and Corporate Finance, *Spring 1969.*

John Fox next turned to a New England corporate neighbor, G. William Miller, president of Textron in nearby Providence, Rhode Island. An Oklahoman by birth raised in the oil boom county of Hutchinson, Texas, Miller brought a wildcatting spirit to the Northeast. Standing all of five foot, eight inches and speaking with a heavy southern drawl, Miller reminded Eli of his first client as a financial advisor for Lehman Brothers, the bombastic "Littlest Texan," Robert Young, who had insulted fellow railroad magnates and made a serious run at reconstructing the transcontinental railroad after World War II before his New York Central Railroad foundered upon the rocks of a brief recession in 1957. Miller stood two inches taller and had a similar accent but exercised far more discipline than his Lone Star compatriot. By 1968, he had served in virtually every executive position available in a company that most on Wall Street called the "granddaddy of all conglomerates."[6] Miller had had a significant hand in creating this reputation, taking Textron from a regional textile company that made parachutes for the Allied forces that stormed Normandy beach to one of the leading aeronautical engineering companies in the world. Although Miller quickly assembled a competitive offer, his shareholders, too, balked at what they considered too high a price for a produce company that couldn't benefit from Textron's manufacturing strength. By December, Miller had withdrawn his bid, complaining that Eli had driven up the price by "pyramiding" debt in his offer.[7] Eli shrugged off the accusation, chocking it up to sour grapes from another beaten competitor.

Fox then threw a Hail Mary pass by courting the Houston-based Zapata Norness, a company that United Fruit executives had considered buying just a year earlier. Zapata's American aristocratic origins belied its namesake, Emiliano Zapata, the Mexican revolutionary who led a peasant revolt in the 1910s. (In truth, the company was inspired by Marlon Brando's depiction of the man in the 1952 film *Viva Zapata!*). Founded in 1953 by future US President George H. W. Bush and former CIA operative Thomas Devine, Zapata also included other Yale alumni who, like Bush, had belonged to the secret society Skull and Bones. Bush had left the company, having won a seat in the US House of Representatives, by the time United Fruit was making its appeal to Zapata, but his old friend and classmate Robert Gow pursued merger opportunities as executive vice president. A petroleum extraction company, Zapata had even less affinity for food production than Dillingham and Textron but its location in Houston, known as the "gateway to Latin America," and its extensive shipping fleet made it a player. It didn't hurt that Gow's father, Ralph, held a seat on United Fruit's board of directors.

As fall turned to winter in 1968, Zapata's privilege and prestige proved to be no match for the persistence and imagination of Eli Black. Behind his black horn-rimmed glasses and gentle smile was a man who relished the opportunity to prove to his well-heeled competitors that he belonged. Investors on Wall Street recounted the time when they overheard Eli calmly warning a challenger, "if you want to play tough, we can be very, very tough players."[8] More often, he beat out rivals by embracing financial arrangements that tested the boundaries of conventional accounting. While Eli's deal for United Fruit had been too rich for Miller's blood, it appealed to short-term investors known as arbitrageurs, operatives willing to take a chance on the new face on Wall Street. Loyal to only themselves, and willing to pull out of a deal as soon as it made sense to their bottom line, these investors provided the upfront funds that more than matched Zapata's offer. "We cultivated them, talked to them from the beginning, tried to make them our friends," Eli told a reporter. Working hand in glove with Goldman Sachs, the investment bank with the most aggressive arbitrage department on Wall Street, Eli approached every short-term investor available, convincing them to back his bid over all others. By early December, he had snatched 370,000 more shares that all but guaranteed victory. Gow admitted, "the deal blew us right out of the tub."[9]

A week after Nixon's inauguration, Eli's chauffeur drove him to the Pierre, a luxury hotel on New York's Upper East Side, where, at a table with views of the bare trees and snowy fields of Central Park, he sat down with a dispirited team from Zapata to claim the remaining stock it had purchased in the struggle to control United Fruit. After a brief exchange of pleasantries, Eli laid claim to an additional 270,000 shares at a price nearly two times what it was going for before the contest began. This final purchase pushed the already inflated price of the deal far beyond any amount most Wall Street observers thought was possible for a seventy-year-old fruit company that had seen its better days.

Eli Black in his Manhattan office, 1972. *Walter P. Reuther Library, Archives of Labor and Urban Affairs, Wayne State University.*

He did not linger, excusing himself to go handle the business that came with being the new banana king. Walking out into the crisp, cold, late January morning, Eli felt invigorated by the moment. He signaled to his chauffeur, Jim Thomas, that he would walk today. He strolled the mile from the corner of Central Park to his office, thinking less about the exorbitant cost of the deal and more about what he would do with his new company.

As he arrived at his building, a reporter met him at the door to ask some questions. Eli invited him up to see the view from his corner office. As they looked out toward Central Park, the reporter asked about the drop in AMK's stock price since the merger and whether he'd taken on too much unsecured debt to close the deal. Standing in front of a series of Shirley's abstract paintings, now joined by a large, three-dimensional, yellow, plastic banana, Eli answered, "the underlying values are there."[10] His confidence would not allow him to think otherwise.

1

TALMID

OF THE 1,174 PASSENGERS ABOARD the steamship *SS Republic,*
arriving in New York Harbor on February 19, 1925, only 84 had paid
the lowest possible fare, $30, for the privilege of sitting out the ten-day
journey on a bench in steerage, packed in below the deck where first-
and second-class passengers had their sleeping quarters, toilets, fresh
air, and meals. Among these was a boy, Eliasz Menasze Blachowicz,
seven weeks shy of his fourth birthday, traveling from Lublin, Poland,
with his mother, Chaje, and sisters, Goldie (thirteen) and Sarah
(eleven). As a third-class passenger, "Eli," as he would come to be
known, felt every motion of the sea, and spent much of the voyage in
darkness. At times the *Republic* rocked so violently that he lost what
little appetite he had for the boiled meat, potatoes, and stale bread the
crew provided, at a cost of sixty cents per passenger per day. Once the
cutter arrived in the harbor, a medical team met it at bay to screen for
the most infectious diseases before allowing it to proceed to Manhattan. At the docks, immigration officials released US citizens and
most of the first- and second-class passengers, and directed Eli, his
family, and other steerage passengers onto a barge bound for Ellis

Island. There, Chaje ushered her son and daughters through a gauntlet of interpreters, who asked them in imperfect Yiddish about their origins and purpose for travel. Satisfied that their stories matched the information on the manifest collected at Bremen, Germany, officials waved them through to their new life in America.

Eli's father, Benzion "Benjamin" Blachowicz, had been the first to leave Lublin, arriving in New York on February 3, 1924. Lublin was known as "the Jewish Oxford" for its yeshiva, a Talmudic institution of higher learning that trained many rabbis, including Benzion and eight previous generations of his family.[1] The city sat at the crossroads of the Russian, German, and Austro-Hungarian empires, all of which had claimed it at one time or another in the nineteenth and early twentieth centuries.[2] The end of World War I and the defeat of the Central Powers had brought the Republic of Poland into being. Despite the creation of its first provisional government, the years of war and deprivation limited opportunities for work in the region and took a toll on its inhabitants. Eli's birth on April 9, 1921, increased costs for Benzion and Chaje, but it also meant they could now contribute another rabbi to the world. With its developed Jewish communities and advanced economy, New York could enable Eli to receive the necessary spiritual guidance, while Benzion could ply his trade as a *shohet,* or kosher poultry slaughterer, to a large customer base. Eli's parents had an ideal image of his future, but it would be their son's relationship to this vibrant, bustling city at a tumultuous time in its existence that would shape his reality.

The Blachowiczes' move came at the end of a century of Jewish migration to the United States that included two waves, the second running roughly from the 1880s until the mid-1920s. Centuries-old antagonism toward Jews in Eastern Europe drove the initial stages of this massive resettlement, which eventually brought 2.5 million Jewish immigrants to America's shores.[3] By the second decade of the twentieth century, the appeal of a new beginning and a prosperous life had become the main draw. Abraham Cahan provided an artful illustration of this desire in his novel *The Rise of David Levinsky*, published in 1917. Cahan's fictional protagonist notes that his forefathers had left their homelands to flee anti-Semitism, but as for his own motivation, it was the lure of a land "of mystery, of fantastic experiences, of marvelous transformations." Later in the story he encounters some successful tradesmen and thinks to himself that only in a country like America could butchers "look and speak like noblemen."[4] As a *shohet*, Benzion would have been impressed by the opportunities available to someone working in the meat trade, and the value of settling among Jewish New Yorkers determined to remain observant of *kashrut*—the laws of their faith relating to food.

Benzion and Chaje made their journey just before a new cycle of anti-immigrant legislation passed. During and after World War I, Congress expanded exclusionary laws, first introduced in the 1880s to limit Chinese immigration, to include bans on categories of "undesirables" such as convicts, prostitutes, anarchists, "idiots," "lunatics," and anyone considered likely to become a public charge. Italian and Jewish leaders saw this policymaking as a veiled attempt to discourage immigration from their countries of origin.[5] For men like Republican Congressman Albert Johnson of Washington, such legislation did not go far enough. In US Senate Committee Hearings on Emergency Immigration Legislation on January 3, 1921, he offered an unvarnished assessment of Polish Jews wishing to emigrate. Johnson believed they were a group "abnormally twisted" by war strains and oppression, and tended to be "filthy, un-American and often dangerous in their habits." Many of them, he argued allegedly, based on prior experience, would prove "unassimilable."[6] In 1921, Johnson lent his name to an emergency quota act establishing a national origins formula. Under this legislation, each nation would be allowed to send a number of immigrants equal to three percent of the total population from that country already living in the US, based on the 1910 census. A few years later, Johnson helped draft new legislation revising the formula downward to 2 percent of the population present in 1890, and fully barring immigration from Asia. This attempt to close the door on further immigration happened just as a final surge of a quarter of a million Jews arrived in the United States.[7] A group of Jewish congressional representatives from New York, in a bipartisan effort (including the Democrat Samuel Dickstein and the Republican Nathan Perlman, both foreign-born themselves), tried but failed to block the bill.[8] President Calvin Coolidge signed the Johnson-Reed Act on May 26, 1924, a little more than three months after Benzion arrived. Eli, his mother, and his sisters were admitted the following year through a provision that allowed for unification of families.[9]

Like many Eastern European Jewish immigrants, Eli's father relied on a benevolent society, or *landsmanshaft,* founded by fellow immigrants from the same European towns to help navigate the challenges associated with coming to the United States.[10] Often linked to one of the hundreds of synagogues located in the city, a landsmanshaft covered the cost of the transatlantic voyage through a low-interest loan taken out by a family member who had already made the journey.[11] In 1924, port authorities noted that an unspecified "society" associated with the synagogue "Lenas Chacedyk," at 232 East Third Street on the Lower East Side, sponsored Benzion's immigration. No synagogue by that name can be found at this address, but many houses of worship maintained a nondescript facade and immigration officials routinely misinterpreted the words of passengers as they filled out the forms. The Hebrew phrase *Linas Hatzedek,* commonly used by Jewish societies offering sleeping quarters to a community's homeless, is perhaps the closest to the name on the manifest, and one used by many synagogues in New York.[12] Although Benzion, arriving with $500, equivalent to approximately $8,000 today, would not have been considered needy, it is likely he would have affiliated with Linas Hazedek Anshe Raztsan Galicia, coming as he did from Lublin, Poland, where Galician Jews resided. Of the few synagogues within walking distance of the Blachowiczes' first home, an apartment building at 75 Columbia Street, this one was just a six-minute walk, across Delancey Street and south of the Williamsburg Bridge.

When Eli arrived in 1925, he joined an established Jewish community in the city where 44 percent of all Jews in the United States lived. Particularly concentrated in the Lower East Side—the twenty-square blocks south of Houston and east of the Bowery—a "Jewish metropolis" thrived, shaped by inhabitants who shared religious and cultural interests. While in 1890 this neighborhood had had the highest concentration of Jewish residents in the world, by the time Benzion brought his family here, middle-class Jews, mainly of German descent, had begun to move out to other boroughs.[13] The departure of older residents of the Lower East Side cleared the way for Eastern European newcomers. In Eli's youth, he would have been surrounded by other new arrivals from Galicia, Poland, Russia, and Romania speaking a version of Yiddish familiar to him. Critical to the family's livelihood would have been its proximity to the meatpacking district in Lower Manhattan, where Benzion could work in the nation's center for kosher meat processing.

The Blachowiczes arrived during a period of expansion for the kosher food industry and its growing importance to the economy of New York. By 1925, most Gentiles consumed meat slaughtered outside of the city and shipped in by refrigerated cars. For Jews to stay within the laws of kashrut, beef had to be soaked and salted (or "koshered") within seventy-two hours of being slaughtered, so kosher producers continued to slaughter live animals in the city to be closer to their Jewish consumers. To give their customers confidence in their processes, owners of packing houses paid prominent rabbis in their neighborhoods to supervise their abattoirs. The rabbis would typically appoint *mashgihim,* or inspectors, to make sure no Jewish dietary laws were broken in the slaughtering process. The employment of an army of *shohatim,* or Orthodox slaughterers, played an equally crucial role. Poultry slaughter, Benzion's trade, grew alongside the kosher beef market during the first three decades of the twentieth century. The number of carloads of live birds coming into New York increased from 1,785,000 in 1896 to 12,513,000 in 1930. In the 1920s, nearly half the poultry sold in the city was kosher, some portion of it through H & L Lire at 343–345 Stanton Street, where Benzion worked.[14]

The kosher business was a mixed blessing. On the one hand, Benzion could provide for his family while performing an essential task for the Jewish residents of the city. He was eligible to join hundreds of other men in a *shohatim* union, the Official Orthodox Poultry Slaughterers of America. On the other hand, the size and potential profitability of the local industry generated substantial corruption. Business owners paid off *shohatim* to classify meat as kosher when it did not qualify as such, and merchants took advantage of customers by charging exorbitant prices, especially during Jewish holidays. The Poultry Slaughterers union, led with an iron fist by Charles Herbert, criminally conspired in price-fixing and violence to expand its power.[15]

Records from Eli's early life give us a fragmented view of his youth in New York City. Benzion and Chaje made great sacrifices to give their son the time and resources to study the Talmud with a reputable rabbi. Where and with whom Eli studied in his youth is unclear, but he would have had plenty of options in the Lower East Side, where rabbis routinely took boys under their wing. Like most girls in their community, Eli's sisters, Goldie and Sarah, worked outside the home to support the family and to fund the religious education of their brother. By the age of sixteen, Goldie had found work as a bookbinder. By seventeen, Sarah was contributing to the household economy as a seamstress.[16] Meanwhile, Eli's reverence for scripture competed with a fascination with life on the streets, where he saw a range of examples of what it meant to be a Jew in America. Although most first-generation immigrants mingled and worshipped among their own, the second generation often rushed out to join a wider, more diverse world.

Benzion tried to cultivate a productive learning environment for Eli by improving the family's living conditions, soon moving from the Lower East Side to the outer boroughs, in search of more space and new opportunities. In the 1920s, the city's Board of Estimate expanded the number of multifamily residences in the Bronx and Brooklyn by eliminating an ordinance that taxed the construction of new buildings planned for dwelling purposes. Benzion saw neighbors move to Jewish enclaves in the Bronx or Brooklyn's Williamsburg neighborhood. In 1927, he joined them, renting an apartment at 1801 Crotona Avenue in the Bronx. Here, Jews maintained their long-standing patterns of group economic, industrial, and social organization, while enjoying the relative spaciousness and modern amenities of a setting then regarded as suburban. Walking the streets of his neighborhood, Eli would have heard the constant clamor of new construction, and witnessed young entrepreneurs choosing the pursuit of capital over the study of scripture. Cahan's character David Levinsky marveled at the transformation of his brethren: "Deals were being closed and poor men were making thousands of dollars in less time than it took them to drink the glass of tea."[17] All around him, Eli saw Jewish immigrants chasing prosperity in trades related to the real-estate boom—living a very different adulthood than the one his parents envisioned for him.

But Eli's time in the Bronx was short-lived. By 1940, and likely by 1935, the family had moved back to the Lower East Side, to 283 Stanton Street, just a block south from their first residence in the United States. Their return might indicate a setback for Benzion, who, like other immigrants, had aspired to move away from the older, poorer, immigrant neighborhoods. From the Bronx, Benzion would have had to travel roughly ten miles each day to get to work in the packing district in Lower Manhattan. The collapse of the stock market likely played a role in their retreat, as well. In 1930, Sarah married Jacob Fuchs and left home to start her own family. Five years later, in 1935, Goldie followed suit, marrying Samuel Simanowitz, a Romanian immigrant living in the Lower East Side. Their departures reduced the number of contributors to the household economy, while the immigration of Chaje's mother, Rachel Schulson, added a new dependent.

The Depression had also triggered an upsurge of anti-Semitism. In the 1930s, some Gentiles questioned why Jews weathered the economic

storm better than non-Jews. Newspapers routinely cited their success
at building a durable business sector as evidence of clannishness and
insularity. During the 1930s, most Americans viewed Jews negatively,
and anti-Semitic violence became more common in the neighborhoods Jews shared with struggling Gentiles.[18] Returning to the Lower
East Side would have saved time, kept the family closer together, and
placed them in a familiar neighborhood, albeit one that signaled downward social mobility.

It was in a time of tumult and political upheaval, then, that Eli entered his teen years. In Benzion's trade he saw how dirty the conduct
of business could be in the United States. By the 1930s, the New York
markets for kosher poultry were so thoroughly controlled by gang-
sters engaging in extortion and price-fixing that stories of murder
and bombings made it into newspapers nationwide. A law enforcement crackdown produced well-publicized arrests and sensational
trials—including of the *shohatim* union's business agent, Charles
"Charlie" Herbert.[19] Benzion may have talked at home about these
scandals, or might have tried to shield his family from them. Regardless, the conversation among neighbors would have been pervasive. It
was, if nothing else, an early glimpse of the wealth to be gained by
dominating a system of food production—and the levels of corruption
such potential could inspire.

Judaism was different in modern America than it had been in
Eastern Europe. Traditional Orthodox rabbis in Europe had warned
immigrants like the Blachowiczes about the dangers of a "godless land"
across the Atlantic, and the loss of faith that so often went along with
assimilation. These concerns seemed to be borne out by the lackadai-
sical religious practices of American Jews in the interwar period. By
the 1920s, a mere one-third belonged to a congregation, and many who
paid dues to a synagogue attended only during the high holidays or
for significant life events like the marriage or death of a close family
member. Eli and his family were among a minority who observed the
Sabbath.[20]

As it grew and evolved on new soil, American Judaism fragmented into competing ideas and institutions. While the Reform Judaism dominant in Central Europe tried to adapt to competition with the modern world, and Orthodox Judaism made its appeal to those committed to tradition, the Conservative movement in the United States offered a third way. Advocates of Conservative Judaism maintained the decorum and aesthetics familiar to transplants from Eastern Europe, while blending it with features and activities common to middle-class Americans. These included coeducational experiences, social activities sponsored by the synagogue, and a greater involvement of women in the maintenance of Jewish tradition. Such congregations gained popularity in the 1930s among those who wanted to remain Jewish while pursuing the American dream.[21]

Eastern European families like the Blachowiczes, who still practiced their faith, became the main targets of recruitment. Benzion would have shared the concerns of conservative rabbis, who worried about Jews straying from *halakah*, or Jewish law in daily life, and given his experience growing up in Orthodox Judaism would not have abandoned the practices he had performed as a young man in Lublin, Poland. To bridge the gap between his experience and the one pitched to his son, he sought a relationship with New York's Kehilath Jeshurun, a synagogue that billed itself as "Modern Orthodox." Founded in 1872 by Rabbi Moses Margolies, it had begun by the early 1930s, under the leadership of Margolies's great nephew and assistant rabbi, Joseph Lookstein, to adapt its practices to the changing mores of its members. Located on East Eighty-Fifth Street on the Upper East Side, KJ (as it was known) was more than five miles from the Blachowiczes' home—but Lookstein's approach made it worth the journey. Existing records do not indicate where the family went to synagogue after arriving in the country, but Lookstein claimed the Blachowiczes as among his congregants.[22] Benzion might have been lured by KJ's exception to the rule against using public transportation on the Sabbath and its strident defense of Judaism amidst a rising tide of anti-Semitism. Both

"Ramaz," as Rabbi Margolies was known, and Lookstein spoke out against pro-Nazi demonstrations held by German Americans on Third Street during the Depression. Their acts of courage and affirmation inspired confidence in their congregants and offered hope that Judaism could survive both apathy from within and anti-Semitic attacks at home and abroad.[23]

Rabbi Lookstein took a particular interest in cultivating the next generation of American Jewry through formal education. Originally from Mogilev, Belarus, Lookstein spent his formative years as a student and a young rabbi in New York City. He attended the City College of New York and took graduate courses at Columbia University, but remained true to his calling, earning his rabbinic ordination at Rabbi Isaac Elchanan Theological Seminary (RIETS) in 1926. He openly worried about the corrosive influence of Adolf Hitler on American minds, including the inclination of some American Jews to downplay their religious affiliation for fear of attracting attention. Lookstein believed that closing the gap between religious and secular education was the most effective way to reach the next generation. It concerned him that parents increasingly said, "I don't want my son to be a rabbi"—and he sought to counter these attitudes by creating a yeshiva day school where children of the faith would not find any conflict between being a Jew and being an American. In 1937, he founded the coeducational Orthodox day school Ramaz, named after KJ's founder.

Eli turned sixteen in 1937, the year Ramaz School enrolled its first class, too old to have been a student but still young enough to learn from Rabbi Lookstein. In correspondence between Lookstein and Eli's widow, Shirley, later in life, the retired rabbi confirmed that he "knew [Eli] from his earliest boyhood," and regarded him as his "very special and favorite student."[24] It had been Benzion who, had determined the course of Eli's studies, but now the boy recognized the threats against Judaism, and saw virtue in following his prescribed path. His father had delivered him to this point as a matter of faith and tradition, along with the imperative of earning a living by serving a Jewish community that cared about observing kashrut. How and why Eli would practice Judaism was more a matter of choice, given the various invitations from interpreters of modern Judaism to change or abandon his practice. As Nazism continued to spread in the mid-1930s, and anti-Semitism threatened the security of American Jews at home, Eli embraced the idea of becoming a rabbi—not just as a matter of his father's will, but a statement of his own faith. In 1936, he enrolled at Lookstein's alma mater, Yeshiva College, where Lookstein was also on the faculty.

Yeshiva had grown from a seminary first chartered on the Lower East Side in 1897 to a multidisciplinary institution at the upper tip of Manhattan, in the Washington Heights neighborhood. Led by Dr. Bernard Revel since 1915, it no longer insisted on religious studies only in Hebrew but offered a more open curriculum, taught in English, to a new generation of American-raised students who demanded more access to the philosophy that animated their faith.[25] By the time Eli landed on campus, Revel had taken Yeshiva from a seminary that focused primarily on training rabbis to the first Jewish institution offering Bachelor of Arts and Science degrees. Revel was a committed Orthodox Jew but nevertheless believed that, for Judaism to survive the process of assimilation, it would have to create a synthesis of Jewish and general studies. Not an old man himself—fifty-one in 1936—Revel employed an even younger faculty of professors who engaged Yeshiva students in debate on how best to preserve Orthodox Judaism in the modern world.

Upon Eli's arrival in 1936, Lookstein introduced him to another young rabbi committed to broadening Yeshiva's constituency. Samuel Belkin had, in his youth, been labeled an *illui,* or genius, and ordained as a rabbi at seventeen. He saw the sixteen-year-old Eli as a protégé who commanded the respect of peers and professors. Belkin would become dean of RIETS in 1940, and Yeshiva's second president in 1943, but before that he would become Eli's mentor. As Belkin's *Talmid,* or student, Eli was only a few years younger, and their relationship was marked by constant but respectful disagreement. Eli attended Belkin's *shiur,* or discourse, five times a week, four hours a day, for two years, on top of the normal course work. Eli always claimed the first bench, and often stood while others sat. "His dialogue with me," Belkin remembered, "created such intellectual excitement and stimulation that the entire student body at times stood on its feet arguing as to who was right, the Rebbe or the Talmid." Belkin wasn't sure himself. "In a greater sense at times I felt he was the teacher and I his student."[26]

Though Eli earned the respect of the campus community, Belkin warned his understudy against *lashon hara*—literally "evil tongue." Insulting speech, even if truthful, diminished the speaker as much as the subject. On campus, Belkin saw Eli as a confident, inspiring figure, radiating *derekh eretz,* a Hebrew phrase that has no exact equivalent in English but translates to "the way of the land." To say someone has this quality is to signal more than a penchant for correct conduct; it also notes that a person harbors a conviction to do good unto others. For Belkin this meant exuding "respect for oneself [and] the dignity of man." A person with derekh eretz was a special kind of *mensch,* someone whose behavior and integrity should be admired and emulated.[27]

Eli pursued extracurricular activities with the same vigor he brought to academics. He was elected to student government, serving as vice president of his freshman class and president in his sophomore year. By his senior year, he led Yeshiva's vaunted debate team, and doubled the number of competitions it entered. The debates he organized challenged contestants to grapple with the questions of the day, such as whether the United States should maintain its isolationism as war raged in Europe, whether President Roosevelt should be elected to a third term, and whether the United States should become a cultural center of world Jewry. Such matters had become more urgent after November 1938, when students read newspaper accounts of Nazis in Germany and Austria smashing windows of synagogues and Jewish-owned businesses in two nights of orchestrated violence. Eli and his peers used debate to bring non-Jews' attention to these events, and to highlight the threat of anti-Semitism in the United States. Eli led a team of three classmates on a debating tour of Eastern States.[28] In his final year at Yeshiva, his peers voted him "most respected" as well as "handsomest" and "most likely to succeed" in their graduating class.[29] Eli's popularity was never a result of being sociable, or the life of the party; he was seen as a deeply serious student. At Yeshiva, where everyone shared an education and a purpose, his peers trusted him and teachers saw in him wisdom beyond his years. Projecting a warm, welcoming spirit, but stopping short of any frivolity, he was a student who "always smiled but never laughed," Belkin remembered. "Perhaps he may have been born old."[30]

From the beginning of his studies at Yeshiva in 1936, Eli traveled ten miles each day from Stanton Street to Washington Heights. On evenings when Eli had to study late, Benzion appealed to friends in that neighborhood to put his son up for the night. Such efforts were a reminder that his education was very much his father's dream, and that Eli was still dependent on family and community to get by.[31] His work never suffered. In the eyes of his professors, Eli had been blessed with "a profound and analytical mind," Belkin said. In his final year as an undergraduate, he delivered an original discourse to the entire class and his teachers, some of whom were regarded as "Talmudic Giants." The lecture, as Belkin later recalled, "was so profound and original that all of them wondered how such a youngster could possess such depth of Talmudic law and such maturity in the delivery."[32] Eli elected to extend his studies at Yeshiva's RIETS for an additional year. By 1941, he was ordained a rabbi.

Eli's years at Yeshiva coincided with a time of power struggles in his home country between the Soviet Union and Nazi Germany. What later came to be called the Second Polish Republic had been cobbled together in the wake of World War I, with its borders finalized in 1922, and had still not settled into a stable society. At least a third of its residents were non-Polish by birth, with traditional affiliations to neighboring countries, and its Jewish population stood as a sizable but embattled minority surrounded by Catholics who viewed Jews with suspicion. As the Great Depression devastated the republic's economy, the effects included stepped-up acts of aggression against Polish Jews, just as the menace of Nazism was emerging in Germany. Eli was in his third year of studies at Yeshiva when Hitler's army invaded his homeland, on September 1, 1939. The collapse of Polish resistance in just a month dispelled any hope of tranquility. The last defense against Hitler's anti-Semitism fell just a year later, when Josef Stalin agreed to the partition of Poland in the Molotov-Ribbentrop Pact, which ceded control of the western portion of the country, including Lublin, to Germany, while Soviet Russia took the eastern half. With Stalin's policy of nonaggression toward Germany and the Allied powers' pre-occupation with the Western Front, Hitler moved to exterminate the Jewish people in Europe. Jews in Lublin were among the first to be forced to live in ghettos in occupied Poland in March 1941. Eli, at that point preparing for his ordination, filled out his draft card for se-lective service to the US military that year. He used the occasion to signal his American identity by crossing out the pre-filled name, "Max Elias Blackowitz," and replacing it with "Elias Max Black"—the shortened surname not a rejection of Poland but an embrace of the United States, now the only country standing in the way of Hitler's plan.[33] Within a year, Nazi leaders established six death camps in Poland—including Belzec, Sobibor, and Treblinka—for the sole pur-pose of killing Jews. By the end of World War II, the Nazis had killed nearly 98 percent of Jewish Poles, the largest percentage of any country in Europe.[34]

All this was happening as Eli finished his schooling and began his career as a rabbi. His role as a religious leader granted him a rare ex-emption from service, a luxury that likely produced more internal dis-cord than relief. In the fall of 1940, when he began at RIETS, the Nazis knocked the British Royal forces on their heels in the Battle of Britain and propped up the authoritarian government of Vichy France on its Western border. The year of Eli's *semicha*, or ordination, news reached the United States of SS troops loading Jewish families onto trains bound for a then-unspecified camp. Eli's decision to become a rabbi had never been entirely his own, but the events in Europe deepened the questions he had about the next phase of his life. He took his first assignment, at the Congregation Sons of Israel in Woodmere, New York, on Long Island, in the summer of 1941. He had been voted "most likely to succeed" by his classmates, but in what? In such dire times, honoring the dignity of man with one's work became a more urgent matter. Never, it seemed, had there been such utter disregard for the dignity of life. Was it enough to pursue a quiet life on Long Island as a rabbi, when his talents by this time were so varied and unmistakable?

He would not have been alone in wondering how best to draw on his faith, education, and ethnic background in a time of armed conflict. The success of the Nazis was emboldening anti-Semitic Americans and triggering a fight-or-flight response in many American Jews. Whereas before the war some drifted away from Jewish laws, lured by assimilation, others were now concealing their identities and denying their lineage, to avoid suspicion or attack. This trend accelerated the debate among rabbis of how best to adapt Judaism to changing times. Yeshiva and RIETS fostered a deep commitment to Orthodox Judaism, but the young faculty entertained discussions about other approaches, including Conservative Judaism, which had become the largest American Jewish denomination by 1941.[35] Eli endorsed shortening prayers and allowing mixed seating among men and women at services— minor concessions that might keep Jews of his generation from leaving the faith. He regarded the transformation of old-world orthodoxy in Europe into modern orthodoxy in the United States as a normal, even ideal progression for the religion. Having watched his father's struggle to climb the ladder, Eli believed that a middle-class existence should never be jeopardized by the faithful practice of religion.

Eli's choice of a conservative congregation suggests he felt ready to define the terms of his own affiliation to Judaism, rather than blindly follow the path of his ancestors and the will of his father. There were other signs of independence. In his final year at Yeshiva, prior to moving to Woodmere, he began to take night classes at Columbia University Business School. It's not clear whether he told his family, but these forays would have been easy to disguise; the Columbia campus was a little past the midway point on the commute to Yeshiva from Stanton Street, near the intersection of Broadway and West 116th Street. The education opened new possibilities. Yeshiva had connected him to a worldwide diaspora of ethical and religious thinkers reaching back in time; Columbia revealed a global system of capital whose growth and development had yet to reach its full potential. As the beating heart of capitalism, New York City provided Eli the perfect vantage point to imagine this future, and his place within it. He might have admired the sway that titans of industry held over the world, even as he questioned whether the mere accumulation of capital justified the respect he saw paid to them.

Columbia University boasted some of the most influential faculty in the country, including scholar-lawyer Adolf Augustus Berle, economist Rexford Tugwell, and political scientist Raymond Moley, all of whom served as members of President Franklin Delano Roosevelt's "brain trust" during the dark days of the Great Depression. The group helped Roosevelt devise the First New Deal in 1933, recommending that the federal government provide a guiding hand in stimulating job creation while checking the power of big business. Berle shaped Roosevelt's policy on corporate influence by advocating voting rights for all shareholders of publicly traded companies, and greater transparency and accountability as to how these businesses were being run by executives. With Harvard economist Gardiner Means, he published *The Modern Corporation and Private Property* in 1932, a book that would influence corporate law for generations. During the 1930s, Berle frequently argued for government interventions that could channel corporate power toward the greater good. Increasing regulation was not the enemy of industrialism but a way of preserving its undeniable benefits, "by balancing economic concentration—specifically, big banks, big corporations, big industrial units—with enough State police power to make them our servants instead of our master."[36] Alongside a more regulatory state, Berle also believed that a rising "corporate conscience" among more socially responsible managers would allow big business to play an enlightening, even redemptive role in a world suffering from economic turmoil and war. It was a message that might have appealed to Eli, who had begun to wonder whether becoming a rabbi had been too narrow a path for him: a corporation could be a powerful force to improve ordinary people's lives, so long as men of virtue controlled it.

Eli's education at Columbia also put him in conversation with other Jewish communities in the city. KJ had exposed him to wealthier Jews, but some of the people he met in and around Columbia belonged to a different class entirely. Here, he found well-heeled "people of the book" who saw their material success as evidence of an ability to balance their occupations with the practice of their religion. At the center of this community stood the Society for the Advancement of Judaism (SAJ), a synagogue at 15 West Eighty-Sixth Street, founded by Rabbi Mordecai Kaplan. Kaplan had been ordained at the Jewish Theological Seminary, a Modern Orthodox institution, in 1893, but came from a noncon-formist family that openly questioned the traditional practices on the Lower East Side. Like Lookstein, he played a role in the religious education offered at Congregation Kehilath Jeshurun, but began to have misgivings about Orthodoxy's relevance to the modern Jew. In 1934 he penned the book *Judaism as a Civilization,* in which he argued that rabbis had an obligation to massage tradition to fit the principles of democracy and equality in America. He believed in the creation of an "organic Jewish community," and saw virtue in the Zionist movement, the creation of a Jewish state. Although his alteration of traditional practices conformed with conversative Jewish intellectuals, he veered toward heresy when he questioned whether Jews were God's chosen people. Among the adaptations Kaplan practiced was extending the coming-of-age ritual for young men (*bar mitzvah*) to young women (*bat mitzvah*), now common practice in America. By 1941, Kaplan had begun to lay the foundation for a new denomination, Reconstructionism, that eventually landed him in the crosshairs of Orthodox rabbis. They excommunicated him in 1945.[37]

The Lubell family, living just a mile from Columbia University, at 789 West End Avenue, had been among the earliest to accept the practice of bat mitzvah. Samuel and Jeanette Lubell encouraged their daughter, Shirley, to participate during the festival of Shavuot at SAJ on May 31, 1933, which Kaplan organized.[38] Shirley's brother, Benedict, attended Columbia University, and likely introduced Eli to his sister at a social gathering. Born on June 20, 1921, she was Eli's age. Unlike Eli's sisters, Shirley had not taken a job to bring money into the household. Samuel, her father, ran a successful shirt manufacturing company in the city, which provided him with the means to bankroll SAJ's founding and expansion over the years. He also spared no expense on Shirley's education. She attended a respected college preparatory institution, the Calhoun School, less than a mile from her home on the Upper West Side. From there, she went to New York University and American University, where she earned a degree in Fine Arts and distinguished herself as a talented abstract painter.

Shirley's faith, education, and artistic pursuits impressed Eli. By no means a modern woman, neither had she been willing to sacrifice her identity to serve the men in her life. When she and Eli began dating, the Lubells represented a different vision of Judaism in modern America. Eli did not share their devotion to Reconstructionism, but he appreciated their support of a traditional community, and agreed that publicly advocating for a strong Jewish presence in the United States and the Middle East offered the best defense against anti-Semitism. These shared values drew Eli to Shirley even as he would now have to invest time courting her on the Upper West Side while living on Long Island.

Shirley R. Lubell, 1943. Aucola *(American University yearbook), 1943, 95.*

In the fall of 1941, Eli relocated to Woodmere in the serene suburbs near the synagogue. Here, Eli walked to his new job, which was a half-mile from his home, listening to birds sing and smelling the salty breeze off the Atlantic Ocean, just beyond Sons of Israel to the south. Eli continued taking courses at Columbia and seeing Shirley, even as he assumed his responsibilities at the synagogue. Over time, he added business classes at New York University.[39]

He embraced the role of mentor to young students, just as Rabbi Lookstein did at Ramaz, paying close attention to their habits and counseling them through the distractions that came with a world at war. Eli was "an excellent, sympathetic man," recalled the head of the school, George Wolf. Noting his work especially with struggling students, Wolf added that Eli "always [kept] in close touch with any children having academic or discipline problems." When the turmoil of the war years threatened the school's ability to pay its teachers, Eli weighed in, challenging Wolf to make good on its commitments. Wolf admitted, "Our pledges were a little behind but we quickly took care of the matter." He took no offense to Eli's complaint, and saw in it only evidence of a genuine pursuit of justice.[40]

Eli's service to the school appeared to leave a positive impression on congregants and his fellow rabbis. When the congregation's spiritual leader took leave of the synagogue in 1942 to serve as a chaplain in the Army, the board of directors unanimously elected Eli to take his place.[41] As the face of the congregation, he was sometimes invited to speak about the war and social issues, along with the usual ceremonial addresses expected of a rabbi. In those rare moments, Eli drew on his business knowledge to offer hope for a thriving and socially just economy after the war. At one such event, hosted by the Woodmere-Hewlett Exchange Club in 1944, Eli advised that the country should create new jobs for the millions of veterans soon to return from Europe and the Pacific. He observed that, during the war, white local workers attacked Black migrants who moved to the North and West to take up labor in manufacturing plants. The conflicts, he said, arose from the erroneous perception that the number of workers exceeded the number of jobs. "Every state, city, and community," he said, "should have a group of capable men ready to cope with these conditions to prevent outbreaks between Negroes and Whites such as have occurred in the past." His analysis downplayed anti-Black racism as a root cause, but his attention to the issue of race relations and economic production showed a willingness to anticipate problems that few in those days would acknowledge.[42] Another time, he addressed the Far Rockaway Chapter of Hadassah, the Women's Zionist Organization of America. His remarks, titled "Palestine at the Crossroads," made the case for the creation of a Jewish homeland in the Middle East.

Privately he lamented the scarcity of such opportunities to engage the community on matters of social importance. Invitations to offer blessings at public banquets, to give the benediction at the local high school graduation, or to observe the start of high holy days, were far more common, and less meaningful.[43] Bernard Fischman—his Yeshiva classmate, lifelong friend, and eventual lawyer—recalled his unhappiness. "He felt his role as a rabbi was very unfulfilling. . . . He didn't think sermons changed anyone's attitude about anything."[44] The invasion of Normandy Beach on June 6, 1944, broke the Nazi stronghold on continental Europe, offering hope that the war might soon be over. The following spring, US troops liberated Jewish victims at Buchenwald, confirming the campaign of genocide that many in the Jewish diaspora already assumed. Up to that point, Eli had obeyed his father, followed the example of Rabbi Lookstein, and fulfilled the expectations of his mentor, Samuel Belkin, but serving a congregation in a quiet suburb on Long Island was not enough, in the face of such inhumanity.

Belkin understood his disappointment. The two men remained in constant contact after his graduation, with Belkin offering a sympathetic ear to his former Talmid throughout the war years. Belkin knew the dilemma now facing all Jews, their outrage and sense of powerlessness, the question of how to engage with a loss so incalculable. He also knew Eli had been exploring business, and encouraged him to exercise that part of himself, even if it meant leaving the rabbinate. "Eli searched to attain harmony in his two domains," he recalled. Through lengthy conversation, he came to know these domains in Eli as a deeper, philosophical split. In him, Belkin saw "Eli the scholar and Eli the man of practical affairs; Eli the visionary and Eli who tried to translate theory into action; Eli the mystic and Eli the man of cold logic." He recognized two tendencies that "do not necessarily supplement and complement each other," and yet, for the love of his young friend and the respect he had for his ability, he supported Eli's choice to leave Sons of Israel "in the hope that his soul may find self-fulfillment."[45] When Eli, on December 9, 1944, took the formal step to legally change his name to "Elias Max Black," he noted on the form that his previous name had been "cumbersome" for him and confusing to his congregants—but perhaps it was more deeply an effort to reconcile these two sides of himself.[46]

In May 1945, Eli tendered his resignation to the board of directors at the Sons of Israel, and proposed marriage to Shirley shortly after. His old friend and mentor, Rabbi Joseph Lookstein, agreed to officiate the wedding, confirming the couple's fidelity to a version of Judaism closer to that of Eli's upbringing. In time, he practiced his own hybridized form of Judaism with secular philosophy mixed in. While he did not convert to SAJ, he was nevertheless supported and unjudged by the Lubell family, who welcomed him with open arms. By this period, Samuel's speculative oil investments in Wichita, Kansas had paid off so well that Shirley's brother, Ben, moved to Tulsa, Oklahoma, to run the family business, Bell Oil and Gas Company. Sam paid for Shirley and Eli's wedding at Kehilath Jeshurun on April 4, 1946, more lavish than anything Eli could have imagined for himself in his youth. He also lent the couple a down payment for an apartment at 211 Central Park West, looking out toward the Museum of Natural History.

Trading the ceremonial white robe or *kittel* of the rabbi for a simple black suit and tie, Eli headed to Wall Street. Lehman Brothers, started by Jewish immigrant brothers from Bavaria in the mid-nineteenth century, took a chance on him. By 1946, when Eli started at the company, Robert "Bobbie" Lehman, the great-grandson of one of the founding brothers, Emmanuel, and the first in the family to be born in New York City, headed its single office at One William Street. In Eli, he saw a serious man, a dedicated worker, and assigned him to some of the less popular accounts in the sales department. Among these clients, the notorious railroad man and "Littlest Texan" Robert R. Young stood out. Born in the Panhandle in 1897, Young distinguished himself as a critic of the New York banking elites and a risky investor who courted disaster. In 1928, Young had quit his job with a famous corporate executive John Jacob Raskob, who believed "everybody ought to be rich," and urged modest earners that year to put money in the stock market.[47] Young did the opposite, short-selling stocks just before the crash in 1929, and made a fortune. With his newly acquired riches, Young chose to take on the bankers who, in his mind, had ruined America's railroads. In 1931, he ignored the advice of his wife by purchasing a controlling interest in the failing Alleghany system, including the Chesapeake & Ohio line, which ran coal from the mines of West Virginia to cities across the East and Midwest. He had refused to share his new plans for the C & O with bankers at J. P. Morgan & Co., earning him the ire of one of the most influential financial houses in America. In 1938, he went further by publicly accusing J. P. Morgan & Co. of manipulating the sale of the most popular lines to cronies, and denying industrious men like him the ability to restore uninterrupted transcontinental passenger service to every American. "A hog can cross the country without changing trains—but YOU can't!," his ads stated. He placed the blame on the "Morgan crowd," who had prevented him from buying the remaining lines. By 1947, when Eli met Young, he had been at war with the banking industry and federal regulators for nearly a decade.[48]

Young's cantankerous disposition and his strained relations with some bankers made his account a job no one wanted to touch at Lehman Brothers—and devising a reorganization plan for Missouri Pacific, which had been in bankruptcy for two decades, depended upon finding terms that different parties with very different interests could all agree on. "Black succeeded when others had been failing for 20 years," recalled his personal attorney, Leonard A. Schine. Young believed in bright, young managers, and he saw potential in the twenty-six-year-old Eli. As well as figuring out how to reorganize the overbuilt Missouri Pacific, or "MoPac"—a 2,500-mile system that extended across much of Texas to Mexico and the West Coast—Eli convinced Young to abandon seldom-used branches to free up capital to invest in the New York Central, another link in the cross-country plan. When the returns on the restructuring began to roll in, Young added him to the restructured MoPac's board of directors. By the early 1950s, Young had the Central in his grasp, and the completion of the transcontinental railroad in his sights.[49]

The success did not change either man. Black remained cool and calculating, while Young continued to fulminate against anyone who stood in his way. Eli watched Young sabotage his own progress, alienating colleagues, clients, and competitors, but he kept quiet. He knew he'd been given an uphill battle, a client few managers could handle, and any success with Young would highlight his talents. Over time, Young became a cautionary figure. What if the power and influence Young had amassed, but squandered through bluster and grudges, could be harnessed by a calm and observant leader and used to do good in the world? Eli hadn't yet settled on where to turn his talents, but his success with Young must have made him more confident that he had chosen wisely in leaving the rabbinate.

In Young, Eli witnessed the heights that one could achieve through sheer determination and the willingness to challenge those who took their privilege for granted. Although born into a family of some means, Young had been an outsider to the New York elites who had chosen to line their pockets with railroad profits rather than reinvest them to build a better system. Young paid himself a salary that was a fraction of his predecessors' and made improvements on his railroad that increased the comforts for the average traveler. That was the virtuous Young—suspicious of inherited power, and sensitive to the needs of the common man. His bombast, however, might have concerned Eli. Young cursed "godambankers" and harangued intrusive regulators. For every mile he gained through will and independence of mind, he lost two with petty grievances and reckless gestures.

Eli began to ease away from Young in 1950, eventually leaving Lehman Brothers for another investment firm, American Securities Corporation. He continued as a director of the Missouri Pacific and member of its executive committee. Shirley had given birth to their first child, a daughter, Judith, on September 27, 1948 and they were now living in a penthouse apartment at 411 Central Park West. On July 31, 1951, Leon, their first son and last child, arrived. Eli was looking for stability, and the opportunity to advise companies that would give him room to grow.

In 1956, when Eli had just begun his own career as a CEO at AMK, Young completed the acquisition of the New York Central, but by that time the public had come to prefer highways and skyways. Always the gambler, Young doubled down—and lost. By 1958, the railroad's stock had plummeted.[50] Eli understood the news had been disappointing for Young, but he had not fully recognized how dire the situation was until he received word that his former client took his own life on January 25, 1958.[51] Young had been found in his twenty-five-room mansion in Palm Beach, where it was evident he had placed a double-barreled shotgun to his head and pulled both triggers. It was rumored he died "close to broke." The day after Young took his own life, the value of Central's common stock registered no marked change from its close on Friday.[52] Sitting in his office a week later still absorbing the news, Eli would have read a *Forbes* account of Young's passing, noting the Texan's favored expression, "to seize opportunity is no sin." He might have compared the words to Robert Browning's "Ah, but a man's reach should exceed his grasp"—and thought about the perils of outsized ambition. Remembering what his spiritual mentors had praised as *derekh eretz*, he might have resolved to keep reaching, but always in a way that sustained his respect for himself and for the dignity of man.[53]

2

AN HONEST BUSINESS

MOVING UPTOWN TO WORK for William Rosenwald's investment office, American Securities Corp., at 590 Madison Avenue, Eli found a mentor well suited to his aspirations and principles. A third-generation American, Bill Rosenwald was carrying forward the legacy of his Jewish, German-born grandfather, Samuel Rosenwald, who had moved before the Civil War to Springfield, Illinois, worked as a clothing store manager there, and lived just a block away from Abraham Lincoln's home. Bill's father, Julius Rosenwald, had built Sears, Roebuck and Company into a national mail-order retailer and later used his considerable wealth to build thousands of schools across the South to serve black communities after Reconstruction. Bill's own philanthropy hewed more closely to his faith and the family's immigrant origins. He created the United Jewish Appeal in 1939, a charitable organization dedicated to providing funds to Jews in war-torn Europe and establishing a Jewish state in Palestine. He also donated generously to support resettlement of Jewish families in America through the National Refugee Service, later part of the Hebrew Immigration Aid Society. In many ways, Rosenwald was a model of

faith-driven influence on the world who could inspire Eli to imagine
having such impact himself.[1]

Rosenwald gave Eli the opportunity to choose from a collection of
the firm's smaller holdings to manage. Scrolling through the company
ledger, Eli landed on American Seal-Kap, its ticker symbol AMK. Decades earlier, the company had carved out a niche in the food industry
after a doctor, Ewald Baum of Natick, Massachusetts, invented a paper
cap for milk bottles. Dr. Baum, paying a house call to a sickly boy, had
spied the probable culprit behind the child's illness: a cat licking the
glass lip of a bottle near the front door where the milkman placed the
family's daily delivery.[2] In 1921, Baum patented a sturdy waxed-paper
cap to cover the bottle's top and began local production of its "SealKapS"
bottling materials and machinery at Baum Dairy Appliance Company
in Massachusetts. In 1926, a group of investors in Long Island purchased Baum's patent and under the new name of Seal-Kap Company
built a factory to take the business to a much larger scale, selling to
companies delivering milk to residents across the five boroughs of New
York City.[3] By the time Eli knew of the company, in 1953, it had sold
millions of bottle tops and its annual gross revenue had reached $5 mil-
lion. Whatever grand visions Eli might have had of influencing the
world through business, his journey would start with this small company and its modest products.

When Eli took his first look at American Seal-Kap in 1953, annual
spending by American households on food had reached nearly $60
billion—triple the $20 billion spent in 1941. Across the same twelve
years the portion of household income going to food had jumped from
22 percent to 26 percent. Although this postwar trend would level off
in the 1950s, Eli believed in the food industry and, more particularly,
thought American Seal-Kap could sustain its position as a supplier to
dairy producers, and even expand profits, in a growing market. That
would require change, however, because the rise of supermarkets was
shifting buying habits away from home delivery of milk. If the company could adjust its operations and offerings to serve the grocery store

trade rather than direct delivery to consumers, it could stay afloat. Fail to adapt, and it could vanish by the end of the decade. As Eli would later put it, this was "a tiny company with huge problems."[4]

Eli first advised management to ramp up production of its products to take fuller advantage of current demand and head off competitors. Longer term, the vision he laid out as the company's active investor and, soon, a member of its executive board, was much grander: American Seal-Kap could transform itself from a reliable producer of dairy containers to a supplier capable of properly packaging anything, including the vast amounts of processed foods that now filled the shelves of American grocery stores. In a short time, American Seal-Kap became the dominant producer of the waxed-paper lids and by 1954, Eli was named its new chair and chief executive, with a mandate to grow the company.[5] The move required him to leave Rosenwald's office earlier than he anticipated, but the opportunity to manage his own company was too good to pass up. The example of Rosenwald's philanthropy still guided Eli. With his first paycheck from American Seal-Kap, he established a student scholarship at Yeshiva University in the name of the Gottesman family, who had funded his own studies there. Naming the gift after his benefactor rather than himself followed an ethic of giving practiced by the Rosenwalds, whose habit was to foreground the causes they championed and the people they assisted rather than themselves. Eli would continue this practice for the rest of his life.[6]

Eli quickly implemented an aggressive plan to expand and diversify American Seal-Kap's business as a premier food container company. He purchased the United Can Company and the Paper Tube Company in New Jersey.[7] He took on rubber and metal fabrication plants that produced washers and precision instruments related to packaging.[8] He bought existing patents of proven container designs and patented new ones developed and tested at his New Jersey facility. And he instructed his research and development staff to focus narrowly on functional design and testing to come up with products that food producers would entrust to American Seal-Kap to manufacture rather than produce on their own.[9] By 1957, the company had all but cornered the market on paper lids, producing 500 million annually, or three lids for every American. It had also established a foothold in the broader food-packaging market, giving it room to grow.

Eli's constant investment in research and development increased American Seal-Kap's ability to cater to a postwar "take-out" and fast-food culture. His transition to a new "die-forming" approach in manufacturing—using forced compression to create commercial objects—created the capacity to produce everything from lids to thumbtacks, although paper packaging remained American Seal-Kap's primary business, accounting for one-third of its sales in 1957. That year, Eli added a line of plastic-coated drinking cups with an eye to challenging the disposable cup market. When a recession hit later that year, Eli's investments in cutting-edge technology helped American Seal-Kap weather the downturn by leasing its machinery to producers across the country, a service that eventually would become a major source of income for the company. After the recession, American Seal-Kap took on established paper cup and container manufacturers Lily-Tulip Cup Corporation and the Dixie Cup division of the American Can Company by rolling out a line of its own. Eli also bought two smaller container companies—Herz Manufacturing Company and Potlatch Forests, Inc.—to improve American Seal-Kap's capacity to produce cups with handles and a collapsible cylindrical container. The latter competed with more expensive and permanent versions on the market. By 1960, American Seal-Kap's sales reached nearly $33 million, up from the $5 million the company had reached in 1952, before Eli took the helm.[10]

Eli's anticipation of changes in food packaging had been the formula for American Seal-Kap's success, but by the early 1960s obsolescence threatened the company's signature product. The rise of supermarkets hastened the end of heavy glass bottles for milk, as consumers increasingly chose to pick up the dairy products they needed along with their other groceries, rather than contract for home delivery. In the interests of reducing weight and fragility, the industry began moving to more durable, lightweight containers made of polyethylene, a thin plastic refined by manufacturers after World War II. Declines in glass bottling directly affected sales of bottle caps, and Eli invested more into manufacturing plastic milk jugs.

The new containers were a success. When American Seal-Kap's contracts with dairies soared in 1964, Eli collaborated with Hercules Powder Company, a major polyethylene producer, to form a subsidiary called Haskon.[11] The team of executives he hired to run Haskon focused on building the machinery to produce the plastic milk bottles as the foundation of their business. Haskon leased property near dairy farms to build its production plants, to save on shipping the new jugs to customers. The company eased dairy owners' transition from glass to plastic as Haskon shouldered the capital investment in the new equipment and their costs for packing, shipping, and bottle-washing dropped. Although larger companies such as Union Carbide and Shell also produced and sold plastic bottles, American Seal-Kap's long-standing relationships with many dairies, and its investments in the National Rubber Machinery Company during the 1950s, gave farmers confidence in Haskon.[12] The price of polyethylene dropped from 47 cents a pound in 1957 to 25 cents in 1964, giving Haskon an opportunity to lower its cost of goods sold, adding to profits. Eli's partnership with Hercules Powder to form Haskon mimicked an emerging trend of conglomeration then catching fire in the US economy. By those standards, Eli's move had been a modest one, but it demonstrated creative, strategic thinking for the benefit of American Seal-Kap. Although neither plastic nor paperboard claimed the entirety of the milk container business at the end of the decade, Eli's commitment to plastic jugs ensured that his company would not die with the decline of glass bottles.[13]

For all his success with packaging, Eli craved a more central role in a booming postwar economy. The unprecedented demand for goods and services by returning veterans and working Americans created a consumer's republic unparalleled in the nation's history.[14] Women played a critical role as workers in this economy—especially working-class women—despite popular impressions to the contrary. In 1953, women constituted 30 percent of the workforce, even as they bore and took primary responsibility for raising the baby-boom generation.[15] A persistent patriarchal division of labor kept women on kitchen duty even as they contributed dollars to household budgets. The food industry grew apace with these developments, discovering new ways of packaging food for quick and convenient meal preparation to meet the demands of dual-career households. American Seal-Kap's proximity to this sector of the economy led Eli to explore new and original ways to feed the working American family and, potentially, a hungry world.

From his office at 122 East Forty-Second Street, one block south of Grand Central Station, Eli contemplated his next move, one that would place him squarely within a dynamic food industry that offered multiple entry points for a man of his talents. Just across the intersection of Forty-Second and Lexington was the Chrysler Building, home of the Great Atlantic & Pacific Tea Company. Known to everyone as A&P, America's grocery leader managed a vast supply chain that kept all its stores well stocked and its sales volumes high. Like most New Yorkers, Eli had become accustomed to shopping at A&P as a young adult. Founded as Gilman & Company in 1859, A&P emerged during the 1940s as the dominant grocery retailer in the United States. By 1964, the competition had caught up, making A&P the subject of takeover rumors by managers who thought they could return it to its glory days. Eli had had a front-row seat to A&P's rise and gradual decline.[16]

A&P led all grocers in developing a market of convenience in the postwar economy, including foods that required less preparation at home, and could be stored in the average American kitchen. Frozen foods increased in popularity as technology in freezing and refrigeration became more pervasive and less expensive for the American family.[17] A&P championed prepackaged, apportioned, and in many cases precooked items that shortened the time of preparation and (in theory) minimized waste. The absence of an extended family and reduction of nonwork hours diminished the appeal of gardening, baking homemade bread, and canning vegetables. Offerings like frozen orange juice, canned peas, and trimmed and packaged beef increased in value, and Americans were willing to spend more for them. The higher prices covered the increased cost of labor, storage, transportation, refrigeration, and assembly that producers built in to processed foods. A&P delivered these products to stores nestled in the neighborhoods where most Americans lived and shopped.[18]

Eli must have marveled at A&P's success, but he also noted its considerable challenges. As the preeminent grocer in the market, A&P spent handsomely in the 1940s and 1950s to repel government attempts to break it up through antitrust suits. John Hartford, its dynamic CEO, had died in 1951 of a sudden heart attack while riding the elevator in the Chrysler Building. His replacement, Ralph Burger, had so far failed to adapt to the changing landscape of retail business. Burger bucked the growing trend of carrying non-food items in stores throughout the late 1950s and 1960s, refusing even to carry toothpaste or shaving cream, insisting that "we have always considered ourselves food merchants."[19] His stubbornness opened the door to competitors that embraced a one-stop-shopping philosophy in their supermarkets. Burger also privileged the Mid-Atlantic marketplace, ceding millions of new customers to competitors, like Safeway, which catered to burgeoning populations in California and the West. He began to abandon Hartford's strategy of having the lowest price on staple items, inviting customers to comparison shop elsewhere. A&P's sales rose 65 percent despite these missteps, but its top four competitors saw their sales grow 200 percent.[20] By 1964, when Eli began looking for new places to invest, A&P had lost more than half its stock value and suffered sales declines of two to five percent on an annual basis, becoming an attractive takeover target.[21]

For Eli, A&P's negatives outweighed its positives as a prospect for purchase. Like other CEOs looking to make their mark, he sought a down-on-its-luck company that could be purchased at a reduced price. Most onlookers viewed the grocery industry without much enthusiasm, but Eli had dealt with such circumstances before, and turned a stagnant business at American Seal-Kap into a diversified and growing one. This had been the appeal of American Seal-Kap in 1953 when it looked as if paper caps for glass milk bottles had seen their better days. American Seal-Kap had been the ideal "backward company in a backward industry," one where a bracing introduction of managerial discipline could dramatically boost its profits and market share.[22] Ralph Burger's mistakes had put A&P in a downward trajectory, but grocery hardly qualified as a backward industry. Eli would be a junior suitor among much better financed investors looking to become the new grocery king. As it happened, it took Burger and subsequent A&P executives much longer to accept their fate, resisting takeover bid after takeover bid until it sold for pennies on the dollar to a German grocer in 1979.[23]

Eli recognized that his ambition to address the world's most nagging problems through business would not be satisfied by a grocery chain concentrated on the East Coast. As he read the financial news, he scanned the horizon for an opportunity that would satisfy two goals simultaneously: acquire a company that could grow along with the current national trends in food consumption; and participate in global healing and postwar prosperity by making food more accessible to more people. A&P had done some of this work, domestically, increasing access to food in the United States, but this benefit had been restricted to the citizens of the richest, most powerful nation in the world. As an immigrant who watched helplessly as his people suffered back home in Poland, Eli looked on with concern at the troubles abroad while making his way in the land of plenty. Two-thirds of the world's population lived without an adequate supply of food, and famine remained a constant threat even amidst advances in agriculture. Examples abounded in the headlines after the war, from severe food shortages in China during the late 1950s and early 1960s that killed millions to starvation in Southeast Asia and Africa in the 1960s due to climate events such as flooding and drought or political conflict. During the 1960s, social scientists steadily warned of hunger amidst a growing global population. Some wrote of "pathological togetherness" in which nations would resign themselves to a constant state of mortal conflict and human degeneracy if the oncoming "population bomb" continued across the developing world. These warnings had reached the financial press. Scenarios of people having to turn cadavers into food to feed the masses of tomorrow haunted the pages of such mainstream magazines as *Fortune*.[24] Such predictions may have created a sense of urgency in Eli to expand accessibility of food more equitably within and beyond the boundaries of the United States.

It was perhaps Eli's brief consideration of the grocery business in 1964 that convinced him it was better to invest in the supply side of the national food system. Supermarkets like A&P had been innovative in selling food to the public but lacked so-called channel power vis-à-vis the suppliers who controlled the quality and presentation of foods and could therefore create an identity that consumers were willing to pay more for. A&P had been the rare exception, and then only with a few products, like tea and coffee.[25] For most other items on store shelves, retailers bought from wholesalers, the middlemen also known as "jobbers." Players upstream from the grocer controlled what they could sell in what quantities, and even when they could take delivery of merchandise. The fact that grocers were numerous while suppliers were relatively few also meant that buyers had little influence over what they paid, and had to accept price hikes by producers and wholesalers. Given their slim margins, they could only pass these increases in price on to customers and hope that they would continue to buy in the same volume to maintain thin profit margins. This lack of control had been the motivation for A&P's elaborate coffee supply chain, which, on this one product, enabled it to become a "price-setter" rather than a "price-taker" by managing every stage of the coffee bean, from its harvest to its roasting, bagging, and shelving in its stores.[26]

Eli found how A&P stocked its meat department most instructive for his next venture. In its heyday in the 1940s, A&P worked with a handful of big national and independent packers that controlled the production and transportation of meat to its many locations. The arrangement relieved A&P of the burden of managing the flow but also made it more dependent on these producers for its supply. While the size of its orders afforded A&P some power to influence quality and price—even establishing a new "Super-right" grade of meat for its suppliers to distinguish the best cuts—the grocer could not exert the same control it enjoyed with coffee. Packers were in charge of sourcing animals for slaughter and how meat arrived at market, usually in bulk to be cut on-site. A&P contracted with some packers to prepackage and brand its bacon before it left the packinghouse but had only moderate success in persuading them to do this with other cuts in heavy demand by modern consumers. The packers' reasons for retaining tight control over cuts, weight, and quality varied, but one barrier frequently cited by management was the role of unions, whose contracts restricted changes to cutting protocols and outdated equipment in the packinghouses. In some cases, packers such as Oscar Mayer did choose to do further processing and packaging of certain products, like bacon and hot dogs, and invested in building brands for these items that consumers would trust and be willing to pay a premium for. Supermarkets had no real input into these decisions.[27]

What frustrated A&P about the meat business would have intrigued Eli. As the son of a shohet, he was familiar with the process of butchering animal carcasses into cuts of meat. He shared A&P's belief that both packer and grocer would come out ahead if the former performed the extra step of breaking down and prepackaging more cuts at the packinghouse, and delivering more meat to stores ready to sell, rather than requiring further processing by an in-store butcher. Eli saw potential in controlling the source of the meat, rather than the point of sale. Although he still had much to learn about the highly industrialized meat business, he saw union contracts and antiquated facilities as mere management challenges to be overcome. Eli regarded packer excuses for not stepping up to grocers' requests as regressive thinking on an industrywide scale, the kind of correctible problem that made the sector a good candidate for investment. If he could find a packer whose shares could be bought in sufficient volume, he would have the ideal conditions of a "backward company in a backward industry"— an acquisition that could be his next step toward a global role in the food business. The right company would also give him assets to leverage for future investments in the food marketplace worldwide.

In 1965, Eli initiated a thorough review of every division at American Seal-Kap, assessing what could be sold to gather the capital he would need to buy the right meat company when he found it. His strategy avoided gutting the company, but it did involve hard choices. In 1956, he had purchased the Chicago Railway Equipment in a bid to expand Seal-Kap beyond its comfort zone of food packaging, but now he decided to sell it to Evans Products Co. in exchange for $3.5 million. He then let go of the entire packaging division, including the cherished bottle caps that had given the company its "Seal-Kap" name—and he renamed the company simply AMK, its ticker symbol. By 1966, AMK had reduced its business to manufacturing lock washers for the railroad and automobile industries; forging steel in an iron foundry in Indiana; and maintaining majority interest in its subsidiary NRM Corp., which made equipment for the rubber and plastics industry. From these divestitures, Eli walked away with $10 million, enough to go shopping.[28]

He had chosen his moment carefully. The early 1960s had witnessed significant changes in the landscape for big businesses, and the time was now ripe for building "conglomerates"—that is, companies made up of multiple subsidiaries operating in quite distinct industrial sectors. The changes in economic policy had been initiated in 1961 with the election of President John F. Kennedy, who entered the White House during a recession resembling the one that had pushed Robert Young to suicide in 1958. Prior to Kennedy's arrival, Democrats had controlled both houses of Congress, but the upper echelons of the corporate world had still had a Republican, Dwight D. Eisenhower, as a sympathetic ear in the Oval Office.[29] Organizations like the American Enterprise Association, funded by twenty-six of the fifty largest companies in America, railed against what it saw as a trend toward "a controlled economy," while the National Association of Manufacturers financed films, comic books, and radio programs promoting faith in free enterprise.[30] Kennedy responded to the economic crisis by departing from his party's conventional wisdom on how to spur growth. Like many politicians of his day, he had embraced the infinite wisdom of Keynesian philosophy—dictating that, in a downturn, a national government should indulge in heavy deficit spending on infrastructure projects to keep employment and wages sufficiently high to maintain robust consumer spending. This time around, however, dropping consumption was not just a national problem but an international one, as American manufacturers had in recent years been experiencing tougher competition in markets around the world. Between their rising costs of goods sold and the ongoing postwar recovery of other industrial nations, US corporations had entered an era of slow growth—and dismal job creation. Kennedy set the goal of reducing unemployment from 8.1 percent where it sat when he took office to 4 percent by the end of his first term.[31]

To accomplish this, the president turned his back on the New Deal policies that had defined the Democratic Party for a generation and embraced tax cuts rather than large-scale government spending to stimulate the economy. As part of these cuts, investors no longer had to pay taxes on the capital gains they accrued when shares they owned experienced a price hike because of an acquisition of a company. Cutting the government's tax revenues would not expand the deficit, Kennedy's administration argued, because investors would put the tax savings to work in ways that would stimulate the manufacturing sector, producing jobs and boosting gross domestic product. Meanwhile, the administration counted on legislation to close loopholes in the tax code that exacerbated wealth and income inequality, but such reforms never materialized. In debates over two Revenue Acts in Congress—1962 and 1964—the business community, influenced by the conservative economist Friedrich Hayek and his Mont Pelerin Society, succeeded in persuading legislators to retain advantages for corporations created by Kennedy's economic policy.[32] The idea that tax breaks for the wealthy could stimulate growth and lift the economy out of recession eventually became an orthodoxy for a good portion of economists across the political spectrum.[33]

Kennedy's assassination on November 22, 1963 may have ended "Camelot," but his policies lived on, giving life to a new American aristocracy of empire-builders. The favorable tax regime for investors created under Kennedy led to the first significant merger movement since the 1920s. During the 1960s, a new breed of business-school-trained managers were quick to recognize how the reduced capital gains taxes would lessen shareholder resistance to acquisitions of companies and began building amoebic, sometimes multinational, conglomerates. This started at the moment of acquisition, in which conglomerate-builders proposed stocks rather than cash or bonds to purchase a company—a method known as "pooling of interest," originally restricted to the merging of two companies of comparable size and power but now available to them. Such arrangements came with the benefit of relieving shareholders of the need to pay taxes on the increased value of their stock in the new company.[34]

The value of these new companies increasingly depended on a fantasy of potential growth rather than a realistic trajectory of development based on historic performance. In the era of the merger movement, market watchers fetishized the price-to-earnings (p / e) ratio, a calculation that reflected a promise to grow rather than actual evidence of growth. A skillful CEO could boost a company's market capitalization by telling a persuasive story that then became reflected in a higher p/e ratio, regardless of whether the company increased production and sales each year.

Eli took special note of how these new business barons boosted the value of the shares of their companies by public tender offers, or takeover bid. Prior to this moment, a potential buyer reviewed his assets and made an offer with the promise to improve a target company's performance based on the combined value of the two. The purveyors of takeover bids, on the other hand, pointed to the bounce in stock prices immediately after the purchase as evidence of their success and a reason why shareholders should trust them with their investment. The bounce contributed to the fictitious value of the new company while the benefit of not having to pay capital gains on the increase made it easy for shareholders to embrace the deal. Before 1966, raising the value of a company was seen as a painstaking process of increasing its bottom-line profitability, whether by increasing revenue, perhaps by improving products, or by reducing overhead costs. Now, the focus had shifted from the income statement to share-price performance and market capitalization.

Changes to accounting rules related to acquisitions also contributed to increased merger activity. Often, the price paid for an acquired company exceeds the fair value of its net assets on the acquisition date. On the company's balance sheet, the difference is termed "goodwill"—a category of intangible strengths, such as its brand recognition or its history of innovation, that justify the premium paid. Under the rules set by the Securities and Exchange Commission (SEC) in the past, goodwill had to be carried forward on subsequent years' financial statements—a reminder that the difference still had to be made up by real growth. Such a burden placed a damper on investment because it hung over the acquirer like an "I.O.U" and curbed investor confidence. Under the new regulations, the two companies simply added up their assets and liabilities without any consideration of whether the acquiring company paid more than the book value for the shares. As a result, the merged company often overstated its immediate earnings per share and understated the value of its assets. Some accountants and economists bemoaned the elimination of goodwill as tantamount to "sweeping liabilities under the rug" but regulatory agencies like the SEC and the Federal Trade Commission looked the other way in accordance with the political interests of the day.[35]

The merger mania of the 1960s often involved aggressive investors moving into lines of businesses that had little or no relationship to the ones in which they were established. Creators of conglomerates or "multi-market corporations" chose this path in part because the Sherman Antitrust Act of 1890 and the Clayton Antitrust Act of 1914, legislation designed to ensure fair competition in the marketplace, made it difficult to grow past a certain point within any given industry. The Federal Trade Commission, created by Congress in 1914 to enforce these acts, carefully scrutinized any mergers aimed at greater "vertical" integration (merging a company with either an upstream supplier or a downstream customer) or "horizontal" integration (often involving acquisition of a direct competitor). Meanwhile, the trend toward the "professionalization" of management had spread the conviction that the principles of business administration were more universal than particular to different industries. This confidence that a portfolio of dissimilar companies could be effectively run by "free form" managers focused on technology modernization and efficiency gains encouraged companies to seek opportunities to expand in all directions. Between 1960 and 1965, 70 percent of mergers and acquisitions involved multi-market conglomerates while only 13 percent were mergers of related businesses.[36]

Eli had already believed in making diverse acquisitions, opportunistically spotting undervalued companies in sectors as different from milk-bottling solutions as railroad car components, iron casting, and industrial machinery for makers of rubber and plastic goods. What he manufactured and how these products served his customers had mattered to him, but now he recognized an opportunity to grow more by concentration than by diversification. By taking advantage of an environment that allowed controlling shares of companies to change hands more readily, he could remake AMK into the consequential company that he had long wanted it to be. Perhaps focusing on a commodity food business also appealed to him at the level of a higher purpose, since it put him firmly in the business of feeding people while making money. In a way that controlling a portfolio of disparate businesses had not, a commitment to food production and distribution would allow him to put his mark on the country and the world, and draw on his personal history and values as he pursued the American dream.

Eli represented a difference in temperament from the new breed of CEOs who made audacious claims of managerial brilliance and dismissed objections to their methods. Businessmen like Ralph Ablon of Ogden Corp., Fred Sullivan of Walter Kidde, James "Jimmy" Ling of Ling-Temco-Vought (LTV), and Charlie Bluhdorn of Gulf & Western aggressively pursued expansion using every accounting trick condoned by the regulations of the decade. While many observers derided the deals as merely "arithmetic mergers" or sterile "mergers by the numbers," and warned of the "chain-letter effect" unleashed when shares with a high price-to-earnings ratio are used to buy a company whose shares had a lower ratio, conglomeration activity continued to skyrocket throughout the decade. In 1968, the number of mergers was ten times greater than in 1950, with much of the growth happening over the previous two years. This "merger movement" forced executives at stable, productive companies to spend time and money fending off potential takeovers. No company, not even the most established, considered itself immune to a trend taking hold "like a strange new virus."[37]

Eli hardly fit the image of a swashbuckling business raider now being celebrated in the press. *Time* placed Jimmy Ling and Charlie Bluhdorn on its cover, while *Fortune* and *Forbes* kept tabs on their latest conquests. Writers who took notice of the up-and-coming Eli tended to see his penchant for academic descriptions of his approach to business and his "egghead" demeanor as evidence that he and those peers were not cut from the same cloth. *Forbes* cited Ling and Bluhdorn's tendencies to exaggerate their accomplishments, while Eli, they noted, maintained a low profile that made him a "man of mystery in Wall Street." Undoubtedly this was intentional, as Eli would have preferred to gain ground by focusing his attention on companies where modern managerial "methods and systems" were lacking and he could make changes to get them operating more efficiently.[38] Publicly, Eli showed indifference toward his peers, although privately he spoke admiringly of them—especially of Jimmy Ling, who had risen from being an ordinary electrician to owning one of the mightiest conglomerates of the decade. Ling acquired Wilson and Company in 1967, a corporation twice the size of his electronics and aerospace company and whose meatpacking, sporting goods, and pharmaceuticals contrasted with the business of LTV. A pending antitrust suit against LTV for its acquisition of similar electronics companies had played a part in Ling's decision to diversify. By the end of the decade, Ling had captured thirty-three companies with combined sales of $3.6 billion. Earnings, however, never caught up with the expectations he had set. By 1970, LTV's disgruntled board of directors ousted Ling from his seat as CEO and he soon faded into obscurity.

The eccentric Charlie Bluhdorn enjoyed far more success and fit the image of the prototypical go-go businessman of the 1960s. "The gauche immigrant boy on the make," as *Fortune* described the Austrian-born chairman of Gulf & Western, generated net earnings of 18 percent or better annually throughout the decade. He achieved this feat using the pooling-of-interest approach.[39] Under Bluhdorn, Gulf & Western maintained discipline in its buying of companies, acquiring only those that promised at least 10 to 12 percent return on investment and avoiding those with substantially higher price-to-earnings ratios than its own. Like Ling, Bluhdorn made a play for a meatpacker—Armour & Co.—but failed to close the deal, a rare outcome for him. By 1968,

Bluhdorn had completed no fewer than seventy-two mergers involving companies that manufactured auto parts, mined Zinc, refined sugar, rolled cigars, and produced movies. He became best known for the purchase of the moribund Paramount Pictures in 1966 and its turn-around based on hits like the 1970 *Love Story,* starring Ali MacGraw and Ryan O'Neal. By the mid-seventies, Bluhdorn's investment in film auteur Francis Ford Coppola, especially his film *The Godfather* in 1972, and his support of Dominican-born fashion icon Oscar de la Renta earned him a degree of celebrity that transcended the business world. In 1983, Bluhdorn died at the age of fifty-six, suffering a heart attack aboard his private jet, allegedly while having sex en route to New York from his seven-thousand-acre resort, Casa de Campo, in the Dominican Republic.[40]

Eli lived a more low-key life but harbored the same passion for making deals, especially in the meat business. Meat processing lacked the glamour of film or the tremendous profit margins in mining and manufacturing, but it possessed some of the qualities that Eli looked for in a good investment. Most management teams in meatpacking companies had lapsed into thinking that they could only tinker around the edges of production processes rather than engage in a complete rethinking of their operations and industry. Many took as a given that no big change could be made in a sector with such formidable unions, the legacy of the labor militancy of butchers and slaughterhouse workers in the 1930s. As an outsider, Eli felt the freedom to break the system to fix it. By 1966, he led both Bluhdorn and Ling to the same conclusion, recognizing the incredible potential of the industry, given the right set of circumstances and a willingness to engage with union leaders and part with accepted traditions in the industry. Shortly before Ling bought Wilson and Bluhdorn sought Armour, Eli had identified a medium-sized midwestern meatpacker, John Morrell and Company, as a likely prospect. His earlier study of A&P had acquainted him with the basic economics of this most expensive item in the grocery store, and the steadily growing demand for it, especially as beef and pork became mainstays of the American postwar diet. Although Eli never touched pork as an observant Jew, he saw no conflict in making money from the sale of it to a hungry nation. Morrell's hog kill department distinguished itself by its production of canned hams and bacon that competed with Hormel, Swift, and other pork producers. If he could secure Morrell, his managerial expertise could re-energize a company that most industry observers thought had seen its better days.

In 1966, Eli took a flight to Chicago, and drove more than three hundred miles to Ottumwa, Iowa, with the intent of evaluating the potential of the company as a possible addition to AMK. When he arrived, he found a city of immigrants that had grown up around the Morrell plant sitting along the banks of the Des Moines River. George Morrell had started out as a small-time grocer in Bradford, England, in 1827 and when he retired, his son John took over a business that was by then thriving and well known for its cured meats. The next generation of the family found itself operating in Liverpool, England, as well as Ireland, then Ontario, Canada, New York, and Chicago, processing increasing volumes of pork through its packing plants. After the Civil War, Iowa emerged as a center of corn-hog producers and packers depending on the Mississippi and Des Moines Rivers as an essential source for ice used in meat storage. Ottumwa, sitting alongside the Des Moines River in Southeast Iowa, became a major packing center starting in the 1860s. By 1888, the company had moved all operations there from Chicago and was fast on its way to becoming one of the leading pork producers in the nation.

Morrell, like most meatpackers, evolved from a family-owned business to one dominated by a union set in a company town. T. D. Foster, grandson of George Morrell and the company's president during the early twentieth century, had worked as a laborer and hog buyer for his cousin in Ireland, and understood the production side of the business. Foster hired the skilled butchers in the Ottumwa plant, showing a preference for workers newly arrived from England, Ireland, and Germany over those who had been in the United States for a while. Hiring wide-eyed immigrants direct from Europe over seasoned residents—many of them from the East Coast, with knowledge of how unions operated there—was a familiar tactic of corporate managers hoping to put a damper on organizing efforts spreading across labor forces. Such managerial maneuvers did not last long as employees discovered their strength in numbers and formulated a working-class analysis of their exploitation. When a group of the most highly skilled workers—the so-called butcher aristocracy—began to question the social control of the company and in 1901 formed Morrell's first union, Amalgamated Meat Cutters and Butcher Workmen of North America (AMCBW) No. 144, Foster tried to dissuade and distract workers from taking an oppositional stance toward the company by hosting elaborate picnics and funding the local YMCA, which encouraged Ottumwans to remain loyal to Morrell.[41]

A second generation of workers threw off the constraints of corporate paternalism and reorganized the AMCBW into Local 236, still affiliated with the American Federation of Labor (AFL) after T. D.'s passing in 1915. A federal ruling in 1918 that affirmed laborers' rights to an eight-hour day, guaranteed forty-hour workweek, paid overtime, and equal pay for men and women gave Morrell employees power to make demands.[42] In 1921, after the company refused their requests for better working conditions and higher wages for the women working as trimmers, Local 236 members walked off the job. Foster responded by hiring African Americans from nearby towns to fill twelve hundred positions vacated by the striking workers, leading to acts of violence by white union members against black strikebreakers that infected race relations in Ottumwa for generations. For his part, Foster appealed to Iowa's governor, Nathan Kendall, to quell the violence with the Iowa National Guard. The effect of three hundred troops arriving in downtown Ottumwa was to restore the status quo but a bitterness toward

Foster—and his son, George M. Foster, who would succeed him as
head of the business—smoldered for years after.[43]

In the 1930s, emboldened by the pro-labor policies of the New Deal,
Morrell workers renewed their fight with management by demanding
their right to collectively bargain for wages and benefits. Drawn to the
more militant Congress of Industrial Organizations (CIO), Morrell
employees began a four-year organizing campaign that culminated in
a successful certification. On May 14, 1937, the international office of
the CIO in Chicago granted to Morrell-Ottumwa its first charter for
packinghouse workers in the United States.[44] Initially named the
United Packinghouse Workers of America (UPWA), and designated
Local Industrial Union No. 32, it was renumbered "Local 1" by the CIO
in 1939.[45] From then on, the union often challenged both Morrell management and the international CIO headquarters, lobbying for more
democratic structures at work sites and within the labor movement.
Locally, leaders of Local 1 frequently used work stoppages and walk-
outs without the consent of the international to control the pace of
work, and demanded compliance from fellow employees who remained on the fence about joining the union. The constant threat of
disruption upset the company management that had little choice but
to agree to the union's terms. Among Morrell-owned packing plants,
Local 1 was the only CIO-affiliated union. Laborers at Morrell's second-
largest plant, in Sioux Falls, South Dakota, remained part of the more
compliant AMCBW.[46]

The consequence of Ottumwa and Sioux Falls affiliating with different union federations meant little until Republicans regained control of both houses of Congress in 1947. That year, Congress passed the
Taft-Hartley Act over President Harry Truman's veto, which, among
other things, granted owners the ability to pursue legal limitations to
strikes, picketing, and boycotts. Local 1 at Ottumwa was among the first
unions to test the new legislation by staging a massive national strike
in 1948, but Sioux Falls remained compliant with the law. When
Ottumwa union members blocked railcars from leaving the plant,

Morrell won a temporary injunction against Local 1, forcing it to reduce picket lines to a maximum of five people. Management eventually broke the union's campaign by hiring replacement workers from
the surrounding countryside and waging a legal and media campaign
that painted the union as violent and destructive to the local economy.
Morrell's president, by then George Foster, chastised the union in
the pages of the *Ottumwa Daily Courier,* complaining that "within the
past five years there have been 42 work stoppages, slowdowns, or
strikes, resulting in 67 days lost." Nationally, the popular impression of
the union's actions mirrored those in Ottumwa, compelling UPWA to
call off the strike and accept Foster's "final offer" of a per-hour increase
of nine cents, far below the twenty-nine cents it sought.[47]

Enmity among employees and management in the meatpacking
business after Taft-Hartley was not unusual, but conditions at Morrell-
Ottumwa stood out among its competitors. The Morrell and Foster
families paid the lowest wages among the five leading meat producers
for decades while constantly pushing for faster kill rates in its plants.
Unionized workers deeply resented management's power and looked
for any chance they could get to regain control of the pace of work.
The antagonism made for a company that, although its revenues grew
with the increased demand in the postwar era, saw its profit margins
sag due to management challenges. Between 1929 and 1953, Morrell's
sales tripled to $296,400,000 but its earnings increase amounted to
just .14 percent of sales. The industry average was not much better
at .80 percent earnings, but Morrell also distinguished itself for its unresolved labor issues. To the average investor, Morrell looked like a
company in constant turmoil with no end in sight. Eli disagreed.
To him, Morrell possessed endless potential in this new food economy
of convenience. Only its decrepit family leadership and failures to
imagine more efficient methods of processing meat had held Morrell
back from what could be a promising future.[48]

Eli's courtship of Morrell began with William Wallace "Mac"
McCallum, the first president not of Morrell family lineage. Having

started his career as an auditor at Price Waterhouse & Co, and then worked as a senior executive at Oscar Mayer, McCallum had accepted the top job at Morrell in 1953, knowing the first priority was to repair relations with the union and the Ottumwa community after two decades of labor tumult.[49] McCallum restored a degree of civic and employee pride in the company with "Morrell Days"—a week-long celebration of the company's presence in Ottumwa that established a symbolic truce between labor and management. His offer of stock options and bonuses lent some credibility to his efforts and encouraged members of the union and the town to support a "Buy Morrell" campaign. McCallum deescalated the battle over the pace of work by focusing, instead, on adjusting Morrell's purchase of livestock to meet real-time consumer demand rather than maintain constant volume at plants. He also shifted from a local to a national promotion strategy and pursued growth through acquisitions. Eli agreed with most of McCallum's moves, which had propelled Morrell past Cudahy and made it the fourth-largest meat producer in the United States, also known as "the Big Four" (Swift, Armour, Wilson, and now Morrell). Still, as long as the Morrell family owned the company, McCallum's interventions could go only so far. After hiring McCallum, A. C. Morrell had relinquished his direct control over operations in the United States but he remained at the helm of Morrell's British subsidiary and still held the controlling financial interest in the entire enterprise. By the spring of 1966, Eli sought to sever the American company from the Morrells for good by making a bid for ownership.[50]

Eli began his pursuit of Morrell through a mutual friend at Price Waterhouse, who arranged an introduction to McCallum over lunch at the luxurious Pierre Hotel in New York City, overlooking Central Park at Two East Sixty-First Street. The setting struck a dramatic contrast with the warehouse district in Chicago where Morrell had its headquarters; it was certainly worlds away from the killing floors in Ottumwa. Eli, sure he could not be the only outsider to spot Morrell's potential value, spared no expense. Despite its tumultuous history, the company had relatively little long-term debt and a low number of common outstanding shares—1,250,000—a figure well below the amount of authorized shares it could sell. This meant that managers had greater latitude to make changes at the company without shareholder interference. It also gave them the option to sell more stock later to retire debt or make improvements at the company. When the two men met at The Pierre in the spring of 1966, Morrell shares had a book value of $42 per share but were selling at half that amount. At that moment, Eli later told *Fortune,* Morrell "looked to me like a great opportunity for someone willing to work hard and apply some imagination."[51] Morrell's low stock price, he believed, reflected its reputation as a troubled company rather than a real threat of collapse. The industry as a whole faced challenges, he also knew, with meatpackers averaging a return on sales of a paltry 1.1 percent.[52] But his faith in taking up slack in operations, divesting underperforming lines of business, and expanding investments that catered to the modern consumer inured him to the gloomy predictions some observers were making. Eli, after all, had taken a bottle-cap company headed for the dustbin of history and made it into a winner. Why couldn't he do the same with Morrell?

McCallum arrived in New York having fielded several inquiries already and was aware of Morrell's appeal to the right buyer. During their lunch together, Eli secured McCallum's trust by being candid about his interest in reorganizing the production schedule, lauding him for his management under circumstances beyond his control, and committing to keep McCallum on as a member of his executive team. He promised that any move would not be "through the back door." Impressed with Eli, McCallum invited him to Iowa to see Morrell's main operations in Ottumwa.

Boarding the small, twin-engine plane to the rural city on the river, Eli must have sensed his own star rising. In many ways, life was good. Shirley had begun to get some attention from collectors for her paintings, while raising their two teenagers in conditions similar to her own upbringing on the Upper West Side. Judy shared her mother's love of art, and fifteen-year-old Leon had begun to show an interest in reading poetry and Jewish proverbs with his father, just as Eli had done with Benzion. Unlike that relationship, Eli sought to give Leon the space to make mistakes and his own decisions about his future rather than impose expectations on him. The best he could do for his son was to pursue an ethical life with purpose. Closing the deal on Morrell promised to give him a national platform to do that along with a nice payday that would support his family's endeavors.

On the ground in Ottumwa, Eli probably fought to avoid letting his eagerness to own the company color his assessment of its potential. By the numbers, the deal looked good. In his brief interactions with the residents of Ottumwa, who had no idea of the purpose of his visit, he saw deeply rooted, hardworking people whose dominant religion may have differed from his, but whose immigrant origins were familiar. The secret visit confirmed his suspicions about the company and inspired him to move forward.

In the months that followed, Eli hosted McCallum for several more lunches without aggressively pursuing the possibility of a takeover. The pace of the courtship built a "feeling of mutual confidence" and an air of expectancy that unnerved but also amused McCallum. "These free lunches are very nice," he finally told Eli in the fall of 1966, "but when are you going to do something?" The question was all Eli needed to start buying shares, starting with a small block on private offer. Over the following months, AMK made purchases on the open market, quietly enough that the price remained nearly steady at $22, until it held nearly 9 percent of Morrell's outstanding stock, a holding worth almost $3 million. Rather than cross the threshold of 10 percent, at which point AMK would have to disclose its intentions to the SEC, Eli appealed to McCallum to facilitate an official tour of Morrell's facilities.[53] He liked what he saw—first, because the "intrinsic values were there," but second, because, in keeping with his search for "backwardness," he was now certain that Morrell suffered from "poor organizational methods and systems." In particular, Morrell stood to make performance gains by centralizing activities like quality control and distribution management rather than running its twenty-seven meat-slaughtering and processing plants as if they were separate businesses. He received little pushback from McCallum, who agreed there were plenty of opportunities for trimming fat and reducing costs.[54]

Eli closed the deal at the end of 1966. AMK made a public tender offer at $27.50, looking to buy 200,000 shares to add to the 9 percent of Morrell's stock it had acquired before November. This was a premium of $2.50 over the current market price of $25. Response was high, and the company ended up buying 300,000 shares, giving it a total of one-third of Morrell's stock. Morrell's management had signaled that it would be comfortable with AMK's purchasing as many as 500,000 shares, but to do so would have required AMK to take on debt, which Eli was unwilling to do. "We had enough shares to put our people on the board," he later explained. "To buy shares beyond that would have been a luxury." Stopping at one-third ownership also helped to maintain the appearance of a "true marriage" of supposed equals essential for the pooling-of-interest method he was employing in the transaction, even though Morrell generated twenty times the sales of AMK. Members of the Morrell board comprised a good portion of the stockholders and enjoyed the benefit of not paying capital gains taxes on their newly improved shares, including McCallum, who was elected to the AMK board and remained part of the Morrell executive team, as Eli promised. On paper, AMK's per share earnings increased 109 percent, pushing its stock price from 12 to 50. To the business press, Eli's acquisition was viewed as the "coup of the year" and heralded the arrival of a new conglomerate wizard on the scene.

AMK claimed seven of the fifteen seats on Morrell's board with Eli overseeing a company that many referred to as "Morrell in disguise."

AMK's sales appeared to soar from $39,442,000 to $840,707,000, but this, too, was part of the illusion created by Eli's pooling-of-interest method. He exploited the rules set by the American Institute of Certified Public Accountants to add Morrell's $799,807,000 to AMK's annual sales of $40,900,000. As a result, Morrell disappeared from *Fortune's* top 500 companies (it had been number 99) while the new AMK entered the list for the first time at 101.[55]

More importantly, the artificial growth improved the capital structure of AMK and increased Eli's potential to use equity to acquire more companies. In mid-1967, Eli made an important move to expand the company by purchasing the other half of rubber and plastics manufacturer NRM, using common and convertible preferred shares now plentiful in the newly expanded AMK. AMK closed 1967 bigger and in a stronger position than it had been at the beginning of the year, even though it had shed many of the businesses that had accounted for its sales in 1966. By the end of 1967, AMK's assets totaled $142 million and its shareholders' equity $64 million. Not having to account for the difference in Morrell's value compared to AMK's eliminated "goodwill" moving forward reduced its long-term debt to $21 million, a paltry figure for a company its size. Eli quickly retired $30 million in debt and used its improved status to acquire the same amount in bank credit for any future purchases he chose to make. In total, Eli entered 1968 with $50 million available for his next purchase.[56]

This cherished position, of course, was a fiction accepted and endorsed by a business world caught up in the throes of merger mania. Some economists speculated about the unsustainability of the financial practices that led to this buying boom, but no one in the government dared call the bluff of a new managerial class that infused the American economy with a false sense of security. For all its productive capacity, US manufacturing had been more than a source of investor wealth; it had provided jobs and a livelihood to millions of workers that built the foundation of the most equitable economy in human history during the postwar era. The fetishization of metrics such as p / e ratios and a company's potential for further acquisitions threatened to lose sight of the fact that many people depended on manufacturing and the goods they produced to enjoy the good life as producers and consumers in American society. Eli may have come to business partly motivated by a desire to shape the postwar world in a way that would avoid the catastrophes that befell his country of origin, but he found that the equation for success could rest more on shareholder profit than the betterment of society. Like others, he took advantage of conditions originally designed to boost growth, probably telling himself that his playing the acquisitions game would lead to improvements that would be spread around to those whom his business ventures touched.

Eli enjoyed the hunt, but was also interested in the operations side of the businesses he acquired. A true believer in the miracles of management, he entered all acquisitions with the faith that he could improve performance by reducing costs, improving quality, and expanding sales. During the first six months of 1967, Eli zeroed in on areas of wasteful spending at Morrell and aggressively eliminated redundancies in the production process that had persisted for many years. The moves had immediate impact on the bottom line. Morrell turned a profit of $5,562,000 in its first year as a subsidiary of AMK, marking a real improvement on the loss it had generated in 1965 and its modest earnings in 1966.[57]

AMK's first annual report after the incorporation of Morrell in 1967 features a quote from the ancient Greek author of *The Iliad* and *The Odyssey*, Homer: "Never blush to tell an honest business."[58] Eli took pride in his successful courtship of Morrell and saw the amicable transition and profitable outcome as evidence of success. Addressing workers on the shop floor in Ottumwa, he tried to allay concerns about personnel changes after the merger by making a series of promises. He assured employees that "performance and capacity form the basis of each individual's opportunity" and that Morrell would strive to reward and promote those who demonstrated superior talent regardless of "race, color, or creed." He also addressed the sore subject of hiring new employees from outside the company to blunt the strength of the union. "Only where no well-qualified person can be found within the Company," he promised, "will selections be made from without."[59] In making this statement, he hoped to put distance between himself and the actions of previous CEOs who sought to curb the power of Local 1 by hiring rural folks who had no experience with unions and would be inclined to side with management in disputes.

Employees at Morrell withheld their judgment. Tired of management's endless criticism of waste at Ottumwa and constant threats of closure, workers at Ottumwa-Morrell looked past his promises and wondered whether his initial moves to shore up quality controls would be the first salvo in a new war over the size of the workforce and the cost of employee benefits or improvements that benefited both company and union. It would not be long before Local 1 got the answer.

3

PYRAMIDS

THE ACQUISITION OF MORRELL at the end of 1967 catapulted Eli into the public's awareness. By this time, he and Shirley had a country home in Westport, Connecticut, and were frequent travelers to Europe, where they visited museums and works of art that inspired Shirley's latest paintings. He had given Judy and Leon strong foundations by sending them first to Ramaz School, where Eli also served on the board of directors, and then on to middle school and high school at the elite, private Ethical Culture Fieldston School. In the fall of 1966, Judy started her freshman year at Barnard College, while Leon began his sophomore year at Fieldston. Eli took pride in affording his children an education that expanded their horizons and gave them the opportunities to pursue their own paths; he was careful not to exert the kind of pressure he had felt from his father from the earliest moments of his life. Until the deal for Morrell, Eli had lived a quiet life, having dinner most nights with his family and staying home on the weekends. Now, with the purchase of Morrell, he was responsible for a company with operations in Iowa, South Dakota, and numerous points west. He had taken the next step toward a position of global influence; now he had to live it.

In the early weeks of 1968, Eli boarded a small plane for Iowa to begin a tour of Morrell facilities as owner. In all, Morrell had twenty-seven plants stretching from the Midwest to the Pacific Coast, but the one that mattered most had always been Ottumwa. Although the company began in England and had its headquarters now in Chicago, Ottumwa had been the place of greatest consequence. The small city in southeast Iowa had served as the company headquarters for most of the twentieth century, and at least three generations of the Foster and Morrell family called it their home. Eli had secretly visited Ottumwa in the lead-up to tendering an offer. Now, he came announced, along with AMK's Morton Broffman and Robert Gallop, with the intent of assessing the long-term viability of the plant in relationship to the other twenty-six. Among those sites, Sioux Falls, South Dakota, loomed large, not only because of its similar scale to Ottumwa but because the workers there belonged to another union, the Amalgamated Meat Cutters and Butcher Workmen, with a less combative history than the United Packinghouse Workers of America (UPWA) Local P-1. Meat-packing had been among the earliest trades to unionize in the United States, and it was not uncommon for different unions to take root in one company at different plants. The AMCBW had been part of the American Federation of Labor (AFL), which had from the start championed skilled craft workers, while the Local P-1 had signed on with the Congress of Industrial Organizations (CIO), which had broken away from the AFL in the 1930s to focus on a more radical agenda of organizing mass-production workers. The two organizing bodies had merged back together in 1955 as the AFL-CIO, but unions under that umbrella retained their deep-seated differences. Born of the Depression and worker militancy, the union in Ottumwa still adopted a more aggressive posture toward management.

Eli had had very limited experience with unions up to this point. As a child in lower Manhattan, he would have noticed some of his father's reactions to the corruption of the *shohatim* union, but in his forays so far into business ownership, he had seen little of the management-labor conflict that characterized industrial production elsewhere. By acquiring Morrell, Eli became the employer of thousands of unionized employees, including 3,500 at Ottumwa alone, who would now give him his first real taste of dealing with organized labor.[1] Would he be up to the challenge?

By 1968, both unions had been worn down by constant struggles with management, but differences remained between the two, most notably in the greater willingness of workers in South Dakota to bow to pressure from Mac McCallum to speed up production and establish new quotas. As McCallum guided AMK executives through their tour of the Ottumwa plant floor in the winter of 1968, he no doubt made it clear that, of all the challenges they would confront, overcoming outdated labor contracts and stubborn union leaders to reduce losses would be the most difficult. Eli's visit carried the weight of an audit from the moment he set foot in the plant. During his courtship of Morrell, he had been pleased to see inefficiencies because they suggested that basic applications of modern management discipline could produce substantial performance gains. Now, as owner, progress depended on going after these cumbersome and antiquated facilities and arcane labor agreements. He especially disliked the way union contracts divided plants into a honeycomb of departments, each with its own seniority-ranked team and strict rules against asking union workers to pitch in on tasks outside the narrow bounds of the jobs they were hired to perform.

As he walked the plant floor in Ottumwa, he imagined a more integrated system with less specialization among employees that would be more productive and increase profits for Morrell. He began to work out in his mind how Morrell might reorient everything from its product mix to its production planning to be more responsive to the needs of its trade customers and the consumers they served. This was a perspective on efficiency he had gained when he studied A&P and the

grocery industry's operations in the early 1960s. With some managerial imagination, the meatpacking company he now controlled could
begin to explore prepackaging cuts of meat at the plant and marketing
luxury and convenience items that catered to a public on the go.

Upon his return to New York, Eli huddled with his managers at
AMK's office on 122 East Forty-Second Street to devise a five-year plan
to double Morrell's value. Among the priorities he set, two labor-related
goals were to eliminate redundant positions and to free Morrell's management from constantly negotiating with unions over production
targets and the division of labor. Eli welcomed McCallum to the AMK
leadership team in New York; they would assign new leaders in Chicago to implement the needed changes at Morrell. One of these men
was an old nemesis of the union, Harry E. Hansel Jr., who had worked
at Morrell since the 1940s. Hansel had a reputation as a hard-nosed
taskmaster who pushed the pace of work on the plant floor in
Ottumwa. He was an engineering-minded manager in the mold of
Frederick Winslow Taylor, the Progressive Era mechanical engineer who
pioneered the field of "scientific management," with its time-motion
studies and elimination of wasted effort. Taylor's principles for boosting
productivity on a shop floor included redesigning work processes and
training employees to work more efficiently. Hansel, like Taylor (and
Henry Ford), believed that in a plant producing a high volume of
output, jobs that had called for skilled craftsmen could be broken into
discrete tasks that any worker could be trained to perform. As the head
of the industrial relations department under McCallum, Hansel had
also persuaded union leaders that it would serve everyone well to institute "gain time" arrangements by which, if laborers finished work
in less than the standard time mandated by the union contract, they
themselves benefited from the time gained: it translated into time off.
As the workforce eagerly responded to this incentive to step up the
pace of their work, the union realized the downside: the sustained
faster performance could now be used as evidence by a management team pressuring union negotiators to agree on new standards

for baseline productivity. The union had grown to despise Hansel, and chased him off to company headquarters in Chicago in 1955 with strikes and work slowdowns.[2] AMK's decision to return Hansel to Ottumwa as the primary site manager signaled its intent to get tough with the union.

Eli's direct engagement with unions had been very limited, but his father's experiences with the *shohatim* union might have primed him to be on guard in any encounters with organized labor. Local P-1 chief steward Virgil Bankson and president Jesse Merrill had not been unethical in their leadership, but they did exhibit a tendency to tack backwards to past agreements rather than look forward to possible new arrangements—changes that might better serve workers while helping the company to grow. Eli might have assumed that, as long as decent pay and good benefits were in place, these men would be receptive to ideas for how labor and owners would mutually benefit from investments in modernization, but if he did, that belief was naive. The conflict he walked into at Morrell had been simmering for decades and would not be resolved by asking employees to trust a new owner. In an act of brinksmanship, McCallum had threatened to close the plant in Ottumwa in 1961 to get out of labor contracts he saw as the chief reason it operated in the red. He had relented when the union backed off from some of its demands. In 1964, however, with the plant still not profitable, McCallum had issued the warning again, and this time relocated executive office staff to Chicago. Ottumwa, no longer home to headquarters but relegated to the status of just another production facility, would feel more pressure to pull its own weight.[3]

Eli disliked the acrimony but understood McCallum's position. In his opinion, Bankson and Merrill disregarded the company's imperative to generate profits. Indeed, some of the positions they took were unpopular even with their own members. He would surely have heard, for example, of the history of sexism at the plant in which union men, bitter about the incursions women had made into their workplace during the war, blatantly used tactics to force them out. The union's fissure along gender lines was laid bare after a strategic decision by McCallum to phase out bacon slicing—the part of the plant with the most women workers. Because the seniority privileges guaranteed by the union applied at the departmental rather than the plant-wide level, women who had worked many years at the plant had no advantage over less experienced men as they sought positions in other departments. Union leadership showed little sympathy for the women. Merrill, for example, later explained, "I've always been a believer that if the man's head of the house he should have the job." Women employees increased their attendance at union meetings to protest such discrimination but had difficulty changing the attitudes and policies of a male-dominated workplace and union.[4]

The distrust between management and the union deepened in 1966 as Harry Hansel was perceived to be using the women's grievances to chip away at labor solidarity. Representing headquarters, he pushed against the discrimination, but some women employees questioned Hansel's motives just as much as they distrusted the male coworkers so actively threatening their continued employment at Morrell. Management, they knew, was mainly interested in having labor costs reduced. As Ethel Jerred, a chief steward in the sliced bacon department, would later put it, "the company would prefer to hire new people from outside town rather than move women with as much as twenty-eight years seniority" into new positions.[5] Hansel played a critical role in these decisions. Ultimately, in April 1966, twenty-one women took control of their own fate by filing a lawsuit against the local union, the national union, and Morrell, on the grounds that all had violated federal law against sex discrimination as set forth in Title VII of the 1964 Civil Rights Act. A federal district court judge dismissed the case against the union on a technicality and gave Morrell time to reach a settlement with the plaintiffs. In 1968, the court ruled that Morrell was now in compliance with Title VII, and the case was closed. It had been many months of disputes that had extended the personal animus between Hansel and the male-dominated union leadership, and now Hansel was back at Ottumwa.

To head up Morrell as its new president and CEO, AMK's board appointed Broffman, already an executive vice president and board member of AMK. Not only a veteran business executive but a Harvard PhD who had taught economics at Rutgers and Harvard, Broffman shared Eli's commitment to modernizing production methods and implementing "tough-minded management." The label captured their strong belief that, whatever operational preferences and protocols might be set by a labor union, it was management's obligation in any business to pursue efficiencies to gain a competitive edge. During their joint visits to Ottumwa and other plants, they had noted that managers in each of Morrell's twenty-seven plants organized their production schedules according to the supply of inputs—that is, the current availability of livestock and local labor capacity, which was dictated by the unions. After returning to New York, they encouraged Morrell executives to stop regarding plants as "individual profit centers" and start managing them as components in a system of production that spanned the entire nation—and that should collectively be driven by market demand. To support this more systemic management, Broffman created three computer centers to coordinate efficient deliveries from production plants to stores within the requisite seventy-two hours. Broffman as president of Morrell played the critical role in instituting this new system and other operational improvements, and in explaining the changes to outside observers as well as employees.[6] Both he and Eli believed that the profits achieved by a more efficient Morrell would justify these changes, and that union leaders would see the wisdom of them once they saw the benefits flowing to owners, shareholders, and employees. Broffman explained to reporters, for example, that meatpackers now sold only three percent of their total "red meat" (beef) production in frozen form but, given the quality improvements possible with new technology, a company willing to adjust its marketing strategy could greatly increase these sales. To achieve that potential, Morrell would package smaller, freezable portions for grocery stores across the country, and the profit margins on these convenient products would be greater.

The business press spent little time following up on the effect of the changes and more time reporting what investment Eli seemed to be turning to next. As with most coverage of mergers during this period, they assumed Morrell's absorption into AMK was for the better and passed along the numbers management emphasized to advance a narrative they wanted to convey to the public. *Fortune* gushed that AMK increased its annual sales from $39,442,000 to $840,707,000, the single biggest jump for any business from 1966 to 1967. Earnings had jumped from $3,020,000 to $7,434,000. Yet the reporter also noted that, without Morrell's results, AMK had earned just $1,872,000 in 1967, and the combined results for the year reflected an acquisition of Morrell that had only been finalized on December 31, 1967. It had been a story of, as the *Fortune* article was titled, "The Sardine That Became a Whale." Most of the earnings gain had come through managerial actions overseen by McCallum. No matter. *Fortune* attributed Morrell's income boost to "suggestions put forward by the new directors"—that is, Eli and his team, who had taken seats on the Morrell board early in the year. Readers could easily take away the impression that AMK's 3,457 percent increase over its 1966 earnings was due to Eli's genius. Shareholders enjoyed immediate gains. For example, whether investors held Morrell or AMK shares on December 31, 1966, they made money, as the former went from $44 to $50 per share, and the latter rose from $12 to $50.[7] The increased value, a mirage in some respect, reflected the market's belief in Eli's promise to increase the fortunes of the two companies combined—and the appeal to sellers of having no capital gains taxes to be paid. Both the new management team and the company's shareholders indulged in the fantasy that it magically became more valuable just by changing hands.

The new rules for acquiring companies in the 1960s fueled this fantasy. Prior to the mid-1960s, a company would draw on its cash reserves or borrow money from a bank to make an acquisition. In theory, the now-larger company would pay off that debt and then some with its greater income. By the mid-1960s, policies of the Kennedy and

Johnson administrations designed to spur economic growth, gave investors like Eli the ability to instead use equity financing, raising the capital needed for a purchase by selling shares of the acquiring company. When share values were inflated by one acquisition, the company had more ability to use equity financing to make further purchases. As always, share prices reflected expectations of future growth, but this so-far unfulfilled promise of profit allowed a company to put off paying the difference in the value of the two companies at the time of the merger (also known as goodwill) in the way that it would have to pay off a debt to a lender. In most cases, whether a CEO could make good on his promise to improve earnings or eliminate goodwill took more than eighteen months to evaluate. Conglomerate builders, intoxicated by the belief that they could squeeze more performance out of any company, sought their next conquests before judgment could be rendered on the validity of their prior promises to increase earnings. The press fueled this behavior by treating these increasingly rich CEOs like celebrities and speculating on their next moves rather than waiting to see if they could back up their words.

Journalists added Eli to their "watch list" of CEOs on the move, even though he kept a low profile and lived a relatively uneventful life. "If your company acquires another that is 20 times its size," the *New York Times* asked in October of 1968, "what do you do for an encore?" Not a year had passed since the acquisition of Morrell, yet the newspapers felt it necessary to describe Eli to the public and ponder what he would do with equity from a company now doing annual sales of $840 million. Business correspondents enjoyed characterizing Eli as a quiet, mild-mannered egghead who wore the same black suit every day and walked the 1.7 miles from his New York City apartment at 799 Park Avenue to his office in midtown Manhattan. The sight of him striding through the city, briefcase in hand, contrasted sharply with other moguls like Bluhdorn, who drew attention for their excesses. They all played a part in an evolving drama full of characters partly constructed by business journalists. Whereas Bluhdorn came across as eccentric and "nouveau riche," Eli was the hardworking immigrant who made good and took nothing for granted. *Fortune* described him as a man obsessed with "systems" while the *New York Times* delighted in describing him as "a quiet, restrained executive whose voice rarely rises in the course of the conversation." Comments by colleagues tended to confirm these impressions. One senior partner described him as "a pretty sober fellow," while another asserted "he's got unusual stability and can't be rocked."[8] No doubt, such characterizations rang true to those who knew Eli but the effect of the reporting was to foster cults of personality around the various men animating the merger mania of the era. In this world, Eli was the measured investor whose life as a former rabbi and self-discipline as an observant Jew conveyed the idea that one should be confident in his decisions.

Given AMK's value after the addition of Morrell, and the expectation of new acquisitions raised by observers, Eli may have felt compelled to stay on the hunt for new companies to purchase. He had confidence in the team he assembled at Morrell, trusting Broffman, Hansel, and other experienced managers to oversee day-to-day operations and introduce new technologies. "After the [Morrell] coup," *Fortune* observed, "an operating man would have immediately turned his attention to tightening up Morrell and fitting it into the parent structure." Eli belonged squarely in the category of dealmaker, content to "leave problems like that to others." *Fortune* concluded that "the operations men may come back into favor another day . . . but in the short run, Eli Black will be riding high as he looks for high-yield investments for his new bundle of assets."[9] That search briefly included a run at the Great American Holding Corporation, an insurance company whose management, in a desperate attempt to avoid takeover by another conglomerate, National General Corporation, encouraged Eli to make the acquisition instead. Unfortunately, before the merger could be consummated, National General managed to buy up 75 percent of Great American's stock, and the opportunity slipped from Eli's grasp. The experience had been a valuable one for Eli. The hostile takeover of the Great American Holding Corporation had taken a course, as *Variety* put it, "unprecedented in the history of American business." Rather than shrug it off as a fluke event, Eli learned from it how not to be beaten again.[10] Eli's modest celebrity and aggressive posture meant that opportunities now found him. In the era of mergers, large holders of stocks wielded influence that could shape the destiny of a company.[11] Individual shareholders rarely amassed such power, but investment brokers did, including those that ostensibly supported the governing regime. A month after the Great American Holding deal fell through, William Donaldson of the brokerage firm Donaldson, Lufkin & Jenrette invited Eli to his office one September morning to let him know that United Fruit had 733,200 shares for purchase. He believed AMK might be the ideal buyer. Donaldson did so on behalf of shareholders who believed that United Fruit's CEO, John Fox, was not making good use of its cash reserves to raise the value of its stock. United Fruit shareholders, it turned out, were not unlike others who consumed news stories of miraculous jumps in the price of shares after new acquisitions. Some had shared with Donaldson their frustration that management had not been more aggressive in pursuing the purchase of additional companies, given the fact that United Fruit had sufficient cash to do so without incurring debt or issuing new shares. In fact, Fox had participated in the merger mania to some extent with the acquisitions of the Baskin-Robbins and A&W retail chains, but these additions failed to appease them or Donaldson. They saw the presence of nearly $100 million in cash and the untapped potential to borrow as much as $300 million as signs of failure and a reason to oust him.

The offer intrigued Eli although he knew United Fruit came with considerable baggage. The company had its origins in an audacious imperial adventure that began in the late nineteenth century. In the 1870s, a colorful railroad tycoon named Henry Meiggs contracted with Costa Rican President Tomás Guardia Gutiérrez to build a railroad from the capital of San José on the Central Plateau to the Port of Límon on the eastern coast, a project that would dramatically reduce the time it took to move coffee grown on local *fincas* to London cafés. Meiggs placed his Brooklyn-born nephew, Minor Cooper Keith, in charge of the rail line spur running from Límon but things did not go well. Constant rains, rugged mountainous terrain, dense forests, and an abundance of virus-carrying mosquitoes made it difficult to secure labor and the project dragged out years longer than expected. At one point, Keith conspired with New Orleans officials to release prisoners if they agreed to be hired by him, allowing the city to empty its jails and send the convicts far away. Of the seven hundred men he "recruited," only twenty-five survived after three years of halting progress on the railroad. Keith drew many other immigrants to Costa Rica including Chinese, Italians, and Jamaicans. Black Caribbean workers previously exposed to yellow fever, malaria, and other tropical diseases endured the challenging conditions far better than others. Approximately four thousand workers had lost their lives by the time the railroad was complete in 1890.

Meiggs died in 1877, but Keith kept the project going. When Costa Rica ran out of funds midway through the project, Keith promised to complete it for free in exchange for duty-free use of the Port of Límon and ownership of approximately 800,000 acres bordering the rail line. Guardia had no option but to accept the deal. To finance the remainder of the railroad, Keith planted the *musa acuminata,* bananas, and sold the exotic fruit to distributors in New Orleans. In 1899, Keith merged his thriving banana business with Boston Fruit, which operated mainly in Jamaica, to create United Fruit Company, the largest agricultural enterprise in the world. Owning a quarter million acres in five Latin American countries, Costa Rica, Cuba, Honduras, Santo Domingo (Haiti and the Dominican Republic), Colombia, and Jamaica, the company fell into the exploitative habits of a monopoly, abusing its power to dominate transportation networks, eliminate competition, and dictate substandard wages and working conditions. It not only suppressed labor unions but, on more than one occasion, installed the government it wanted in countries where it operated. In Colombia, when thirty-two thousand workers organized for basic rights, asking for health care and more humane living conditions, United Fruit and the US State Department conspired with a faction within the Colombian government to crush what they interpreted as a communist uprising. On Sunday, December 6, 1928, when three thousand striking workers filled the square in Cienega, Colombia, and defied the order by their provincial leader, a military general, to disperse, the Colombian army opened fire and killed many. Subsequent United Fruit executives pushed the notion further that demands by banana worker should be linked with the specter of communism. Samuel Zemurray, for example, spent two decades at the company's helm, from 1932 to 1951, and in that time forged a strong working relationship with the US State Department. His efforts paid dividends for the company in 1954, when the CIA conspired with United Fruit and Latin American opportunists to overthrow the democratically elected government of Jacobo Árbenz in Guatemala. What was Árbenz's crime? He had expropriated land owned by United Fruit to institute a peasant farmer program.[12]

By the time Eli made a play for United Fruit in the late 1960s, its dark legacy had been cemented in the views of many across the hemisphere. The company's "sins," *Fortune* reported, were so numerous "that it would hold even the prurient eye of a browser in a Times Square bookstore." Those "evil days" had earned it the moniker of *el pulpo,* the octopus, a label reserved for a select few companies that extended their reach deep into a host nation to benefit their shareholders. United Fruit's CEO since 1960, John Fox, had done much to shed this ignominy by paying the highest agricultural wages in Latin America and building schools, hospitals, houses, and laboratories throughout Central and South America in the early 1960s—especially in Honduras, where the company maintained its regional headquarters in La Lima. Other changes had been forced upon it by the US government, which had brought an antitrust suit against the company in the 1950s and won a judgment against the company compelling it to divest assets for the

Eli Black (center) touring United Fruit's floriculture project in Campin, Honduras, 1972. *Walter P. Reuther Library, Archives of Labor and Urban Affairs, Wayne State University.*

creation of a new competitor. By the time Donaldson appealed to Eli to buy shares in United Fruit, the resolution of the case was still pending, but seemed inevitable. Even with these changes, United Fruit still had to live down its reputation, well earned in the first five decades of its existence, as "a dirty young man full of *macho.*"[13]

United Fruit's outsized position in the marketplace and its accumulated wealth made a takeover worth considering for Eli. Besides the sizeable assets that could be leveraged to make acquisitions, as current shareholders wished, United Fruit possessed a brand in "Chiquita" that was known throughout the western hemisphere and associated with the most popular fruit in the United States. Eli liked the idea of trying to wring more profit from staple foods through branding, as A&P had done with its coffee, and Oscar Mayer with hot dogs. While United Fruit's centrality to the economies of its Latin American hosts—and manipulation of their governments—had inspired the epithet "banana republics," Chiquita's successful marketing had put a brighter face on a product consumers might associate with US corporate colonialism. As singers imitating Brazilian film star Carmen Miranda sang the delights of Chiquita bananas in company commercials, United Fruit's unsavory history receded to the background of the public imagination. The opportunity to take control of a product and a brand possessing such influence might have struck Eli as his best chance to build a major, multinational corporation focused on food. As with Morrell and AMK before it, Eli saw United Fruit's past blunders and backward management as evidence of a company ready for a bold program of modern technology and managerial techniques.

Eli would also have had a prominent model of a leader capable of combining modern industrial management and the pursuit of large-scale social benefit in David Eli Lilienthal, then at the height of his fame based on his high-profile leadership of the Tennessee Valley Authority, then the US Atomic Energy Commission. Lilienthal was born an American, in Morton, Illinois, on July 8, 1899, but his parents' Austro-Hungarian immigrant origins and his Jewish faith would have made him a familiar figure to Eli. In his long tenure at the TVA, he had led the ambitious Depression-era project undertaken as part of the New Deal to bring hydroelectric power and regional economic development to the rural areas of the Tennessee River Basin. If, in his days taking classes at Columbia University, Eli had been intrigued by Adolph Berle's theories and advocacy of government intervention in the economy, the public corporation structure of the TVA offered him a view of them already in action. During the 1930s, the TVA arose as a controversial bulwark against the private business that would otherwise invest in extracting the region's natural resources, and built the capacity—at the behest of the federal government—to supply electrical power and control its distribution from the Midwest to the mid-Atlantic. Like Berle, Lilienthal believed a harmonious hybrid of public and private enterprise could be established and maintained to do most for the betterment of society. TVA had to generate sufficient revenues to cover its costs, just as a for-profit enterprise would, but with no private shareholders it was under no pressure to distribute a high return on investment. Instead, what Lilienthal called "the people's dividend" was TVA's impact on the lives of average Americans, who benefited from the many private businesses that flourished as a consequence of this massive investment in infrastructure.[14]

The United States as a whole realized more dividends from Lilienthal's work when it declared war against the Axis powers in 1941 and needed to ramp up industrial production of munitions, aircraft, and other materials. TVA rose to the occasion, including by boosting its production to the point of being "the ninth largest producer of power in the Western Hemisphere."[15] In 1946, Lilienthal left the TVA to accept President Truman's appointment as the first chairman of the new Atomic Energy Commission. In his confirmation hearings, an old nemesis, Tennessee Democratic Senator Kenneth McKellar, hinted that his Eastern European background might predispose him to communist sympathies. Lilienthal responded forcefully, agreeing that no such sympathies should be tolerated but cautioning that "while we seek fervently to ferret out the subversive and anti-democratic forces in the country, we do not at the same time, by hysteria, by resort to innuendo and smears, and other unfortunate tactics, besmirch the cause that we believe in."[16] His performance in the role would later see him hauled before a congressional committee to answer harsh criticism by Republicans that the Commission's mounting expenditures were evidence of "incredible mismanagement."[17] The Democrat-dominated committee cleared him of any malfeasance but, in February 1950, he resigned his post and left the federal government's employ to embark on a new phase of his career, applying what he had learned about regional economic development as a private consultant.

Eli would have been aware of Lilienthal's leadership of the TVA and Atomic Energy Commission, but may have taken greater inspiration from this last stage of Lilienthal's working life. After a brief stint consulting to Lazard Freres & Co., a leading investment bank involved in many postwar rebuilding projects around the world, Lilienthal founded his own consultancy, Development and Resources Corp., to advise major public works projects overseas. Throwing himself into projects with potentially transformative impact on societies, he knew that "management requires a humanistic outlook on life rather than merely mastery of technique." In his view, the "manager-leader of the future should combine in one personality the robust, realistic quality of the man of action with the insight of the artist, the religious leader, the poet, who explain man to himself."[18]

Insights like these might have resonated with an Eli hoping to create a balance between intellectual and spiritual pursuits, as his mentors Rabbi Lookstein and Rabbi Belkin taught.[19] Lilienthal, it seemed, had not only succeeded in discovering a productive and fulfilling mix but had become an advocate for it as a way of life.[20] He saw an important role for himself and his colleagues in building foundations to facilitate more private development—investments by private enterprises in infrastructure and other forms of economic capacity building. In their first consulting assignment, Lilienthal's group advised a project in Colombia's Cauca River Valley similar to the TVA, sharing their expertise not only in water reclamation and hydroelectric power generation, but in preparing local communities to take advantage of the new opportunities presented by the change.

To Eli, Lilienthal's consulting projects represented the realization of his ambitions and the ideals articulated in President John F. Kennedy's Alliance for Progress. Kennedy's principles were twofold: provide economic development throughout the region as an alternative to Communism while avoiding the exploitative practices of past US businesses in the hemisphere. Lilienthal strove to be a leader in this public-private partnership by using D&R to improve the infrastructure of his host country while turning a profit. When considering Donaldson's offer to buy United Fruit stock, Eli recalled Lilienthal's assessment of the company up to that point: It had, he said, practiced a "form of colonialism" that was "ethically wrong and self-defeating" for the company and the United States. Here, Lilienthal's thinking departed from Berle, who, as an aggressive anti-communist in the 1950s, advocated covert military action in Latin America to the benefit of US corporations like United Fruit. Berle lived to regret the CIA overthrow of Árbenz in Guatemala at the behest of United Fruit executives, asserting that "We eliminated a Communist regime—at the expense of having antagonized half the hemisphere."[21] Berle's dubious contention that Árbenz's communism had justified the coup notwithstanding, both could agree that undermining the sovereignty of a Central American neighbor did not age well.

Private companies, some of them Lilienthal's clients, who hoped to do business in Latin America after such foreign policy blunders embraced Kennedy's new approach in the region. "The private corporate investor," Lilienthal asserted, "must get rid of its reputation as an exploiter of resources." He added, "It must come in as a good citizen and identify its own goals with those of the community, state or nation in which it operates."[22] In Colombia and Iran, Lilienthal developed hydroelectric dams and irrigation projects with heads of state to address what he identified as one of the two great challenges of his time: world hunger along with the escalation of military conflict. Like Eli, Lilienthal saw farming as a business with rich potential if managed properly, and not as an enterprise paid for primarily by an assortment of government agencies. He eschewed calls for land reform and the proliferation of small farms in favor of large commercial enterprises served by private-public partnerships that delivered natural resources to its clients. His faith in the power of the administrative state to control nature and society placed him in the pantheon of what political scientist Jim Scott calls "high modernist" thinkers.[23] Men like Lilienthal saw management as a salve for the world's ills, identifying what people want and building a complex structure to deliver it to them. By 1968, Lilienthal regretted the vulgarities of capitalism in a previous generation but believed that men of conscience and science could make the system work to the advantage of everyone. As "the manager-leader" of the future, he exported his vision of large-scale commercial farms to Latin America and the Middle East to conquer hunger, redeem corporate America, and defeat communism.

Probably even more than Lilienthal, Eli believed that business leaders should take more responsibility for providing forms of social support that would otherwise be administered by a bureaucratic government. This was the message of a brief article Eli published in the pages of the *Harvard Business Review* at a moment when the Nixon administration's plans to dismantle many social welfare programs created, in his view, "an opportunity to regain the loyalty of employees and the esteem of the public." Equally, with regard to the other countries hosting his business, he might have believed that "enlightened self-interest must now be identified with the public good" and that "socially conscious programs, designed to improve the quality of living of employees, are indeed the legitimate concern of business."[24] In United Fruit, he had the power to seize this opportunity and pursue it with vigor.

Perhaps taking a lesson from the failed Great American Holding Corporation to act without delay, Eli skipped the courtship of his target and went straight to purchasing United Fruit stock. Within three days of Donaldson's invitation, he phoned his bank, Morgan Guaranty Trust, to borrow $35 million for the acquisition. On September 24, 1968, the third-largest trade ever on the floor of the New York Stock Exchange scrolled across its ticker, although the identity of the buyer was not revealed. Only Donaldson, Eli, and his bank knew that AMK had just purchased nearly ten percent of United Fruit for approximately $41 million. Within another three months, Eli sealed the deal. In an interview about the acquisition, he noted that the intense interest by others in United Fruit did not afford him the luxury of courting John Fox the way he had Mac McCallum at Morrell. The sure-footed Eli won over Fox anyway with a gentle but confident demeanor and a commitment to incorporating United Fruit's executive team in the new company. "Black had been saying right along that the [other companies] would drop out, and he was right," Fox told *Fortune,* adding that "I finally came around to his view that our companies would do well together." It was Eli's reputation as an asset manager rather than an "operating man," the magazine noted, that made him an especially good fit for United Fruit.[25]

Eli's conquest of United Fruit may have impressed his conglomerate-building peers, but it raised concerns among union leaders at Morrell that their company had been leveraged to complete the deal. They anticipated that Eli would now look to cut jobs to recover from the high cost of the merger, and perhaps worse, renegotiate hard-fought labor contracts that protected the rank and file. Representing approximately five thousand employees, Local P-1 of the AMCBW leveled a trenchant critique of the merger in a newsletter to its members, taking note of the "dizzy pyramid of bank loans, bonded indebtedness, and printing-press stock" that now undergirded their jobs. The union observed that AMK issued $317 million in convertible debentures, or IOUs, to secure United Fruit. They also noted that AMK offered United Fruit shareholders company stock at the price of $46 per share, well above its $34 price prior to the merger. The union assumed that AMK would now make up the $12 difference by squeezing more productivity out of Morrell workers, or worse, eliminating jobs that management regarded as redundant. As the union saw it, "the AMK Corp has, therefore, obligated itself to pay off a $300 million debt at 5½ percent interest."[26]

The numbers and financial instruments Eli used to complete the merger may have been beyond the grasp of most employees, but the immediate consequences of it were not. During the merger frenzy of the late 1960s, most workers witnessed an erosion of benefits and job security even as jet-setting CEOs claimed that the changes had been for the better. While Eli avoided the excesses of his peers, his consolidation of departments and expectations of increased productivity at Morrell in the first year of AMK's control conformed to the formula employed by this new group of managers. The union provided an explanation to changes that had already been felt on the shop floor, especially in Ottumwa where workers felt the effects of Hansel's influence. In a letter to Eli that they shared with the rank-and-file, union leaders observed that AMK would have to exceed earnings well above what Morrell or United Fruit had accomplished over the previous decade to achieve the level of profit necessary to cover the cost of buying United Fruit. "Orders to sweat super-profits out of the Morrell workers have already brought a ten percent cut in the work force at the plant in Ottumwa, Ia., and with it a demand for more production from less workers," they wrote. Spoiling for a fight, the union warned, "Morrell workers are willing to pull their own weight, but they are not going to be browbeaten or frightened into building an empire to rival the ancient Pharaohs of Egypt for the benefit of AMK."[27]

Eli paid no attention to these criticisms. He regarded the increased profitability of AMK in the first year after the incorporation of Morrell as evidence of his success, even though the company's gains resulted from cuts rather than increased sales. Many of the cost-saving measures, moreover, had begun under McCallum. Chief executive since 1953, McCallum had presided over some bad years, but had recently taken Morrell from a loss of $345,000 in 1965 to a modest profit of $696,000 in 1966. In 1967, Morrell's profits climbed to $5,500,000; the following year, it did even better as an AMK subsidiary. Efficiency gains both before and after the merger were boosted by the elimination of jobs, although Eli accelerated the process. Business journalists wrote glowingly about Morrell's supposed transformation, reinforcing the narrative of Eli's genius. Eli was only too happy to claim some credit. "Proper marketing and controls work in every business," he told *Fortune,* and, "the meatpacking industry is not exempt."[28]

The ups and downs of the meat business should have given Eli pause. In previous decades, meatpackers had been at the mercy of variable livestock supplies, prompting companies to invest in rural plant construction to be nearer the animals as they became ready for slaughter. Morrell's first move from Chicago to Ottumwa in 1887 was guided by this same logic. By the mid-twentieth century, decentralized production in rural plants across the midsection of America required shop managers to coordinate their schedules with a complex national network that delivered meat to customers across the nation.[29] These sites of production fostered varying work cultures and union agreements, even within a single company, that made the management of meatpacking a balance of farmer schedules, union contracts, consumer demands, and shareholder expectations. Although meat sales had come to dominate the grocery list of most Americans, meatpackers struggled to come up with a profitable operating model.

Eli would have seen the potential pitfalls with a cursory study of the historic "Big Four" meat producers. In the 1950s, Cudahy—the company Morrell passed on its way to becoming the fourth-largest meat company in the United States—spent $6 million to raise the productivity of a large plant in Omaha, Nebraska. The company lost hundreds of thousands of dollars annually after the investment, forcing management to sell off the huge complex to its competitor, Armour, for $2,300,000 in 1967. Its quick reversal of fortune following the addition of facilities should have shown Eli that the cost of such growth must be recouped soon after the investment. Cudahy, also a producer of pharmaceuticals, focused its meat industry operations solely on dry sausage and was caught and passed by Morrell that year. Meanwhile, the biggest of the meatpackers, Swift, struggled to rationalize its sprawling system of meatpacking plants and distribution centers scattered around the country, ultimately deciding to shutter 250 of them. The write-off of these assets meant that, in 1968, the company lost $42 million on sales of $2.8 billion. Even without that hit to the income statement, Swift would have achieved a mere 0.5 percent return on sales. Asked by a reporter about the write-off, Arnold La Force, a member of Swift's board, admitted, "we took a real bath." He and his fellow directors hoped the changes implemented by Swift's new CEO, Robert W. Reneker, would turn the company around by investing in product development and branding and divesting from underperforming businesses. Swift would "eliminate losing businesses," Reneker said, "either by being astute enough to turn them into a profit, or by being realistic enough to discontinue them."[30] Regardless of their position in the rankings, leaders of the industry struggled to modernize operations and fend off the aggressive conglomerates and hungry competitors that wanted to devour them.

While Eli and Broffman would have learned from the cautionary tales of Cudahy and Swift's recent history they were probably more inspired by the shining example of a new kid on the block, Iowa Beef Packers. IBP, as it came to be known, achieved early success by revising everything from how cattle were purchased to how meat was preserved and shipped to customers. Formed in 1960 by Currier Holman and Andy Anderson, IBP fully embraced efficiency models of production that cut out middlemen and incorporated automation. Holman had worked for Armour and Swift, learning from the giants of the meatpacking business before striking out on his own. Anderson, who had started his work life in one of Henry Kaiser's famous shipyards, building World War II liberty ships, applied his engineering skills to meatpacking. Together, they revolutionized the dissembling of animals into meat and its preparation and packaging into more market-ready products. Their innovation started with the purchase of cows direct from farmers rather than at terminal markets where jobbers controlled the wholesale price. This approach allowed IBP to influence 85 percent of the flow of cattle on an hour-by-hour basis. The constant demand for beef in a healthy consumer economy freed IBP from worrying about swings in the market that might leave them saddled with too much beef. The constant movement of animals to their abattoir pens reduced the typical loss of weight or injury that came with herds of newly purchased cows waiting for slaughter. "We know our profit or loss on every head," bragged Holman. Cutting out the middleman allowed Holman and Anderson's cattle buyers to offer "grade-yield" pricing to their suppliers, paying higher prices for better animals rated on an individual basis. The range of price points constituted a powerful form of feedback to cattle producers, training them to raise cows in ways that would yield better beef.[31]

On the production side, IBP dramatically altered the process of slaughtering animals by introducing automation to its plants and re- ducing its labor costs. In two plants in particular, the innovations highlighted IBP's differences from a major competitor, Armour. After IBP acquired through a 1967 merger a pork plant it did not need, it made a deal with Armour to swap that asset for two recently built beef-processing plants in rural areas, one in Nebraska and another in Kansas. Armour had spent $2 million each to construct these small, modern plants in 1963, but had not yet managed to operate them profitably. Now in Anderson's hands, the plants were substantially enlarged and redesigned for greater efficiency. For example, he elimi- nated a traditional feature of slaughterhouses—the "gut buggies" used by workers to remove offal and other by-products of the butchering process—and replaced them with moving belts. He devised machinery to remove the cloth shrouds used to retain moisture in the carcass after slaughter and before butchery. For preservation of beef, Anderson in- vented a new refrigeration system that minimized the loss of moisture in hanging carcasses. These and other improvements reduced the plants' dependence on labor while increasing the number of animals they handled per week from the 2,500 Armour had been processing to 8,000. IBP's redesigned approach catapulted it into *Fortune's* 500 largest US corporations and made it the company to watch within the meatpacking industry.[32]

IBP's innovations in the packaging and shipping of meat were its greatest contributions to the industry and the approaches Eli most wanted Morrell to emulate. Holman and Anderson questioned the industry convention of selling dressed carcasses, or hanging beef, to grocery stores, where skilled butchers then produced fresh cuts for customers. Instead, IBP broke the carcass down into smaller cuts that could be vacuum-packed and shipped more easily and efficiently. These changes reduced dependency on specialized couriers who drove sides of beef from plant to grocer using a network of rails, hooks, and pulleys located in the processing plants, trucks, and back rooms of grocery stores. IBP also began to circumvent the counter butcher at the point of sale by hiring several "knife men" to fabricate steaks and other popular cuts on an industrial scale at the slaughterhouse. Consumer purchases of home freezers increased the appeal of frozen foods and allowed meatpackers to think beyond the fresh meat counters that had dominated grocery shopping for nearly a century. Although most meatpackers had begun to adjust to this new reality, IBP stayed on the cutting edge of the trend by investing in "quick freeze" refrigeration that preserved the freshness of the beef soon after it was cut. IBP committed to mass production of ready-to-cook beef for supermarkets, restaurants, and food service companies, and these markets became responsible for a third of its sales by the end of the decade.[33]

Most of all, Eli surely noticed how the stock market rewarded Iowa Beef Packers for its innovation. In 1967, IBP stockholders earned 26.8 percent on their investment compared to 6.6 percent for Swift and 6.4 percent for Armour. Such returns reflected growing confidence in IBP's business model—although, like other companies during this era, including Morrell under AMK, the returns told only part of the story. For example, in 1968, IBP increased its net operating earnings 13 percent over the previous year, but actual profits totaled $534 million, or just 1 percent on sales. These numbers were consistent with the industry's overall profit margins in 1967, a good year in which meatpackers saw net earnings of $192 million for a return on sales of 1.1 percent.[34] Like other companies, IBP partly built its success on a story directed at investment bankers and business journalists that celebrated its efficiency and reduction of labor costs.

Seeing what IBP had achieved in a short period of time, Eli may have believed he could do better. He had wanted to push the branding of the most desirable cuts just as he had witnessed in some of A&P's specialty items. He was also determined to take up operating slack in

Morrell's production and develop new profit opportunities in frozen foods beyond what IBP had accomplished. He would do this, he told McCallum, by centralizing the production process and persuading union leaders to support changes for the good of the entire company. Bloated and redundant departments within the Ottumwa plant would be collapsed, but increased productivity and profits would benefit employees as Morrell thrived. Eli thought a logical plan for improved performance would overcome whatever initial union pushback the changes provoked. The gains made in Morrell's first year under AMK had helped to make the case. He saw the increased profit as evidence that he could leave the task to his experienced and educated managers in Hansel and Broffman. Besides, bigger challenges lay ahead with United Fruit—the target that became his idée fixe after 1968.

Eli's confidence in his business model blinded him to an important difference between Morrell and IBP. As a new company born in the sixties, IBP had less history of union contracts and labor activism in its company. The notion of a "closed shop"—the condition in which an employee was expected to belong to the union to work at the company—did not exist at IBP, whereas it had been the rule at Morrell for more than four decades. Much had changed since the Congress of Industrial Organizations had ushered in a union (eventually known as Local 1) at Ottumwa more radical than the craft-oriented union at Sioux Falls in 1937. In 1955, the American Federation of Labor merged with the Congress of Industrial Organizations, which closed the political gap between Ottumwa's Local 1 of the UPWA and the AMCBW local at Sioux Falls. By 1968, UPWA and AMCBW had consolidated into one packinghouse union, with Ottumwa's union changing its title once again to Local P-1, under the new AMCBW.[35] Eli's management team had to meet with AMCBW at the bargaining table every time it chose to eliminate a department or position at its processing plants. Although the unions at the two sites had become more aligned with one another by the time AMK took control of Morrell, Hansel and Broffman attempted to exploit Sioux Falls' historic willingness to speed up production to break the resolve of Ottumwa union leaders, who remained wary of management's plans.

At the end of 1969, Hansel and Broffman began implementing a modernization plan for Morrell that would set the company on a profitable course in the coming year. Eli's confidence in the two, and his preoccupation with incorporating United Fruit into his emerging business empire, meant that he would not tend to the day-to-day changes in Iowa. His past experience in adjusting American Seal-Kap's production line by studying the broad outlines of the container business gave him confidence that the same could be done in the meat industry. Systems, he argued, mattered more than individual skills or departmental tasks.

Eli, instead, spent most of his time tending to the overall structure of the conglomerate. Morrell had been an important part of his plan, but United Fruit was the jewel in the crown of his new company. In 1969, Morrell constituted 59 percent of United Brands' sales and 15 percent of its total income. United Fruit's banana revenues amounted to 37 percent of United Brands' sales and 76 percent of its total revenue. In September 1970, Eli reorganized the management organization chart to reflect this reality, appointing himself chief executive officer of the United Fruit division of the company and relegating Jack Fox to president. Eli and Fox would also serve as chief executive and president of the overall conglomerate, honoring Eli's commitment to retain Fox as an executive—although everyone on Wall Street knew United Brands to be Eli's. In his first annual report after renaming the company, he assured shareholders and the public that "the creation of United Brands . . . is indeed a fresh beginning, and even more important, a major act of progress and renewal."[36] The notion of "renewal" had been clear, but what "progress" meant to Eli was not defined. Certainly, he planned to deliver greater returns for his shareholders, but that had been the goal of any of United Fruit's suitors. Was he thinking of other ways in which the most notorious US company doing business in Latin America should move forward?

Answers began to come early in Eli's tenure as CEO of United Fruit. In September 1969, Hurricane Francelia, a category-three storm, had devasted United Fruit's primary site of operations in Latin America, La Lima, on the North Atlantic Coast of Honduras. Soon after, United Fruit executives had negotiated a new contract with the union representing its banana workers, the Sindicato de Trabajadores de la Tela Railroad Company (SITRATERCO), and based on it implemented wage reductions and job cuts. The union president, Oscar Gale Varela, saw United Fruit's actions as a betrayal of its employees and a reversal of its stated goals not to place profit ahead of the needs of its employees and its host nation. As Eli came on the scene and learned about worker grievances, he found himself agreeing with Gale that United Fruit had fallen short of its obligation to employees.[37] Unfortunately, negotiations had concluded prior to the official announcement of the merger.

When Gale returned to the plantation in 1971 to renegotiate the contracts, Eli's people were ready. Robert Trumbull, Eli's primary negotiator, worked with Gale to reach an agreement that honored the labor of the nearly ten thousand unionized workers at La Lima. Gale, determined to avoid the kinds of "unnecessary and unjust" cuts made in 1969, had prepared a number of demands, including a "seventh day wage" that guaranteed workers overtime pay at twice their normal rate once they exceeded forty-four hours in a week. Trumbull saved him the trouble of making the pitch. "We offered it before [Gale] asked for it," Trumbull told a reporter.[38] The new deal promised to increase company expenditures on wages by eight percent in the first year of the contract in 1972, resulting in a cost of $6.5 million for United Fruit over the three-year period to follow. In addition to the overtime pay, Gale won a modest increase in the minimum wage for pickers from $.35 to $.375 per hour, higher Christmas bonuses, and increases for dock and salaried workers. All totaled, the agreement pushed United Fruit's overall expenditures on wages up an additional $2.5 million over what Eli's predecessors had agreed to in 1969.[39]

Gale also won several benefits related to insurance, housing, and education programs. He asked for, and received, a $2 million disability and survivor assistance package for workers killed or injured on the job. The agreement required United Fruit to match one percent of worker salaries deducted from their paychecks and a 1 percent contribution from the Honduran National Security Institute to cover the total cost. The company also contributed $1 million to a national skills training program, $2 million to assist workers seeking to buy union-built homes in Honduras's second largest city, San Pedro Sula, near La Lima, and a half million to extend a commitment to support primary education up through sixth-grade for children living in the Sula Valley. In total, the new contract increased United Fruit's obligations by an estimated $15.5 million over the next three years. Eli made the deal despite the ill effects of another hurricane, Edith, in September of 1971 that had limited full production. Taking stock of the apparent generosity of his new boss, La Lima manager Houston H. Lacombe told visiting reporter Georgie Ann Geyer, from *Chicago Daily News*, "We are paying $2 in social benefits for every dollar earned." Clearly bothered by the equation, Lacombe added with a grimace, "That's our problem."[40]

The negotiations played out just as Eli had hoped, even if some of his lieutenants in the field and executives in Boston disagreed with his approach. Herbert Cornuelle, second in command under Fox, had written in the company's 1968 annual report that any attempt to improve United Fruit's image would be futile. He had been an advocate of the associate growers program, which placed cultivated lands owned by the company back into the hands of peasant farmers in Honduras. The tepid response from local officials disappointed Cornuelle, who wrote, "No matter how successful we are in this process, we will still be perceived . . . as a threat to national independence and sovereignty."[41] Eli rejected this dreary prediction by doubling down on the program and raising the stakes with his generous pay and benefits package in 1971. When Geyer published her piece, one line in it, declaring that

United Fruit "may well be the most socially conscious American company in the hemisphere," especially pleased Eli.[42]

Geyer's compliment had meant to call attention to how differently United Fruit operated than it had in the past. At the same time, it captured Eli's plan for the future, to make United Brands a beacon of social responsibility in the Americas. He seemed to be taking to heart Adolph Berle's lectures at Columbia University, urging corporate leaders to embrace their responsibilities to society and not just their obligations to shareholders. Such an approach, Berle had argued, would also help earn the trust of consumers and defend America's system of free enterprise against a chorus of critics. Berle's obsession with communism in Latin America, however, had drawn him into domestic affairs in Central America that tainted the liberal cause he supported. More recently, leaders like David Lilienthal had advocated similar attention to the social well-being of host nations but with a stronger emphasis on partnerships between business and government to achieve company and political goals. As a newcomer to the multinational corporate world, Eli had a chance to carve out his own path, starting with acknowledging the wrongs of United Fruit's past and working in concert with leaders like Oscar Gale Varela to build a more just future.

The failure to show a profit at United Fruit after a year of owning it complicated Eli's narrative. As he approached the first anniversary of the merger, he came face to face with the harsh truth that banana sales had been weaker than he anticipated. He wanted to believe that the industry would rebound, but had no way of knowing whether disruptions to his rosy predictions, whether political or environmental, would subside. Under these conditions, his reliance on other subsidiaries in United Brands—namely, Morrell and the still-unproven lettuce business, Inter Harvest—would have to carry the weight. Whether Hansel and Broffman could restructure the Ottumwa plant and win over the rank-and-file members of Local P-1 remained unclear. Meanwhile, a new challenge, the rise of the United Farm Workers in California, would test his resolve to build a new type of food corporation committed to social responsibility and financial gain.

4

SHADOWS

ONE EVENING EARLY IN 1971, Eli sat down alone in his study at 799 Park Avenue to review the draft of his "letter to shareholders"—the gloss he would put on the annual report making public United Brands' performance in his first full year as the chair. Staring at the blank page, surrounded by the vast, high-ceilinged rooms of the apartment and the abstract images on Shirley's canvases, he replayed this pivotal year in his mind. By this time, Shirley was living mostly in Westport, where she could paint in her custom-built studio. Shirley's love of art had carried forward to Judy, who earned a degree in Art History from Barnard in 1970. Judy, the oldest child, had chosen a conventional path, starting with an early marriage to Allen Nadler, on September 24, 1967, just one year into her studies. Al's Dartmouth degree would have impressed Eli; Leon had chosen the same school. Eli had spent a portion of every sabbath reading philosophy and history with his son, in hopes of inspiring a fidelity to critical thought and reflection on the world's affairs, but Leon seemed to be heading in a different direction. "Every newborn is a messiah," he quipped in his Fieldston senior yearbook in 1969, adding, "it's a pity he'll turn out a common rascal."[1]

Judith Black Nadler, senior photo. Mortarboard *(Barnard College yearbook), 1970, 46; BC12-01-Mortarboard, 1894–2018, Barnard Archives and Special Collections, Barnard College.*

Leon Black, 1969. Fieldglass *(Ethical Culture Fieldston School yearbook), 1960, 131.*

However troubled he might have been by his son's impudence, Eli himself had strayed far from his father's intentions. By 1971, Eli and Leon could no doubt enjoy the humor of the parallel, confident that they were both destined for bigger things.

The numbers Eli was reviewing, however, were dispiriting. The audited financial statements showed a loss of more than two million dollars in United Brands' first year. Eli had created the company on December 31, 1969, knowing that he could fall back on substantial cash reserves, but the poor performance shocked him. He had spent the past year in charge of the United Fruit Company division and overseeing the parent corporation's transition from a conglomerate of diverse, mid-sized manufacturers into a more focused pairing of two major food-industry players. The problem had not been with Morrell, where Morton Broffman—before handing the CEO job off to his successor, Elias Paul—had achieved a nearly 75 percent increase in earnings and the most profitable year in company history. Those gains were offset by United Fruit's miserable performance, weighed down by natural disasters and a poorly timed banana harvest. The company had been in recovery mode since a devastating hurricane in September 1969, which hit just as Eli was working to secure the deal. The category-three storm, Francelia, had carved a perfect path through the midsection of Central America, crossing over the Bay Islands of Northern Honduras before crashing into the northern coast, and inundating the San Pedro Sula airport, where Eli flew in and out of the country to evaluate his operations. The flooding washed out four bridges between La Lima and the coastal ports used by Fruit's "Great White Fleet" of steamships traveling back and forth to the United States and beyond. Flooding ruined 50 percent of the banana crop, and caused damage of nearly $5 million, from which it had taken two years to recover. By the time Eli sat down to write his shareholders letter, fifteen thousand damaged acres had been replaced, but in the rush to get back up and running, United Fruit had overplanted, and the subsequent harvest arrived at a time of historically low demand.

The rude welcome was a lesson in how unpredictable agriculture can be, especially when a crop is grown outside the country, and in the path of hurricanes.[2]

Eli's predecessors, Jack Fox and Herbert Cornuelle, had begun to invest in other businesses to limit United Fruit's exposure to the risks inherent in the banana business—and to grow the company even as the US antitrust regulators' consent decree forced it to divest a large portion of its banana operations. The two had responded to criticism from United Fruit shareholders, who wondered why management had not leveraged its significant cash reserves and the absence of debt to create new revenue streams. In the years leading up to the merger, not every acquisition United Fruit attempted worked out. For various reasons, Fox and Cornuelle failed to pull off takeovers of Winchell's Donut House in 1966, Del Monte in 1967, and a Puerto Rican hotel chain named Swiss Chalet in 1968. Yet their intensive drive for diversification had worked out on several other fronts. In 1966, Fox and Cornuelle had celebrated the acquisition of J. Hungerford Smith, a maker of soda fountain syrups, and its subsidiary A&W Root Beer, the drive-in restaurant that was at the time the second-largest restaurant chain in the United States. In 1967, they had acquired Baskin-Robbins, the California-based ice cream maker and retailer, and Clemente Jacques, Mexico's largest producer of canned goods. Their 1968 investment in vegetable production in California, acquiring several farms across twenty-two thousand acres and merging them into a business called Inter Harvest, had potential on another level. Eli wondered: Could the lettuce business be expanded to the same scale as the banana business? In 1970, Eli committed significant time and resources to make this idea a reality.[3]

The waning performance of United Brands' banana operations confirmed that Eli would need an additional revenue source to meet the growth he promised investors. How United Fruit would diversify its business had been in question since 1954, when the US Justice Department filed an antitrust suit against the company, charging that it had monopolized the banana trade. By 1958, the two parties had come to terms with a consent decree compelling United Fruit to come up with a plan, by late 1966, to sell a large portion of its operations to a capable competitor—probably by establishing a new company itself and setting it up to succeed as a spinoff. By 1968, a plan was in place but the new company, Sovereign Fruit, was not yet doing business. By complying with the consent decree, United Fruit would lose 17 percent of its banana business, a decline that would strengthen the position of its main competitor, Standard Fruit, itself now a subsidiary of Castle & Cook.[4] As it turned out, United Fruit would fulfill the court's request in 1972 by selling the company's Guatemala division to Del Monte, a new entrant to the banana business. Eli might have seen a silver lining in the situation, in that it could only help the company's reputation in Latin America to put more distance between itself and a country where, less than twenty years earlier, it had played a role in a CIA-induced coup. In the years since the 1954 overthrow of Árbenz, United Fruit had shifted the bulk of its operations to La Lima plantation in Honduras, where government officials were more congenial, and the company was held in higher regard by the local population. With United Fruit's operations cut down to size, Standard Fruit, its main competitor, briefly dethroned United Fruit that year as the top exporter of bananas to the United States.[5]

As he surveyed the many subsidiaries that composed his new company, Eli looked to Inter Harvest, the company's recent combination of California produce grower-shippers, as the best prospect for boosting United Brands' profits in the coming year. From an outsider's perspective, lettuce, known locally in Salinas Valley as "green gold," appeared a safe bet. The industry had evolved during the Depression years, creating minor fortunes for the earliest firms. What had been a mostly regional market dominated by Japanese immigrant "truck farmers"—growers who produced crops on a large scale to transport to markets at some distance—became a national produce business with the transportation revolution of the 1930s. Shipped on ice aboard transcontinental railcars, lettuce on the earliest trains took up to three weeks to travel across country and, even with rail stops along the way to replace the ice blocks, often spoiled before it reached its destination. Improvements in the rail system shortened the time of delivery, while other innovations helped the product last longer. Salinas Valley grower Bruce Church, for example, advanced vacuum cooling and bred more durable varieties that could withstand the journey. Early grower-shippers like Church took note as the New York City market called the most durable variety of California lettuce "iceberg," highlighting its difference from the other "butter" lettuces grown seasonally in New England and the Mid-Atlantic states. To capitalize on this early form of produce branding, Church and three other large growers—Russell Merrill, Ken Nutting, and Gene Harden—jointly founded a business, Grower's Ice, to provide ice-packing services for their own produce and shipments by other fresh vegetable growers. Now, iceberg lettuce from California could be enjoyed on the East Coast year-round.[6]

World War II transformed the industry, introducing new investors and technologies that changed the method and scope of lettuce cultivation in the West. Former fighter pilots returned from the front lines to Salinas with flying skills that could easily be adapted to the cultivation and delivery of product to market. Most of them owned small, twin-engine airplanes that gave them the freedom to range across the American Southwest—from the Salinas Valley inland from Monterrey Bay to the Mexican border and Arizona—where lettuce production thrived. Men by the names of Charlie Huston, Hank Garin, Jim Mapes, and Murphy Malgin surveyed and acquired land for the cultivation of new crops. Perhaps their success in the theater of war had steeled them against any risk they might encounter in the produce business as they expanded production and developed household brands. Famous for mixing in gambling in Las Vegas and golf in Southern California with business across the region, these men organized the Grower-Shipper Vegetable Association of Central California, which functioned primarily as a lobbyist for lettuce growers in Sacramento, Phoenix, and Washington, DC.

Born at the right time to be at the vanguard of California lettuce, these men also took advantage of two government directives more than a decade earlier: the publicly funded water projects in the Colorado River basin and the internment of Japanese American citizens. In 1928, the US Bureau of Reclamation received authorization to build Hoover Dam as part of the Boulder Canyon Project that would eventually deliver fresh water to the desert southwest. The All-American Canal, which the bureau completed as part of the project in 1942, irrigated California's Imperial Valley bordering Mexico, making it possible to replace dry-farm crops like cotton with more lucrative vegetable crops, especially lettuce. Profits from these initial reclamation projects turned large grower-shippers into power brokers in the West, who lobbied the federal government for more irrigation projects throughout the mid-twentieth century—leading to, for example, the Central Arizona Project initiated by President Lyndon B. Johnson in 1968. Government-subsidized water ensured profits for these early landholders and guaranteed a future for the lettuce industry.

In places such as the lush Salinas Valley, where coastal fogs moderate dry inland temperatures, immigrants from Japan had taken the first steps, in the decades prior to World War II, toward growing vegetables to truck to a burgeoning Bay Area. In the aftermath of Pearl Harbor, however, and the United States' declaration of war on Japan, President Franklin Delano Roosevelt ordered that all Japanese Americans be rounded up and held in detention camps for the duration of the conflict. *Issei,* first-generation arrivals, and *nisei,* their second-generation children, had paved the way for the industry, but were now forcibly removed from their farms. The prolonged period of internment made it possible for non-Japanese growers to acquire their land at fire-sale prices. When World War II finally ended, Japanese American growers found it nearly impossible to reenter a business that had in the meantime become one of the pillars of the California economy and a focus of speculation by investors outside the Golden State.[7]

United Fruit's investment in lettuce production contributed to a corporate land rush in California that worried local growers even as they stood to profit from the increased attention. A 1964 report from the US Department of Agriculture predicted expansion of US food production to meet the presumed population growth by the end of the century.[8] Such projections echoed concerns about "population bombs," especially among the poor, but, at the other end of the class spectrum, corporate leaders interpreted concerns about food shortages as an opportunity to make money.[9] By the end of the decade, corporate investors with scant history in farming started buying up small farms, including Uniroyal, Boeing, Kaiser Industries, American Cyanamid, Getty Oil, and a few insurance companies. Among these companies, Purex, maker of bleach and laundry detergents, moved most aggressively to acquire land in California. Companies aligned with food production, such as Del Monte and premium-priced food distributor S.S. Pierce, became major players in California, as well, the latter acquiring the strawberry grower Pic 'n Pac Foods.[10]

United Fruit's long history as a banana producer placed it squarely in the business of agriculture and made it a much more credible investor in a state that accounted for 35 percent of US agricultural output. Fox asked United Fruit executive Bill Decker to lead the charge in assembling a market-dominating organization out of what had been independent lettuce grower-shippers. Decker promptly traveled to San Francisco for the annual convention of the United Fresh Fruit and Vegetable Association, which included every lettuce producer in the state. While he found the major grower-shippers whose operations dated to the postwar years to be a closed and guarded community, Decker got more traction with two relative newcomers to the industry, Tom and Bob Nunes. Their father, an immigrant from the Portuguese-speaking Azores Islands in the mid-Atlantic, had been a part of the earlier generation of grower-shippers, but only in the 1950s did the brothers begin to make a name for themselves. They were children of immigrants on both sides—their mother was a woman of Portuguese ethnicity born on the island of Kauai before Hawaii was a state. Tom had worked with his father on the family's Toro Farms while Bob attended Stanford University. After graduation, Bob Nunes worked first as a bookkeeper for a large grower-shipper, then in the sales organization of a produce distributor, before joining the team at the Growers Exchange, a new grower-shipper his brother Tom and some partners had founded in the mid-1950s. When one of those founders retired in 1959, Bob bought into the partnership. In 1966, Tom and Bob went on to found Nunes Bros. of California, and Bob in particular began trying out innovative marketing approaches. In its first year, for example, Nunes Bros. struck a co-promotion deal with Lawry's Seasoned Salt by which it printed a coupon on its lettuce wrappers. It was another promotional investment—the production of a ten-minute film about the company—that drew the attention of Decker. When he saw it at the San Francisco convention, he sensed that Nunes Bros. could be the cornerstone of United Fruit's plan to enter the lettuce market.

After months of resistance and two unaccepted offers, the Nunes brothers agreed to a deal that kept their name on the new subsidiary and kept them in management roles. Jealousy among the other grower-shippers who were party to the deal, and United Fruit's plan to apply the Chiquita brand to their lettuce, forced a compromise that gave Bob and Tom Nunes control over production but no say in marketing. The new business would be known as Inter Harvest, a corporate name with no reputation behind it but showing no favoritism among the independent farms coming together to form the new subsidiary.[11]

The creation of Inter Harvest had not been Eli's idea, but he regarded it as a source of tremendous potential growth. He agreed with the plan set by Fox and Cornuelle to sever the Nunes brothers from marketing decisions so that the Chiquita brand could be extended from bananas to lettuce and other vegetables produced by the new company. The approach mimicked the trend in the meat business, where traditionally generic products like wieners and dog food were now brand-labeled, advertised, and gaining levels of customer loyalty that allowed them to fetch a better price. Bananas had become the rare food commodity for which consumers associated a specific brand—Chiquita—with a reliably higher level of quality. The Nunes brothers had been clever in many ways in their packaging and marketing of lettuce, and had discussed building a distinctive and well-known brand for their product, but had not yet invested in doing so. Eli was enthusiastic about the prospect of this now happening under United Brands' direction. By keeping the Nunes brothers on as operation managers, Eli believed he could have the benefit of their talents while depending on his marketing team in New York City to devise a sales strategy.

It was also true that Tom and Bob Nunes had plenty on their plates to do without also being responsible for marketing decisions. There was the challenging task of integrating the operations of what had been separate growers to accomplish. "We had to coordinate different planting schedules, standardize equipment inventories, adopt common color schemes; we had to equalize salaries, create an organization chart that actually worked, and standardize reporting procedures and supply and container purchasing," Bob Nunes would later recall. "We both felt as if we were riding a tiger."[12]

Eli's decision to shift marketing and other business functions to United Fruit managers at headquarters was typical of corporations' approaches to post-merger integration. It was, first, a way to achieve some of the efficiency and synergy expected from a combination. Another benefit was that, by merging staff performing the same kind of "overhead" work in different divisions, a large corporation could develop greater depth of expertise and experience in a realm that could be tapped as needed by its various business units. Also part of the rationale was the belief that these professionals' skills were generic— that, for example, business acumen could just as easily be applied to one type of marketplace offering as another. As Eli himself had put it after the Morrell acquisition, "proper marketing and controls work in every business." For him, the differences in selling lettuce, meat, and bananas may have appeared so negligible that there was no downside to pursuing scale efficiencies across the food businesses of United Brands. Inter Harvest should take advantage of its parent company's strengths.[13]

Such an approach was not without its critics. With the rise of agribusiness on a huge scale in the 1970s, observers of the decline in family farms warned that corporate asset managers like Eli Black underestimated the value of small landholder's local understanding—and commitment to success. The variability of weather, soil, seed, and yields required a longer view of a piece of land's productive capacity than publicly traded corporations could take. In a picturesque phrase, one writer called it "the shadow of the owner on his land" that kept fields producing, through the sheer persistence of farmers, despite all manner of setbacks. Not only veteran growers but agricultural economists recognized the difference it made to have people personally invested in farms making decisions amid the uncertainty that plagues agriculture day to day, season to season, and year to year. An "active" owner, with more at stake, would be less inclined to throw in the towel and accept defeat in the way a conglomerate owner might, figuring it could write off losses and that the risk was in any case hedged by other, unrelated revenue streams. Finally, given the complexity of farming, with its highly variable inputs and processes to manage, it was unlikely that a remote owner could manage the dynamic decision-making required. Having vested, "on farm" managers made for higher profits per unit of land because of real-time adjustments based on a host of considerations, including the cost of field labor. As agricultural economists had been able to show, once the size of a farm gets beyond the ability of the on-site manager to stay on top of operations, economies of scale give way to diseconomies of scale—meaning, further expansion of production erodes profit margins. Salinas Valley grower-shippers were able to finetune their operations in a way that was imperceptible to a corporate managerial class that arrogantly believed they could optimize inputs and outputs better.[14]

Several out-of-state corporate newcomers had already come face-to-face with this reality and been humbled by their forays into agriculture.

S. S. Pierce, based in Boston, badly miscalculated its ability to consolidate and improve major strawberry production under its subsidiary,
Pic 'n Pac. Executives believed they could expand production on a
two-thousand-acre megafarm, created from the purchase and consolidation of five independent farms in the Salinas Valley. The company
subdivided the property into blocks of five hundred acres, disregarding
the fact that local farmers had always grown on hundred-acre blocks. In
just two years, the company lost $4.5 million on sales of $10 million due
to production cost overruns and mismanagement. Over that period,
Pierce replaced Pic 'n Pac managers three times but saw no improvement
in performance. By 1972, Pic 'n Pac fell $3 million in debt, forcing Pierce
to assume control of the day-to-day operations of the subsidiary.[15]

Eli had faith that United Brands would be different, and that Inter
Harvest would reap the benefits of being part of a multinational corporation. In the first few months, he encouraged Bob and Tom Nunes
to bring their considerable knowledge to bear on the new subsidiary.
"I recall [Eli Black] saying to me, after we signed the acquisition papers and management contract, that our mistakes should be ones of
commission, not omission," Bob Nunes later recalled. The point was
to encourage them to keep thinking like entrepreneurs and experimenting with innovative ways of doing things. As Nunes interpreted
it, "he wouldn't fault us for making mistakes, but he would for being
too conservative."[16]

Tom and Bob's deep knowledge and commitment to continuing
the success of their company through the new subsidiary compelled
them to make suggestions even when their opinions fell on deaf ears.
Repeatedly, the Nunes brothers confronted what Bob called a "strong
corporate culture" that made it less open-minded than the grower-
shipper community in California. "They'd hear my explanation," Bob
later remembered, "then disagree with it!"[17] Among the many mistakes
Tom and Bob witnessed, the most disruptive was headquarters' determination to use United Fruit's longstanding network of distributors, or
"jobbers," rather than the brokers who had sold the Salinas growers'

produce to supermarkets across the country for decades. From an efficiency point of view this seemed only logical: United Brands had thirty-three sales offices strategically placed around the country, and strong relationships with key distributors. Lettuce was simply an additional grocery product for them to push through their existing channels. As the Nunes brothers predicted, however, the traditional lettuce brokers, who were in a position to push whatever producer's lettuce they wanted to their buyers, retaliated by promoting competitors' lettuce over the Chiquita brand. United Brands, surprised by the drop in buying, then reacted with price promotions—undermining its own goal to stabilize the price of Inter Harvest lettuce and achieve the predictable sales volumes that make for efficient production schedules. Before long, the company's actions had reverberated up and down the supply chain and the market was temporarily flooded with lettuce so that the whole industry suffered a price collapse. Adding to the mayhem, other grower-shippers interpreted the glut of Chiquita brand lettuce as an underhanded attempt to drive them out of business and they filed suit against United Brands. Bob Nunes recalled that "Tom and I were blamed" by the other Salinas growers, even though the brothers had nothing to do with the situation.[18] Fortunately, everyone eventually figured out that the burst in supply had been caused by United Brands' incompetence rather than an abuse of its clout, and the suit was dropped.

The challenge of resentful jobbers might not have been impossible to overcome, but there were other ways in which using United Fruit's system compromised the quality of lettuce produced by Inter Harvest. As Tom and Bob Nunes tried to convey to decision-makers in New York, lettuce is simply more perishable than bananas. Indeed, the existing network was optimized for a product that *improved* in transit: bananas are harvested green and continue to ripen for many days after picking, reaching their optimal sweetness and softness just before going bad. Lettuce, by contrast, only deteriorates from the moment it is harvested. Anticipating more in-transit spoilage, the Nunes brothers worked overtime to make sure that lettuce packed in the fields in California surpassed the standards of the industry. But by 1970, despite the efforts of experienced *lechugueros* (lettuce workers), the decline in quality had become so evident to consumers that United Fruit's logistics planners had to admit they could not achieve the speed and care required to maintain a dominant position in the industry. In some regions, buyers were learning to expect better quality from Inter Harvest's competitors. By 1971, United Brands was seeing such problems that it decided to suspend the use of the Chiquita label for Inter Harvest produce, rather than tarnish a brand United Fruit had spent decades building.[19]

This was the already challenging situation in Salinas, then, when another formidable threat arose: the arrival of Cesar Chavez and his United Farm Workers union. In a period when Eli's rise was being charted on the business page, Chavez had been capturing the front page. His insurgent organization, begun in the early 1960s, was a determined effort to raise the wages of impoverished field workers—most of them Filipinos and Mexicans whose ability to organize and engage in collective bargaining had always been impeded by their migratory lives and the guest-worker programs that made them too easy to replace. In 1962, Filipino field workers had begun a push toward unionization, walking out of fields up and down California, while at the same time Chavez and members of the National Farm Workers Association were methodically building political capacity among Mexican farm workers to change their own lives. These two movements coalesced into the United Farm Workers Organizing Committee, the force behind the famous Delano Grape Strike of 1965 to 1970. Through its sustained efforts to publicize a years-long boycott of table grapes, and especially after it succeeded in gaining pay raises and health protections, this underfunded multiracial, multigenerational, and multidenominational movement entered the consciousness of the American public. Using tactics and messages not commonly employed by unions, it gained serious momentum as not only a labor movement but a civil rights cause.

In an accident of history, the UFW's most powerful tool, the boycott, was only first tried because of the particular conditions of the time and the labor group involved. Back in 1935, when Congress had passed the National Labor Relations Act allowing workers to engage in collective bargaining, it had explicitly excluded farm workers. Carving this group of workers out, however, also meant the group was not subject to the Taft-Hartley Act passed later, in 1947, which rolled back some of organized labor's gains—including the ability to use secondary boycotts. Farm workers, it turned out, were uniquely permitted to put pressure on an employer by trying to suppress sales of its product by vendors, through picketing stores or other nonviolent means. Typically, Chavez could be heard decrying the fact that farm workers had been excluded from the landmark federal legislation, but privately he also saw opportunity in this loophole to do something other unions could not. The triumph in Delano, California, had begun with an experimental boycott of grapes in 1965, and from there grew into the full-blown offensive that took *la causa*—the farm workers' cause—out of the fields and into urban America.

Five years later, the tactic used first as an experiment had been honed by creative UFW organizers into a reliable game plan—and one that was especially powerful against growers of produce as highly perishable as table grapes. On July 29, 1970, Chavez signed contracts with the majority of Delano grape growers that recognized the right of workers to be represented by the UFW in all labor decisions. That same summer, Eli Black was awaiting final approval from the US Securities and Exchange Commission for the purchase of United Fruit, unaware that the news stories he was reading about Chavez would soon become highly relevant to his own business interests.

The success of the United Farm Workers sent other sectors of California's agricultural economy scrambling—especially the lettuce

growers, whose Grower-Shipper Association had devised a contain-
ment strategy for Chavez even before the historic agreement with grape
growers was completed. Years earlier, in 1961, one of its members, Bud
Antle, had signed an agreement with the Teamsters union enabling it
to represent haulers and drivers on his farm—an act that at the time
had been denounced by his peers as a betrayal of the industry. Now
the Teamsters, as a somewhat more grower-friendly union than the
radical *Chavistas* of the UFW, looked like the least bad choice—and
its foothold in Antle's operation could allow it to claim prior jurisdic-
tion. As the UFW was finalizing its arrangements with grape growers
in Delano, the Salinas grower-shippers worked out an agreement to
have the Teamsters also represent field workers, effectively preempting
UFW's campaign to organize the lettuce industry. On July 27, 1970,
thirty-five members of the Grower-Shipper Association, including
Inter Harvest, signed contracts with the Teamsters without farm
workers' knowledge or input.[20]

The lechugueros, who had been closely watching developments in
Delano, resented the unilateral actions of their employers and prepared
for a fight in Salinas. On August 2, 1970, thousands of workers marched
out of the fields to signal their preference for a Chavez-led union.
Chants of "Viva Chavez!" and "Viva La Causa!" rang throughout the
Salinas Valley as they flocked to a stadium at Hartnell College to listen
to the labor leader speak. Chavez assured them the time had passed
when "a couple of white men can sit in their Taj Mahal in Burlingame,
California (Teamster Headquarters) and determine the future of black
and brown workers."[21] The lechugueros roared their approval while
UFW organizers circulated membership cards. By the end of the day,
the union had collected 650 cards registering workers' preference for
the UFW. Testimony from broccoli workers at H. W. Mann Packing
Shed revealed the extent of the support for the union. When supervisors shared the news that the owner had agreed to contracts with the
Teamsters and asked them for their approval, workers resisted. "We
told them we had already signed with the union of Cesar Chavez."[22]

Such acts of resistance encouraged Chavez to move forward despite the wealth and influence of both the Grower-Shipper Association and the Teamsters.

Tom and Bob Nunes looked on with a sense of foreboding. Writing later, Bob recalled, "I never met Cesar Chavez, but watching the United Farm Workers in operation, I often wondered what the ultimate objective was." From his vantage point, the union was acting like it "wanted to break the back" of the lettuce industry.[23] The Nunes brothers agreed with the Grower-Shipper Association's decision to thwart Chavez by signing contracts with the Teamsters. But like others in the industry, they could only guess how United Fruit would react to the ongoing threat from the United Farm Workers. As the largest producer of lettuce in California, Inter Harvest offered Chavez an obvious target for a boycott. Aiming for the top had been Chavez's strategy when it targeted grape growers: the UFW had singled out John Giumarra, the largest producer in the table grape industry, and by drawing him to the negotiation table, Chavez was able to get 85 percent of his peers to follow suit. To Chavez, Inter Harvest would have looked like a similar mark, although its corporate profile, with headquarters in New York and Boston, made it less certain that other lettuce growers would follow its lead.

Chavez saw other reasons to single out United Brands. When the UFW began experimenting with the boycott in 1966, it discovered that targeting corporations sometimes offered the most direct path to victory. Prior to taking on table grape growers, the UFW had waged a campaign against Schenley Industries, a producer of wines and spirits based in Chicago, New York, and Delaware that sourced most of the grapes for its wines from California farms. Schenley's owner, Lewis Rosenstiel, mindful that its national brands, including Cutty Sark, Seagram's, and Roma, would all be tarnished by bad press, decided to raise pay for field workers and to coordinate with Chavez to manage hiring on California farms rather than fight a protracted war with the union. This early agreement, achieved four years prior to the table grape contracts, set the UFW on its successful path and served as a model for how to begin the lettuce campaign.[24]

Chavez instructed his now well-oiled boycott department to dissect the assets and vulnerabilities of Inter Harvest's new corporate parent, United Brands, a company whose name had been adopted on June 30, 1970. In addition to Inter Harvest, the union identified numerous subsidiaries held by Eli Black, including United Fruit Company, John Morrell Meat Company, A&W Food Services, and Baskin-Robbins. The corporation also claimed Revere Sugar Refinery in Massachusetts; Surrey Shipping Co. in Bermuda; radio, telegraph, and telephone services throughout Central and South America and parts of Western Europe; and additional agricultural subsidiaries in Guatemala, Costa Rica, Spain, and Italy. The appearance of a diversified portfolio belied the fact that United Brands depended on sales from two primary entities, United Fruit and Morrell, for its health. Despite Inter Harvest's unproven performance, its 60 percent share of lettuce production in a state where the United Farm Workers possessed its greatest influence made lettuce and United Brands critical to the union.[25] Having sorted through the possibilities, UFW decided the best way to exploit United Brands' vulnerabilities would be to threaten boycotts of not only Inter Harvest lettuce but also Chiquita bananas.

Chavez revved up the boycott machine across America and drew on useful contacts in key cities, none more important than Anna Puharich in New York City, a philanthropist and consummate friend of the union. Anna belonged to the ranks of volunteers who never picked fruits or vegetables but cared enough about the injustices suffered by farm workers to devote substantial portions of their lives to Chavez and the United Farm Workers. Born Ann Levy on February 6, 1934, to a Jewish immigrant father and a Catholic mother in Brooklyn, Puharich took an indirect route to becoming the influential fundraiser and socialite she became in the late sixties and early seventies. At sixteen, she married Shelly Wollman and became a mother, having four children by the early 1960s. Unfulfilled by her marriage and seeking more in life, she started taking classes toward a college degree and, in 1962, went to work for a young trust-fund philanthropist, Stewart Mott, at the foundation he and his siblings had set up, Spectemur Agendo, to fund programs that were "unconventional, controversial, and unacceptable to traditional sources of foundation support." Within a year, she met and married Irving Israel, one of the foundation's lawyers and twenty years her senior. So effective was she in her role that the Motts made her executive director of the foundation, a position from which she cultivated relationships with high-profile people from Andy Warhol and his "superstar" Baby Jane Holzer to Attorney General Robert Kennedy and former New York Mayor John Lindsay. Hosting parties in the upscale apartment overlooking Central Park that she shared with Irving, Anna raised funds for such controversial projects as sex education in public schools, mobile medical clinics for prostitutes, and the first suicide hotline in New York City.

Anna met Cesar Chavez at Bobby Kennedy's funeral in June 1968 and began raising funds soon after to buy a brownstone at 331 West Eighty-Fourth Street on Manhattan's West Side to house UFW workers in town to stage pickets. By 1970, she had left Irving Israel for Andrija Puharich, an independent scientist and inventor focused on extrasensory perception and other psychic phenomena. As Anna Puharich, she threw herself into the farm workers movement, working alongside Chavez whenever and wherever he needed her.[26] She continued to host fundraisers in New York City where she brought young, earnest students together with sober business types to be wooed by Cesar Chavez. Her work resulted in donations to the United Farm Workers union totaling over $30 million. During this time, she introduced writer and environmental activist Peter Matthiessen to Chavez. Matthiessen became so smitten with the labor leader that he followed him for a year and wrote a biography, *Sal Si Puedes: Cesar Chavez and the New American Revolution.* By the start of the lettuce workers campaign, Chavez regarded Puharich as an indispensable soldier in the movement who could cross boundaries and facilitate relationships like no other.[27]

Cesar Chavez with Anna
Puharich (holding "Boycott
Lettuce" sign), early 1970s.
*Walter P. Reuther Library,
Archives of Labor and Urban
Affairs, Wayne State
University.*

Cesar Chavez speaks
to UFW donors in the
Manhattan apartment of
Anna Puharich. *Bob Fitch
Photography Archive,
Department of Special
Collections, Stanford
University Library.*

In August 1970, Chavez responded to the Grower-Shipper Association's preemptive agreement with the Teamsters by dispatching Anna
Puharich to United Brands' headquarters in hopes of striking a deal
with Eli. Chavez understood that boycotting Chiquita would initiate
a battle that would likely drag the union into another global campaign
on the heels of a grape boycott that stretched the union's budget and
volunteers' energy. As he later recalled, "I knew that if we ever started
a public boycott against them, it would be very hard to turn off."[28]
Chavez noted that United Fruit's checkered past would make it easy
to rally support for the boycott, but acknowledged "there were other
ways of applying pressure." He must have wondered whether Eli, having
come from outside of California, and whose business interests included
multiple subsidiaries, might see the virtue of circumventing a protracted war with the UFW by agreeing to terms separate from his
lettuce growing peers. He hoped that Puharich, a skilled matchmaker
of moneyed interest and needy causes, would be able to persuade Eli
to side with the most celebrated workers in the country at the time.

Cesar had witnessed firsthand Anna's unique abilities to convey *la
causa* to the wealthy—and with Eli, she would be in familiar territory,
as the child of a Jewish immigrant to New York and the wife of an af-
fluent Jewish man. Through her work in the philanthropy world, Anna
might have known of Eli's charitable giving, which had grown with his
rise as a conglomerate builder. By 1970, he was a reliable supporter of
the American Jewish Committee, Federation of Jewish Philanthropies,
Jewish Guild for the Blind, and the Jewish Museum of New York. In
addition to contributing large sums of money, he volunteered as a
member of the board of trustees for each of these organizations. His
work on the American Jewish Committee included a term as the chair
of the publication committee for *Commentary,* whose formidable
editor, Norman Podhoretz, was the son of Jewish immigrants from the
same Central European region of Galicia as Eli's parents. *Commentary,*
having shifted under Podhoretz's leadership from a liberal to a neo-
conservative stance, gave voice to American Jews like Eli who sought

to fortify US support for Israel. Eli was also on the board of directors of another magazine, the *Saturday Review,* whose longtime editor-in-chief, Norman Cousins, later observed that "Eli's insight, leadership and sense of conscience created an exciting and new ideal for the multinational corporation." Eli was also a big donor to cultural institutions, as a trustee of the Lincoln Center for the Performing Arts and member of the Business Committee for the Arts.[29]

Anna Puharich placed the cold call to United Brands in August 1970, only to find that Eli was touring in Europe with Shirley. She pressed forward anyway, making her case to Eli's assistant, Burke Wright, that his boss needed to tend to an urgent matter in California. "When I left Salinas," Anna informed Wright, "[UFW officials] were having a meeting about boycotting Chiquita." The provocation spurred Wright to phone Eli, who promptly instructed Maury Kaplan, chairman of United Brands' Executive Committee, to set up a meeting with Puharich. The next day, Puharich strode into United Brands' offices at 200 Park Avenue, confident that she could persuade Kaplan to act. "I don't know what they expected," Anna would later recall, "but they didn't expect me." Chavez agreed: "I'm sure he didn't expect to meet someone as sophisticated as Anna and as beautiful, or that they had a number of mutual friends." Kaplan listened attentively to her assessment of the potential for a boycott against United Brands and how it would disrupt the company's reputational makeover. By the end, Kaplan had shared his home phone number with Puharich, and asked her to keep in touch. He also called Eli, who instructed him to investigate her claims immediately. "If it's true what she's saying," Eli told Kaplan, "Then let's sit down and let's work, do everything we can to negotiate and sign with them. We'll worry about fighting the Teamsters later."[30]

When Eli returned to the country he met with Puharich and, like Kaplan, was struck by her intelligence and determination. He came away confident that she could broker a productive relationship with Chavez. Having recently come from a visit to California, she spoke passionately about the farm worker struggle there and shared her impressions of the UFW leader, whose vision for social justice, she believed, fit with Eli's own priorities to do good through his new company. Later she would learn it also fit his children's values. "Black and Kaplan told me about how they had been boycotting grapes" in their own homes, Puharich recalled. "Their children were in college and were very into it, too, especially Black's." As she understood it, when Eli told Judy and Leon about the situation, they had reacted strongly, "like, he'd better sign. They never expected it to hit them."

Eli told Anna of his intention to work with Chavez and professed his sincere respect for Chavez's commitment to integrating spirituality into his movement. Chavez famously made use of Catholic symbols like the Virgin de Guadalupe and practices like the *Peregrinacion* (Pilgrimage) in union campaigns, blurring the line between labor and civil rights. It was one of those strategies, inspired by Chavez's understanding of mass movements, that initially frustrated other labor leaders accustomed to the more hard-nosed tactics traditionally employed by unions. Chavez proved his critics wrong by reaching many ethnic Mexican workers who were not inclined to draw a distinction between their faith and their passion for justice, and inspiring them to upset a system that placed them at a disadvantage. Eli must have appreciated the courage and fortitude Chavez showed in asserting the relevance of religion in the daily life of workers, and recognized his public expressions of piety as an effective tactic both to disarm enemies and to cool the passions of any in his movement who contemplated violence against their opponents. Some of these tactics were now aimed at United Brands, yet Eli's admiration for Chavez compelled him to work out an agreement.

Eli was also impressed with Anna Puharich, whose movie-star looks, warm smile, and infectious laugh had the same effect on him that it did on so many others. As a daughter of immigrants who had spent her entire life in New York, Puharich understood Eli's community and possibly some of his motivations. She saw his hope to build a company with a conscience as more genuine than the typical pronouncements made by executives giving away money to burnish their reputations or gain entrée to important social and political circles. Eli's giving had closely hewed to his faith and honored those who had given much to him; his gifts of time and money to Jewish organizations had honored institutions that mattered to his father and mentors, Rabbis Joseph Lookstein and Samuel Belkin, as well as the benefactor whose sponsorship had put him through school. Like his former boss, William Rosenwald, he supported Zionist projects and Jewish immigrant relief agencies.

Eli's level of giving may have impressed Anna, but she also sought to nudge him outside of his comfort zone by exposing him to the very timely cause of a different group of people being treated unjustly—and a set of remedies which would have immediate impact on the business of food and United Brands' daily operations. In just two short years since meeting Cesar Chavez, she had moved from raising money for the United Farm Workers union to working alongside him, relocating for months on end to California to be close to the action. She had become convinced that the farm worker struggle offered Eli an opportunity to be on the right side of history, not just as someone who gave to an organization but as a CEO who built his business model around the notion that social justice and profitability could both be advanced through more enlightened collaboration with organized labor. Over the next four years, the two confided in one another about their hopes and plans, and how they could achieve them by working together. Although thirteen years her elder, Eli found he could talk to Puharich easily. He wrote frequently to Anna, even as she remained loyal to the cause that threatened his company.[31]

Eli made good on his promise to work with Chavez by instructing members of his executive team to rescind its agreement with the Teamsters and, instead, pursue a pact with the UFW. Inter Harvest had been a United Fruit subsidiary prior to the AMK acquisition, and John

Fox, in United Fruit's historic home office in Boston, assembled the team to handle the thorny transition. United Fruit Vice President Will Lauer would represent the company in its three-way negotiations with Bill Grami, organizing director of the Teamsters' Western Conference; Herb Fleming, president of the Grower-Shipper Association; and Jerry Cohen and Dolores Huerta, lead lawyer and lead negotiator, respectively, for UFW. Always contentious, the exchanges at times became hostile, and took place in an atmosphere of brewing violence among farm workers, Teamsters rank-and-file, and growers in the fields, byways, and public establishments across the Salinas Valley. The National Conference of Catholic Bishops in 1969 had formed an Ad Hoc Committee on Farm Labor, and it served as mediator in the dispute, assigning Monsignor George Higgins to shepherd a peaceful outcome to the conflict. Chavez's use of nonviolent tactics like fasting proved to be less effective and sustainable than during the grape conflict, given his weakened state from months of struggle in Delano and the brazen aggression practiced by rogue members of the Teamsters in Salinas. On August 18, 1970, Chavez abandoned a prolonged fast on orders from his doctor and began a slow recuperation at the St. Francis retreat, a facility near the historic Mission San Juan Bautista, forty miles south of San Jose. Higgins and members of the UFW team kept Chavez abreast of the situation.

Lauer confronted several challenges, none more vexing than the internal struggle among growers. In a secret meeting among members of the Grower-Shippers Association on August 20, 1970, Lauer tried to persuade his peers to release the Teamsters from contracts they had signed earlier in the month. The Teamsters were fine with this; Grami of the Western Conference had been instructed to cede representation of the farm workers by his boss, Teamsters president Frank Fitzsimmons, who was at that time trying to repair damaged relations with the AFL-CIO, the organizing body with which the UFW was affiliated. The growers, however, resisted a move that they knew would cost them more. Lauer walked out of that meeting as a strong signal that Inter Harvest would break ranks and unilaterally rescind its contract with the Teamsters.

The next day, Herb Fleming held a press conference to issue a public reminder that the growers' contracts with the Teamsters were legal and binding. "They have assured us that they will honor these contracts," Fleming declared, "and we intend to do the same."[32] Meant to create the illusion of solidarity among growers, Fleming's announcement also served as a declaration of war against Inter Harvest and its intention to sign with Chavez. Lauer pressed on anyway, aware that Grami had been seeking a convenient exit from the conflict, and knowing that an agreement with the UFW would honor the will of Inter Harvest's employees.[33]

On August 22, 1970, Lauer, Cohen, and Huerta met at the Highway Center Lodge, one of the many motels lining Highway 101 running through the heart of the Salinas Valley. Lauer arrived with a sense of relief that negotiations with the Teamsters were behind him and an agreement with UFW could now be secured quickly. An election could be held allowing Inter Harvest workers to confirm what Cohen and Huerta had been claiming: that the majority of them supported the UFW. Chavez's team, however, impatient for negotiations to start, wanted to skip a formality whose result was a foregone conclusion. "It's too late," Cohen declared. Huerta agreed the workers had already been forced to wait a week and it would be "impossible" to hold an election: "we just ran out of time." Frustrated by this new resistance to a step he considered "fundamental"—even "critical"—Lauer proposed that Monsignor Higgins come in as mediator.

Higgins also believed the union's assertion that a strong majority of Inter Harvest field workers preferred the UFW to the Teamsters, but he appreciated Lauer's need for proof. He also understood that verification could come in another form—not through an election but by making an official count of the cards signed by workers indicating their preferences. If it used a so-called card check, the UFW could simply turn over the cards collected at the Hartnell College rally earlier that month. As well as being quicker and incurring no expense, this would head off any attempt by the Teamsters or growers to influence the outcome. "That's not exactly what Chavez wanted," Huerta hesitated. "He told me no card check." But Marshall Ganz, another member of Chavez's team, offered assurance that the union held 856 authorization cards favoring the UFW—a number representing 95 percent of Inter Harvest's machine and ground crews. Lauer was comfortable with the card check approach. The important thing was that he be able to show others at his company hard evidence that this was the will of the workers. "You signed with the Teamsters without a majority," Huerta shot back. Lauer admitted that that decision had been a mistake, one that they could not repeat. "We need elections for a matter of morality and principle."[34]

The union's negotiating team had no other choice but to ask Higgins to do the counting—and they insisted he do it alone. "I had never conducted a card check on that scale," Higgins remembered. He counted deep into the night, struggling to sort out the identities of workers whose names overlapped with others or whose signatures took time to verify as authentic. Throughout the fourteen-hour ordeal, United Fruit's vice president of industrial relations interrupted Higgins frequently to see if he needed anything. Sensing the man's anxiety, Higgins began to wonder if United Fruit was trying to intervene in some way and finally asked, "What are you looking for?" It turned out the man's sympathies were with Chavez and his team. "For God's sake, brother, they've got to win!" he said. "We've got to negotiate!"

The union remained on edge, too, as Higgins neared the end of the process. When Higgins emerged, Huerta demanded that he convey to the public that 95 percent of signed cards were in UFW's favor, but Higgins refused. "Dolores," he said, "I think, in fairness, I should not reveal the numbers to either side." Huerta flashed her familiar anger at him, but Higgins didn't give in, knowing that the union had fallen short of the majority both sides had hoped for. In the end, Higgins told Lauer and Chavez's people only that the card check had proven sufficient worker preference to proceed with negotiations and saved the truth for the archives.[35]

Whether or not Eli was kept apprised of developments in any detail is not known, but it must have pleased him to know that progress was being made in the negotiations. In the week that followed the card check, the Teamsters and growers further discredited themselves with acts of violence, one of which landed Jerry Cohen in a San Jose hospital. The aggression would only have deepened the rift between Eli's team and the local growers. Lauer continued to work through disagreements with the UFW delegation, dealing with frequent blow-ups by Dolores Huerta, who insisted that foremen be covered by the new contracts and that the company defer to the union-controlled hiring halls for the dispatch of workers. Over the next fortnight, the two sides battled in their motel of choice along Highway 101, each trying to pry concessions out of the other.

By August 25, 1970, it looked as if a breakthrough might be near. Anticipating success, Fox flew to California to lock in the agreement. He and Lauer dispensed with motel diplomacy and headed straight to the St. Francis retreat where Chavez was regaining his strength. The two entered the mission-style complex and headed for the library, the most ornate room at the Franciscan retreat, with chandeliers and richly paneled walls. As the sun set, casting shadows on the stained-glass windows, Chavez greeted the chairman of the board and chief executive officer of United Fruit. "They opened by saying they were 1,000 percent in accord with what we were doing," Chavez recalled, and they intimated that they had heard he was a reasonable man—while also hinting that "Dolores wasn't reasonable." Chavez immediately felt he should make clear that he was no less adversarial than his trusted negotiator and top ally: "I opened up by telling them that they couldn't get away with what United Fruit had been doing in Latin America for all these years." The two men defended the company, reminding Chavez that United Fruit had pursued a new relationship with its primary host country, Honduras, and welcomed collaboration with the premier union in Central America, SITRATERCO, even before Eli Black added to the reforms that were changing the company's reputation. "Of course, they didn't come in with hostility," Chavez remembered. He later said. "I just wanted them to know that they were not going to get an easier deal from me than they would from Dolores." The two organizational leaders having met and expressed a mutual desire to come to terms, it would be up to their teams to return to the negotiating table and continue to work toward an agreement.[36]

The next morning Chavez doubled down on his pressure on Inter Harvest by instructing volunteers in Boston to picket United Fruit's headquarters. "Concentrate on Chiquita," he told them in a phone call. "Hit the buyers today, the brokers tomorrow, and we announce the boycott publicly Friday!" The protests were a lesson to Eli and Jack Fox in how much influence a tired but determined cadre of UFW volunteers could wield. Lauer took umbrage at the press quoting Chavez saying Chiquita was "running scared" and broke off negotiations. When Huerta reported his intransigence that evening, Chavez had her call Lauer back. After she had spoken for a time, Chavez grabbed the receiver himself and issued a warning: "We have no choice but to boycott if talks are not resumed." Within moments, Chavez was yelling at Lauer, "Damn right we're singling you out!" Recalling the nerve he had hit when he brought up United Fruit's history a few days earlier, Chavez added, "Your company has been exploiting our brothers in Latin America for a long time, and we won't let you try the same dirty corrupt politics here!" The outburst had been a departure from the stoic, peaceful warrior Chavez had projected during the fast, but it produced the desired results. When the two sides met at the mission-style Travel Lodge along Highway 101 on August 29, 1970, they had something to trade. In exchange for the UFW's calling off the boycott against Chiquita products, Lauer would agree to two-year contracts that included pay raises for machine and field workers, the creation of union-managed hiring halls, the inclusion of foremen, and some regulation of pesticides. Chavez remained concerned with the possibility that Inter Harvest might invest in automation to replace workers, but Lauer offered his assurance that no such plans were in the works. For now, Inter Harvest workers would see an immediate bump in their per-hour wage from $1.75 to $2.10, with another increase to $2.15 in 1971. The agreement exceeded the Teamsters' proposed rate, which would have jumped to $1.85 and climbed to only $2.08 in the final year of the contract.[37]

Chavez claimed victory the next day, while United Fruit managed the fallout of the decision with fellow growers and some of its own staff who resisted the agreement. As Chavez had hoped, some corporate growers followed suit—notably Freshpict, owned by Purex, which also sued for peace with the union. Inter Harvest remained the biggest and most important defection from the Grower-Shipper Association, which maligned it as an outsider and a traitor. "They're from Boston," was the reaction from local grower. "It's a conspiracy to put the local grower out of operation. Inter Harvest has no interest in the valley, just in making money."[38]

Eli would have understood their anger but disagreed with their strategy. Their attempts to substitute the UFW with the Teamsters had been a failure to recognize the legitimacy of Chavez and the appeal of the farm workers movement. The union had proven itself a worthy adversary, beating a long-established grape industry that failed to overcome the boycott over five punishing years. Now running a multinational corporation, Eli had to think differently about the significant exposure his product lines had in the marketplace. Conversely, most of the growers in Salinas marketed vegetables that they had had a hand in growing themselves. As an organization dominated by family-run, multigenerational companies, the Grower-Shipper Association saw the industry as an expression of their cultural heritage, which could not be compromised through concessions to outsiders. To them, Eli's decision to work with Chavez was a betrayal of that heritage and a confirmation of his own outsider status. For Eli, working with Chavez not only made good business sense but also offered an opportunity to demonstrate the social responsibility for which he wanted United Brands to be known. In the end, he believed, carrying Chavez's eagle emblem alongside the Chiquita name on every package would signal to his customers the superiority of his products in every way, from the quality of the lettuce to the happiness and security of the workers who harvested it. Eli also made a few friends in the deal. In the coming months and years, he worked through Anna Puharich to arrange several visits with Chavez on both coasts.

Eli's choice to work with Chavez produced significant criticism from within the company—most importantly, from Tom and Bob Nunes, who had to implement the new arrangements with UFW. The deal to create union-run hiring halls essentially transferred the responsibility of assigning workers to the field from growers' hands to those of inexperienced UFW representatives. As Bob Nunes recalled, "Tom and I disagreed with the decision to sign and made our objections known." As sons of immigrants themselves, they claimed to have "the highest respect and sympathy" for farm workers but had their misgivings about Chavez and believed no good would come of working with the union. United Fruit drew a hard line with the brothers, forcing them to "go along or step aside."[39] Feeling they had already compromised too much, Tom and Bob Nunes walked away from the company, taking with them the last vestiges of a local managerial class that existed among the original, independent farms. In their place, a United Brands senior vice president Richard "Dick" Johnson, was assigned to oversee the relationship with the UFW, while Harold Bradshaw, president of Inter Harvest, worked to coordinate hiring and marketing with the union in California.

By the end of 1970, Eli must have felt he had made more enemies in one year than he had in his entire career. The Teamsters tried to punish United Brands for its agreement with Chavez with an ill-conceived appeal to wholesalers in Los Angeles and San Francisco not to unload Chiquita lettuce carrying the UFW eagle on its packages. While the

Teamster's campaign failed, it underscored the level of enmity that Eli's organization had attracted, and the degree to which he had become embroiled in a conflict that had been peripheral to him when he began his pursuit of United Fruit. Anna Puharich, who now traveled with Chavez in California, tried to reassure Eli that he had made the right decision but the lack of profits and the disarray of United Brands in its first year required an act of faith—and some creative writing to shareholders—to get through. He chose an approach that mixed hard truths with optimism. "The year 1970 was a poor one for the Company and for the economy as a whole," he wrote in the first line of that year's letter to shareholders. Yet, after reporting the disappointing news from Honduras about banana production, the difficulty of negotiating a new contract with AMCBW at Morrell, and the strikes in California that had undermined profits at Inter Harvest, Eli turned to the underlying financial strength of the company's future. "The creation of United Brands is indeed a fresh beginning, and even more important, a major act of progress and renewal." With a new, younger group of executives on the job, including himself, he promised a "freshness of vision" and "vitality" that would see United Brands through these difficult times.[40]

Indeed, Eli had youth on his side for the time being, given that his company in its new form as United Brands was less than a year old. Yet, no amount of positive talk could reverse the trends he now witnessed. The acquisition of United Fruit was supposed to lead to bigger and better things. He comforted himself and others with the thought that these bad numbers were "caused in large part by uncontrollable, natural disaster," and unexpected labor disputes that had cut into production and consumed management attention. He told himself that these unusual conditions would pass, but he would now have to work hard to ensure such an outcome. "The actions we have taken and are taking," he concluded, "should be the basis for the turnaround of 1971."

5

ISRAELITE

AMONG THE MOST PRECIOUS benefits of Eli's growing wealth was the privilege it afforded him to host a generous Passover Seder at his home in Westport each spring. The ritual feast commemorates God's delivery of the Jews, the "Israelites" of biblical history, from the bonds of slavery in ancient Egypt. As someone deeply educated in his faith, and as a parent, Eli took special pleasure in this festive holiday and the opportunity the Seder presented to teach the history of the Jewish experience and its modern relevance. He often invited people he particularly respected, those he wished to weave into the fabric of his family life.

On April 9, 1971, the people new to his circle included Cesar Chavez and Anna Puharich. Circumstances in Salinas forced Chavez to decline Eli's invitation, but he would come a year later. On this evening, Anna attended for the both of them, honoring a growing friendship and the relationship between United Brands and the United Farm Workers. Although she lived just across Central Park from the Blacks, her arrival on their doorstep marked a culmination of sorts, after nearly a year of trips between New York and California, numerous phone calls, and occasional meetings in Manhattan. She had been the first liaison between Eli and Chavez, helping them recognize that they had a basis for collaboration rather than conflict. This work also drew Anna and Eli closer to one another, opening a relationship that had become increasingly important to him. Now, a joyful Eli took her hand to proudly introduce her to other guests.

It is not uncommon for Passover Seder to involve readings from the Haggadah, a printed booklet laying out the time-honored order of a gathering designed for Jews to impart to their children the ancient story of oppression and liberation. Like many families, Eli's selected readings of their own to supplement the traditional text, some from secular sources. Shirley chose "Unseen Buds" from Walt Whitman's *Leaves of Grass* to add to the 1971 Haggadah, the cover of which she designed. Judy offered a reading from John Stuart Mill's *On Liberty*. Leon, by then studying philosophy and history at Dartmouth, chose two short passages, one by Herman Hesse, the German-Swiss poet and author who had opposed Hitler, and another by Austrian philosopher Martin Buber. Eli chose to quote an even more contemporary voice, Henry Merritt Wriston, a former president of Brown University, advisor to the Eisenhower administration, and president of the Council on Foreign Relations. Wriston's speech explored the connection between human dignity and freedom, a subject that had interested Eli since his studies at Yeshiva. Eli believed that leaders in society had a responsibility to reduce obstructions to people's freedom as much as possible. Wriston had spoken critically of "corporate policy" that avoided "taking controversial positions on public questions" or stifled employees' participation in a political party "not favored by the management." As Eli read the passage, he may have shot a knowing glance to Anna, who understood the sacrifices he had made to support the lechugueros and the United Farm Workers.[1]

In the conversation and the breaking of the matzah that followed, Eli would have spoken confidently of the decision he had made, voicing his empathy with the workers and sharing insights he had

ISRAELITE   127

gained about Chavez. On an evening full of reflection on Jewish forebears escaping the bonds of servitude, he may have reached a deeper understanding of what it meant to support California field hands in their fight for freedom from exploitation. Generations of Eli's people, like Chavez's, had labored hard and traveled long distances seeking better lives. Now, as the employer of tens of thousands, he was in a position to affect the lives of many who struggled. He had the opportunity to disrupt the notion that labor and management must always be at odds, and to create a profitable company that honored the dignity of everyone whose lives it touched. As he said his goodbyes to guests that evening, he promised Anna they would stay in touch, and asked her to give Cesar his regards and communicate the Blacks' wish to host him the following year.

Spring is often a time for renewal and reflection, and this one must have been especially so for Eli. Coming off an intense and financially disappointing year in 1970, he felt good about the outcome of negotiations with the United Farm Workers, and the fact that Inter Harvest was given credit for a more enlightened approach to labor relations in California agriculture. Much remained unresolved, especially the question of whether the UFW could follow through on their commitment to hire field workers for the lettuce harvest that summer, but Eli knew that his company's dealings with Chavez had clearly shown it stepping up to a higher level of social responsibility.

United Fruit's reputation for undermining sovereign governments and extracting profits from its host country had made it an easy target for derision during the labor negotiations with the UFW, but by the same token, the company represented a high-profile opportunity to convince doubters about the effectiveness of a more conscientious business model. Eli took ownership during a time when the public's skepticism about the ability of big business to improve society was very high. The antiwar movement was taking aim at US companies that profited from the war in Vietnam, and not only the makers of missiles and tanks. When the UFW researched how California grapes were still being sold in high volumes amid a powerful boycott, it found huge shipments going to Vietnam—a clear indication that the US government was using military purchasing to protect growers' businesses and undercut the union. In Latin America, especially Central America, United Fruit's name had become synonymous with exploitation and manipulation, an octopus taking hold of every aspect of citizens' lives. Eli had agreed that the company could and must reverse this history by making operational decisions that would benefit its host countries and not just its own bottom line. Such priorities ran counter to the emerging business orthodoxy voiced by Milton Friedman, who famously believed that "the Social Responsibility of Business is to Increase its Profits."[2] By caring about United Fruit's legacy in Latin America and its influence on society, Eli took the bold step of siding with those who thought the time had come for business to respond to the needs of employees and consumers as much as to shareholders.

Eli had made the usual investments in public relations to reshape the image of United Fruit, and his first annual report for United Brands, written in the spring 1971, concluded with an in-depth discussion of "United Fruit Company in Latin America." It acknowledged the "strong winds of nationalist aspiration" sweeping across countries where United Fruit and other foreign businesses owned so many productive assets: "The desires of these nations to control their own destinies and reap a larger return from their national resources and their gross national product are understandable." It claimed that "all of the Company's policies for investment, land utilization, social reforms, labor relations are geared to the rising expectations of our host countries." Countering the popular image of United Fruit as exploiter of land and labor, a charge raised during the UFW negotiations, it offered assurance: "The company's operations are not extractive. *They create rather than deplete a national resource.* For every dollar in profits in an average year, United Fruit has left more than seven dollars in its host countries," in the form of wages, taxes, local purchasing, and capital investment.[3]

At the same time, Eli recognized that the work of building a new narrative of corporate responsibility should include an acknowledgment of the sins of the past. To make these points more legible to the public, he agreed to spend $25,000 on a company film in the works when he arrived. Called *Yanqui Go Home,* it offered a candid assessment of United Fruit's history of bad behavior in Central America while highlighting its recent decisions to work cooperatively with host nations and United Fruit's labor union, SITRATERCO. The film was released to positive response. When *Business Week* asked United Brands' public relations representative, Thomas McCann, about it, he commented that "most P.R. guys hate it because it's too frank"—but added, "the payoff is that people are viewing our company in light of current events rather than past history."[4]

Eli recognized that his campaign would have to be accompanied by real, measurable changes in management practices. "Public relations, as an end in itself, is dangerous," he told the reporter. If it wasn't matched by reality, the hypocrisy would be exposed. But, he added, "P.R. as a constructive tool for telling a story—if there is a story to be told—is effective."[5] To overcome the cynicism of reporters and the public, Eli backed up his rhetoric about a new, improved United Fruit with a range of substantive improvements. In his agreement with union president Oscar Gale Varela, set to take effect in 1972, he rejected the usual piece-rate compensation for banana harvesters by establishing a set rate of $95 per month based on a forty-four-hour week. Additionally, he made each employee a shareholder by including bank stocks as part of their wage structure. Such compensation represented the best in Honduras, amounting to $22 million in salaries paid there per year by United Fruit. For the first time in the company's history, field workers had ten paid vacation days per year.

Whereas previously United Fruit would import managers from North America, the company now hired Honduran nationals for these positions. By 1972, of the 325 residential managers at La Lima, three hundred were Honduran and only five came from the United States.

In another departure from the past, the company ended its practice of bringing in workers from neighboring Central American countries, especially from Guatemala and El Salvador. Hondurans now made up 99 percent of the workforce on plantations supplying United Fruit. Eli took pride in offering full-time employment to banana workers, noting that it marked a "sharp contrast to agricultural employment generally, including the United States."[6] When asked how their working conditions compared to previous ones, workers at La Lima confirmed Eli's narrative of change. Alberto Reyes, a veteran picker at United Fruit, told a *New York Times* reporter, "I worked from 6 AM to 6 PM. We never dared complain. They would bring in Guatemalans and others to pick the bananas. The Americans had all the good jobs then. All that is past."[7]

Eli extended investments in Honduras's health and education infrastructure. La Lima maintained a 235-bed hospital with eleven full-time physicians and the capacity to perform major surgeries. United Fruit workers and their families paid 25 cents to use the facility, while those not employed by the system also benefited from an aggressive campaign against malaria and polio, which the hospital effectively eliminated from the region within three years. The company paid $500,000 per year to support the school system serving the La Lima community. The school employed 210 teachers who were in 1972 educating over eight thousand students up to sixth grade. United Fruit provided $50,000 in scholarships for students to finish high school or college without any obligation to return to La Lima as employees.[8] Eli rejected the notion that these provisions for workers had been acts of charity. "For an enlightened and progressive company," he wrote to shareholders, "they are the necessary costs of doing business in tropical areas that had to be converted from virgin jungle to productive large-scale agribusinesses with integrated farming and transportation operations."[9]

Eli also advanced the approach to land ownership that Jack Fox had been implementing. Although United Fruit controlled significant acreage in nearby Costa Rica, Guatemala, and Panama, the greatest share of its landholdings were in Honduras—amounting to nearly 200,000 acres. Prior to the merger, the company had initiated the transfer of land ownership from United Fruit to local planters under what it called the associate growers' program. "*Since 1952*," the 1970 annual report announced, "*the Company has divested itself of 65 percent of its holdings in the four countries.*"[10]

In Honduras, Eli intensified this program, arranging for United Fruit to return 135,000 acres to the Honduran government to be broken up into eighty-six separate groves of fifty acres each for independent planters. As well as claiming a noble purpose to put land in the hands of Honduran farmers, the company benefited as the voluntary forfeitures deterred calls for more sweeping expropriations of lands it owned but had not cultivated. The program also offloaded some of the risks and costs of growing, allowing United Fruit to redirect some of its own resources to controlling disease in the groves and building the Chiquita brand worldwide. By the early 1970s, the program enjoyed popularity in Honduras as participants were realizing earnings of between $1,200 and $7,000 per year.[11]

Regarding matters of national governance, United Fruit executives professed no interest. As a general manager on the ground in Honduras told the *Boston Globe,* "We realize we have to work with whatever party is in power. . . . We have no political opinions."[12] Such a position stood in stark contrast to a past when the company had been happy to exert influence, even to the point of causing the United States government to intervene, to keep the kinds of politicians out of power who would dare to crimp the flow of cash from its banana plantations.

Changes in policy may have produced good storylines for the company, but they did not improve financial performance. United Fruit, with Eli now running the business directly as CEO, suffered another dismal year in banana revenues in 1971, due to low market prices for the fruit—the result of an oversupply thanks to companies' overzealous replanting in the wake of Hurricane Francelia's destruction. Eli tried to put a positive face on the situation by celebrating the sales growth of United Fruit's UK subsidiary, Fyffes Group, and its non-banana activities, such as the cultivation and sale of African oil palm in Central America, the raw material used by its Numar subsidiary to make margarine, shortening, and other oil-based products. Performance was heartening, as well, at Baskin-Robbins, A&W Root Beer, and other subsidiaries of the company. Plastics production for the packaging and labeling of lettuce and bananas offered an especially bright spot and encouraged Eli to seek new investments in this area.

The bits of good news, however, could only do so much to soften the blow of another bad year. Overall, United Brands had improved its net sales by less than $1.2 million, but had taken extraordinary losses of $22 million, largely through Eli's decision to dispose of some nonproductive properties and decommission a number of vessels in the company's famous "Great White Fleet"—a costly step in the current year, but one that would reduce overhead costs going forward. After accounting for these charges against income and taxes, United Brands overall had lost $24 million, which on a per-share basis translated to a net loss of $2.43 per share. Although Eli continued to reassure investors that "our financial condition remains strong," the company's position rested primarily on cost-cutting rather than a dramatic increase in productivity.[13] He offered the indeterminant promise that "the banana industry will correct itself as it has in the past," but without any certainty of when that might happen.[14]

Among the greatest disappointments was the performance of Inter Harvest. Despite the agreement with the United Farm Workers, stoppages and worker slowdowns in lettuce production persisted. Eli had hoped that siding with the farm workers would eliminate interruptions in the harvest and benefit sales of Inter Harvest lettuce against its competitors, but neither came to pass. Part of the problem had been the muddled message of the stakes in the labor fight. During the grape boycott and the strike in Delano, the battle had been starkly drawn between growers and farm workers. In the case of lettuce and Salinas, the three-way struggle among growers, the Teamsters, and the United Farm Workers confused a public that had difficulty distinguishing one union from another. The Grower-Shipper Association proved to be a much more worthy opponent than the grape growers, and spent handsomely to overwhelm news of Inter Harvest's defection with ads claiming unity among lettuce growers.

Not all the failure to capitalize on the agreement could be attributed to grower or Teamster actions. Reviewing the outcomes of recent mergers and acquisitions in California agriculture, *Fortune* claimed that "the shadow of Cesar Chavez" hung over corporate investors, causing many to falter. By signing with the United Farm Workers, the authors argued, corporate farms paid between 25 and 30 percent more for labor than their smaller nonunion competitors. Farm managers expected harmony and efficiency in exchange for working with the union. Instead, they found a union ill-prepared for the bureaucracy of labor management and upset workers who took their frustrations out on the employer. *Fortune's* observation that the United Farm Workers union was "critically short of leadership at the shop-steward level" matched the perception by many, including within the UFW, that the union lacked the influence it needed to direct workers to where they were needed. In many cases," the magazine argued, "only Chavez himself can persuade workers to live up to the terms of the contracts."[15]

By early 1972, several corporations either folded operations or diversified their crops to reduce exposure to Chavez and the UFW. In the case of Tenneco, an oil company that had diversified into agribusiness (in grape and lettuce crops, both subject to UFW influence), the company sold seventy thousand acres of farmland and invested in a subsidiary, Heggblade-Marguleas-Tenneco, to move more aggressively into marketing rather than production. The vision was of a future where it would become the principal distributor of massive, low-margin crops raised by independent farmers. Building the "Sun Giant" label became its main objective. The company continued to cultivate rare, out-of-season specialty crops on twenty thousand acres, but for the most part, embraced its new identity as a packer and marketer, not a farmer.[16]

Eli shared the frustration of his peers and suspended use of the Chiquita brand label for Inter Harvest lettuce, but refused to give up on Chavez and the union as partners.[17] In his shareholders letter in the United Brands 1971 annual report, published in the spring of 1972, he noted the expiration of contracts with the United Farm Workers in August and promised to resolve the quality issues caused by the mismanagement of hiring halls.[18] He renewed his invitation to Cesar and Anna to attend the Passover Seder at his home and was pleased to learn that Cesar would make the trip this time. At the celebration on March 29, 1972, Eli included in the Haggadah a speech by James F. Oates, Jr. called "The Contradictions of Leadership." Oates had led two companies, first the Peoples Gas, Light, and Coke Company in Chicago, and then the Equitable Life Assurance Society of the United States. In both these roles Oates had distinguished himself as a manager who promoted and cultivated talent within his companies and invested in communities, including through urban renewal projects in Pittsburgh during the late 1960s. Reading to a packed house in Westport, Eli raised Oates's central dilemma for the CEO during a time when inequities and rebellions had increased the "moral sensibility of American society" and demanded a clearer vision of how businesses served their employees and society in general: "Does the successful business try first to profit or to serve?" Oates's question spoke to Eli's concerns in this moment. Oates had noted that the easy answer was "both," but that the true dilemma had always been how to do that, and at a scale that meaningfully benefited both company and society. "As we raise our sights and enlarge our moral expectations," Oates argued, "we become more sensitive to the inequities of our society, its corruptions, and its unrealized potentials for a humane life."

Eli agreed with Oates that a willingness to compromise "moral principle" for the good of the company or the accumulation of wealth was "no longer judged good enough" for the business leaders of their time. Eli gave his guests something to ponder with the final line of Oates's speech: "More and more Americans are stirring themselves out of the complacency induced by affluence to ask the harder questions: affluence for what? And for whom? And what beyond affluence?"[19] Eli, a man who had risen from poverty to become a wealthy businessman, had grappled with such questions for some time. How should he honor the lives of the people affected by his company? How might his actions influence the moral context of his time, now that he had achieved his goal of presiding over a major multinational corporation?

As he read, his eyes fell on Anna and Cesar. Their ongoing work offered perhaps his best chance to fulfill the promise of United Brands to make the world a more humane place. His selection of Oates's article conveyed to his esteemed guests the moral dimensions of his decision to side with the farm workers in Salinas and his intention to continue that commitment. For Chavez, a trip across country was not made lightly, but the assurances he got from Eli that evening must have made this visit worthwhile. He, more than most people in that room, would have identified with Eli's humble origins and known the burden of responsibility that comes with success. He, too, had struggled with the moral question of what to do with power once he gained it. Perhaps in Eli's rabbinical background, he saw an authority that, like his, was inseparable from a religious upbringing and faith that caused him to lead in a different way than others of his time. The victory in Delano, and persuading Eli to sign contracts with UFW, now required him to be a manager of other people's lives and business—something he was not prepared to take on years before when he began his rebellion as a community organizer. Although he espoused the notion that creating a union would solve many of the farm workers' problems, he understood that this was easier said than done, and that he needed Eli's patience and cooperation to fully succeed. It must have given Chavez some peace of mind to know that Eli understood and appreciated the moral and ethical dimensions of their work together, and was willing to stand by the relationship. When Eli and Chavez said goodbye that evening in Connecticut, they still represented two opposing sides, but the two men trusted that they could work together through future conflicts.

On July 26, 1972, Eli went along with two of his senior vice presidents—Dick Johnson and Will Lauer—to a meeting in California to renegotiate contracts with Chavez and his cousin Manuel Chavez. Johnson began by identifying two challenges plaguing production: a general lack of discipline among workers represented by UFW, and their inability to complete specific tasks. Johnson noted "a very noticeable deterioration in the attitude of workers toward the Company" because of poorly organized hiring halls. As evidence, he shared the case in which the UFW managers assigned work to a man and woman, both sixty-eight years old, which was too strenuous for them to perform. This incident fit a more general pattern of hiring hall managers dispatching "substantial numbers of [workers] who do not have the required skills, physical ability, or necessary capacity" for the jobs they were hired to fill. Lauer added that when the company reassigned employees, workers engaged in work stoppages that union officials failed to quell. The involvement of hiring halls in transferring workers from one job to another added an unnecessary layer of oversight and resulted in delays. Eli and his team strongly recommended that the process be streamlined and that the union resist micromanaging the production of lettuce and other vegetables. Johnson cited union interference in the harvesting process by encouraging workers to question the authority of working foremen in the field who took instruction from crew foremen in charge of training and farm-level supervision. "Almost every attempt to pass on instructions" from crew foremen, Johnson observed, "meets with strong objections." In one case, a work crew "refused to finish off a field" to complete an order even though the crew foremen noted that they had more time remaining in the day. According to Johnson, the workers "unilaterally established" a seven-and-a-half-hour workday even though their contracts called for nine-hour days. When the company tried to enforce the contract, union officials had backed up workers by threatening the company with "more trouble than it can handle." Johnson cited an "air of tension" and a "lack of pride" from union supervisors and workers alike. From the company's vantage point, the conditions violated "the spirt of our collective bargaining agreement" and compromised the competitiveness of Inter Harvest lettuce.[20]

On a personal level, Eli contributed funds to the union's National Farm Worker Service Center to aid UFW families in distress and served as a trustee of the UFW's Martin Luther King Fund created to support educational services for farm workers and their children. Such dedication of money and time was an important way of expressing his support and friendship to Chavez. These individual investments complemented the commitments to these endeavors written into Inter Harvest's contract with the UFW. Yet, even these issues came under scrutiny during the negotiations in July 1972. Eli raised the issue of the UFW's Robert F. Kennedy Medical Plan, to which United Brands contributed half a million dollars over the first year. The company argued that the same health benefits could be covered by a private company for much less, saving the UFW and United Brands as much as $170,000. Eli also questioned whether the $250,000 that United Brands and Freshpict had contributed to UFW's Economic Development Plan was actually improving opportunities for the farm workers' families the program was meant to serve.[21]

Chavez acknowledged some of the problems but cited grievances of his own. He told Eli and his managers that "workers were treated like serfs" and faulted the company for not laying out the number of hours at the beginning of the day. This failure, he argued, showed that the company "doesn't honor [the] contract" and communicated to workers, "if they can break it so can we." It wasn't a reaction he supported. In fact, he said, "We are trying to teach people if the company breaks [the] contract we shouldn't do the same." A lack of trust between company and union, Chavez noted, made it difficult for the UFW to balance assignments across the grape and lettuce industry, given workers' preference for grape harvesting. "We don't want work stop headaches, but there are problems that are deep rooted and have to be explored," Chavez said, but quickly added, "It's very easy to blame the union—we're not going to be held responsible for the competition problems."[22]

Cesar and Manuel Chavez worried, too, about the emergence of a new front in Florida, where United Brands, under the subsidiary Floriculture Inc., raised tropical houseplants for the US market after importing seedlings from Honduras. In 1972, the United Farm Workers began organizing employees on citrus plantations owned by the Coca-Cola Company in the Sunshine State that produced orange juice for its subsidiary, Tropicana. During the union drive, Manuel Chavez had heard from Floriculture workers who welcomed the UFW that they had been threatened by foremen with dismissal if they joined the union. Both Cesar and Manuel appealed to Eli to rein in these foremen and embrace the union across all United Brands production sites within the United States. It was an argument that Eli resisted. "We were a logical first choice in lettuce," he admitted, but added, "we're just pipsqueaks [in Florida horticulture]." Eli claimed that Floriculture had yet to make money. "[If you] attack the leader in that industry," Eli promised Chavez, "we will hand you a contract on a silver platter—I give you my word." Chavez responded that the other companies would sooner meet increased wage demands from employees than agree to contracts with the union. For this reason, he argued, the size or market influence of Eli's company was less important than his willingness to sign contracts. Will Lauer interjected, "our position has always been [that] we want a union." In the end, Eli promised to consider contracts in Florida if the union focused on improving the poor quality of lettuce coming out of Inter Harvest in California first. He added, "It's in our best interests for both of us."[23]

Despite their differences, Eli honored his intentions of continuing his collaboration with Chavez and the UFW at the July meeting in California in 1972. Within days, Johnson followed up with a recap of the company's main concerns and a note of optimism that the UFW and United Brands could overcome its differences. Johnson noted that "during the past two years both the Union and the Company have solved many problems through mutual cooperation," and expressed his belief that they could do this again "to the advantage of all concerned." Aside from the specific problems confronting Inter Harvest and Floriculture, Eli recognized that he and Chavez shared some common enemies—specifically, owners of industry who refused to accept the presence of the United Farm Workers in agribusiness. Although Eli expected concessions from his friend, he continued to support Chavez in his pursuit of a more just workplace for farm workers. By the end of the week, the two sides had agreed to a three-year contract extension.

The agreement came just as lettuce growers were ratcheting up the pressure on the United Farm Workers by supporting Proposition 22, an initiative on the California November 1972 ballot that would restrict the union's use of the boycott. Chavez put Eli's loyalty to the test by asking him to intervene on behalf of the union with his peers, many of whom were helping to finance the Prop 22 campaign. Even in normal times, such a request would have been a tall order for Eli, who had been publicly maligned and sued by his fellow growers in 1970. At an industry meeting among lettuce growers in November 1972, Eli defended his decision to renew contracts with the UFW to avoid a harmful boycott. He also declined to support his fellow growers' advocacy for Proposition 22 and urged them to accept the outcome of the election as the final word on UFW's right to use the tactic. In her reporting to Chavez of what happened at the meeting, Anna shared that Eli convinced his peers of his "truthfulness, honesty, and integrity" but declined "to tell them how to run their businesses." He encouraged

Puharich to channel Chavez's energies toward defeating Proposition 22.[24] In the end, the union beat back the challenge at the ballot box, but conflict between the Teamsters and the *Chavistas* raged in the fields of California well into the following year.

Eli regretted the continued warfare and the constant travel back and forth to California, but seemed to enjoy seeing Anna Puharich on a regular basis. Anna had been present at most of the meetings that involved face-to-face negotiations between Eli and Chavez, since she had been the person who brought them together, and she now played a more prominent role in managing the affairs of Chavez from within La Paz, the UFW headquarters. She remained married but had grown apart from her husband, Andrija, who had become increasingly consumed by his interests in Uri Geller's purported telekinetic powers and the mind-expanding potential of psychedelic drugs. She was flying frequently now between California and New York City, running herself ragged in the process. Eli identified with this nomadic life, having to shuttle between the United Fruit headquarters in Boston and the United Brands offices in New York City, with stops in Connecticut to see the family on the weekends in between. By the fall of 1972, Anna had been suffering from an undiagnosed ailment, perhaps caused by the stresses of her travel schedule, but continued to facilitate meetings to strengthen the alliance between United Brands and UFW. "Get a pair of old pants ready for your farm visit," she wrote Eli on September 23, 1972. The trip, which involved visits to a farm worker village, also included a meeting with Chavez in mid-October. The two had developed such a comfortable rapport that Anna felt free to advise Eli on how to present himself: "Please don't get a haircut until you return from California!" Her jest had been aimed as much at the West Coast hippie culture as at the conservative look of her corporate friend. The trip had been more of a social call on the part of Eli, but every meeting between him and Chavez deepened the bonds of trust they would need for their collective venture to succeed.

Polaroid photo of Eli Black with unidentified farm workers in California, 1972.
Anna Andreini-Brophy Papers, box 2-folder 55, Walter P. Reuther Library, Archives of Labor and Urban Affairs, Wayne State University.

When Eli traveled abroad in October and November, his correspondences with Anna increased in frequency and intensity of feeling. During his visit to United Fruit's British division, Fyffes Group, in London, Eli wrote to Anna expressing concern for her health and relief that she was finally on the mend. "I was delighted to find when I telephoned last that you absconded to an unrevealed Shangri-La to rest and recuperate," he wrote. He kidded, "knowing you, as I think I do,

I was unable to credit you entirely with such a display of good sense and I feel quite certain that the admonitions of your doctor must have influenced you strongly to take this most sensible step." Striking a gentler tone, he added, "I hope he did not alarm you unduly."[25] From London, he had proceeded to the Canary Islands off the coast of northern Africa, where he toured fruit and vegetable plantations owned and operated by United Fruit. He reported, with a mix of pride and awe, that "we seem to own an abundance of both magnificent beach property as well as mountainous regions."

His travels also took him to business in Germany and a wedding in Geneva for a son of Chaim Herzog—the chief of intelligence for the Israeli Armed Forces who would become Israel's sixth president in 1983. Herzog was also the brother-in-law of Abba Eban, whom Eli had known well in New York before Eban left for a career in politics in Israel in 1959. He admitted "a lingering feeling of discomfort" in Germany and resisted flying direct on the German-owned Lufthansa to avoid patronizing a company that had served the Nazi regime during World War II. Yet he could not complain about how he was received and joked, "I even met a few Germans with a sense of humor!" Arriving back in London two days later, he felt more in his element. "I love England," he told Anna, and "think the British are still the most civilized people in the world." Although he spent the better part of his two-page letter reporting on connections made and business acumen shared, he returned to his opening sentiments of concern for her. "Back in the States week of [October 9] when, I hope, you will be fully restored to complete health and physically able to cope with your insatiable curiosity and your penchant for getting yourself deeply involved in your beloved causes—and everything else."[26]

Anna's replies show sincere affection for Eli but also a desire to learn more about United Brands' business. She frequently requested financial information from him to help the union construct its negotiations strategy with the company. For example, during his visit to California following his trip to Europe, the two traveled together aboard his Beechcraft Queen Air, a small twin-engine airplane. While flying across the state, the two discussed how the company and the union might further close the gap between them. In addition to securing the use of the pilot's camera to capture the visit, she asked Eli to send a copy of United Brands' recently issued third-quarter earnings report and information about the sunglasses maker Foster Grant, in which United Brands had just taken a thirty percent ownership stake, signaling Eli's next takeover. Anna passed on the information to Jerry Cohen, who used it to calibrate how far the union could push United Brands on issues of compensation for workers and contributions to the National Farm Worker Service Center.

Eli knew well that whatever information he shared would make its way to UFW contract negotiators, but there was no harm in making Anna aware of company updates that by law had already been publicly disclosed. While seated on the plane close to one another, the two fell into conversation about how their lives had been transformed since their friendship began. For Eli, Anna had ushered him from contributing money to a social cause to shaping it through the policies he instituted at United Brands. The partnership with Chavez had been the clearest manifestation of his new business ethos of social responsibility, which also doubled as a market strategy for distinguishing the company from its competitors. For Anna, Eli's friendship made it possible to move from courting wealthy donors who wanted to give to left-leaning causes to building and sustaining a partnership between business and labor. Until meeting both these men, her role at Spectemur Agendo, a philanthropic foundation launched by Stewart Mott to support radical causes, had been enough. With the discovery that she might work with the two men to build a different model for doing business motivated her to move some of her life to California at the end of 1970 to work for the union and create this unusual partnership. By the fall of 1972, the two friends had invested so much in one another and spent so much time together that they no longer questioned the sincerity of their feelings for one another.

Eli's trip to California in October had mostly been an opportunity to see Anna and Chavez again and celebrate the conclusion of another long-term contract with the United Farm Workers. In November he turned his attention to United Fruit, where the recovery from natural disasters and the economic woes of his host countries threatened to deepen the financial troubles of his banana business. Anna continued to offer a sympathetic ear to his fears and aspirations, even as he traveled to Colombia and Central America with Leon to evaluate United Fruit's operations. Leon's presence pleased Eli tremendously since his son's Dartmouth graduation was coming up in June 1972 and he had been weighing his options about what to do with his life. "It will be fun doing all this with Leon and valuable experience—now that he has decided to go to Harvard Business School," he wrote. Eli was surprised to see improvements in crop cultivation and high morale among workers whom he addressed in his imperfect Spanish. The presidents of Costa Rica, Panama, and Colombia hosted him for meals at their homes in a "most friendly and cordial atmosphere." Eli overflowed with confidence in his description of these meetings, noting that he "would say 'I told them how to run their countries and they listened attentively,' but that sounds presumptuous, so I won't say it." He boasted that one president had told him "he had not received as many valuable and productive ideas from all his ministers and advisers" as he did in just four hours of conversation with Eli. With Anna as his audience, Eli betrayed a vanity that he certainly could not have displayed to those heads of state—unless he wanted to perpetuate the image of the imperialistic US capitalist.

Among the countries he visited, he deemed Colombia "the most primitive and perhaps most beautiful and exotic of our divisions." Set in a lush jungle in a remote part of the country, United Fruit's property played host to diverse flora and fauna. "Only some of the people are more fascinating," he remarked, including his manager, Ira Hubbard, whom he described as "a mountain of a man hewn out of solid granite." Although the trip entertained Eli, it revealed the superiority

Eli Black with President José Figueres Ferrer of Costa Rica and guests, 1972. *Anna Andreini-Brophy Papers (LP002659), Walter P. Reuther Library, Archives of Labor and Urban Affairs, Wayne State University.*

of La Lima in Honduras over other United Fruit plantations throughout Latin America. He promised to share "a very exciting new idea for C.C. [Cesar Chavez] in the plan outlined for La Causa," before closing with "wish you were here" and recalling their time together aboard his private plane in California.[27]

When Eli returned to the United States in December, he sent Anna an unexpected token of his esteem—a bracelet, accompanied by a blank card but clearly from him. The gift was not one that Anna was comfortable receiving. Her handwritten reply was gracious, but short and direct. "Thank you from the bottom of my heart for the incredibly elegant bracelet," she opened, assuring him that the gift and the thought behind it had made her day "brighter." Still, "I'm sorry I can't accept it," she informed him. "Please try not to think of me ungrateful and / or rude. Because if you do it will sadden you—and us."[28]

Whether he meant it to be or not, Eli's gift had been a presumptuous act—capping off a year of calculated risk-taking, including gambling with the future of Inter Harvest by doubling down on its relationship with the United Farm Workers. Eli wasted no time in responding to Anna's rejection. "I think I understand," he wrote on personal stationery labeled "Memo From E. M. Black." Because she had noted the mysterious blank card that came with the bracelet, he had an opportunity to say that the wrong card had accidently been enclosed: "The one I wrote was, 'may your most cherished hopes be fulfilled in the coming year." And with that, he changed the subject, inquiring whether Cesar had received a note he had sent, and signed off in his usual fashion, with "all good wishes."[29]

Eli had just missed Chavez, who came to Manhattan to appear on the Dick Cavett Show, Wednesday, December 13, 1972, taping on West 58th Street. "Hollywood needs new talent desperately," Eli joked with him, adding, "and you may yet get an irresistible offer." Although Eli had left for a few days in Boston, finalizing United Fruit's budget for the forthcoming year, he offered to meet up with Chavez later that week in New York. He also renewed an earlier offer to have Cesar join him for that year's Agribusiness Seminar at Harvard Business School as his personal guest. Eli had attended and spoken at the gathering in previous years. He told Cesar, "I believe you would find it interesting and instructive."[30]

Eli noted the uncharacteristic silence from Cesar who had, up until then, been very responsive to him. Since the signing of the contracts with Inter Harvest, Cesar had been consumed by the renewed battle with the Teamsters who had attempted another run at organizing farm workers in California. Although the Teamsters initially backed off from their intentions to replace the UFW in Salinas, the dysfunction of UFW hiring halls encouraged grape and lettuce growers to invite them back. Grape growers had been the first to get burned by the UFW mismanagement of hiring halls, with many of them regretting they had signed three-year contracts set to expire during the summer of 1973. By the summer of 1972, most had had enough of the UFW and, in some instances, taken over the dispatch of workers themselves, in violation of the contracts.[31] Many of them imagined seeking common cause with lettuce growers who introduced the idea of substituting Teamsters for the UFW. In 1972, President Richard Nixon, who had spent years representing California in Congress and was very familiar with the politics of Chavez's social movement unionism, encouraged the Teamsters' president, Frank Fitzsimmons, to disrupt it by offering to organize field workers again in violation of his pact with Chavez to leave them alone. Fitzsimmons, sensing new leverage in his on-again, off-again war with Chavez, began entertaining offers from grape and lettuce growers that summer to become the union of their choice.[32]

By the close of the 1972 growing season, many of the United Farm Worker organizers recognized that poor management of the hiring hall system had jeopardized the union's ability to hold on to contracts. Fighting the labor war on two fronts—grapes and lettuce—had overextended the union and caused Chavez to move skilled negotiators to Salinas while neglecting the contracts in Delano. The agreement with Inter Harvest and encouragement from Eli had been a rare glimmer of hope in an otherwise resistant lettuce industry that sought to block the boycott in court and invite the Teamsters into their fields. Jerry Cohen, the head of UFW's legal team, understood the urgency of reorganizing the hiring halls, not just to honor Eli's expectations but also to save the union from the loss of the Giumarra Ranch in 1973, which had been the first grape grower to sign contracts with the union. Cohen led a team of skilled union organizers to come up with remedies to the union-controlled hiring system rather than scrap it. To his chagrin, "Cesar never bought into [the agreement]," contributing to a fractured union going into the critical year of 1973.

Under the pressure of the moment, Chavez began to retreat from the frontlines into a self-imposed exile where he engaged in practices that demonstrated his anxiety about a loss of control. His fasts, which became more frequent, moved from an attempt to quell the passions of potentially violent followers to obsessive behavior that, he claimed, cleared his head and made him more focused.[33] The distance and infrequent meetings with Chavez made changes in his character less visible to Eli, but those who worked with him sensed something was wrong. His closest confidantes quietly questioned these claims and began to wonder whether he was losing his way. Many within the union also criticized his moving the headquarters from Delano to a former tuberculosis sanitarium high up in the Tehachapi Mountains donated to the UFW by a wealthy donor. From there, Chavez grew more distant from the rank and file of the union. Organizers and lawyers tried to keep his focus on the emerging battle to maintain the contracts. Chavez resisted these appeals and became less responsive to the needs of workers and the critical partnerships that had given the union a fighting chance to succeed.

Although Chavez secured a new agreement with Eli, the stress of fighting on two fronts came to a head during the renegotiation of contracts with the grape growers in April 1973. Despite Cohen and others' efforts to rectify the problems with hiring halls, Chavez abruptly objected to growers allowing "whores in the camp" where many aging Filipino workers resided, shifting the direction of the meeting. Cohen struggled to get Chavez back on point, but he would not have it. "That's one of the first strange things Cesar does," Cohen remembered.[34] Chavez never resumed serious negotiations and allowed the talks to break down. Instead of agreeing to necessary adjustments to the hiring system, he announced a strike against grape growers and an expansion of the boycott. Although he confidently asserted that "this industry has no way to go but with us," growers of both lettuce and grapes proved him wrong as they appealed to the Teamsters to supplant the UFW.[35]

The continuing chaos prevented the UFW from resolving many of Eli's concerns even as his company sought to capitalize on its relationship with the union. Inter Harvest redoubled its efforts to associate its lettuce with the UFW eagle symbol by expanding the size of the image on each wrapper and increasing the percentage of heads wrapped from 20 percent to 50 percent.[36] The pressure of in-time, in-field wrapping stressed an already distrustful workforce that continued to express its discontent with unauthorized work stoppages and slowdowns. Cesar wrote Eli personally, promising to resolve the problems, but solutions never came.[37] The union's failure to reengineer the hiring system led to a continued slide in quality, which offset whatever gains the company made by identifying its vegetables with a just cause. The UFW further strained relations when the union failed to distinguish Inter Harvest lettuce from its competitors in its advocacy of the boycott. An angry St. Louis grocer wrote executives at the company: "How the hell can we promote Inter Harvest lettuce when the United Farm Workers put ads in the paper" demanding a universal boycott regardless of brand? Harold Bradshaw, the president of Inter Harvest, turned the question over to Chavez, citing other examples of the union's failure to exempt the company's lettuce from the UFW ban. "We consider the ad," Bradshaw wrote, "a completely irresponsible act in complete violation of our collective bargaining agreement regarding boycotts by the Union."[38] Inter Harvest spent significant money running ads to counter the message from the union, but the damage had been done.

In the months that followed, the failure to make Inter Harvest profitable forced Eli to scale back his expectations for a relationship with the United Farm Workers. What had been anticipated to be a contributor to United Brands' market share and a socially conscious partnership that would burnish the reputation of the company became a headache and an embarrassment. Eli promised a resolution to the difficulties each year in his annual report but never showed progress.[39] In 1973, he was still reporting disappointment with the subsidiary's performance, after heavy rains in Arizona and the Salinas Valley caused significant losses in vegetable sales. The unpredictable weather led to an overabundance of lettuce, celery, and cauliflower at a time when customers were buying other products. Such overproduction suppressed prices and sacrificed profits. Meanwhile, protest and internecine union warfare contributed to the company's swoon. The renegotiation of contracts with Chavez spared Inter Harvest the wrath of an erratic UFW boycott but made it a direct target for the Teamsters. In mid-summer, at the height of an already disappointing growing season, Teamsters truck drivers and haulers walked off the job for three weeks. Eli responded by dramatically reducing the company's dependence on the unpackaged fresh produce market and emphasizing the consumer-ready, source-packed lettuce and celery sales. Such production represented just a fraction of the overall fresh produce market and United Brands' overall output.[40]

Eli also withdrew much of his time and support from the United Farm Workers. In June 1974, when Chavez requested another contribution to the National Farm Worker Service Center, a separate entity from the union designed to address non-work-related assistance to field workers such as housing and food aid, the company refused, citing budgetary constraints.[41] Later that year, Eli wrote Chavez with more bad news. In September, a category-three hurricane, Fifí, had struck Honduras, destroying 95 percent of the country's banana crop, including many plantations supplying United Fruit. The considerable loss of life and the destruction of property forced Eli to concentrate on Central America. "Because these problems will continue to absorb my time and attention for many months to come," he informed Chavez, "I have reluctantly concluded that I will have to resign as Trustee of the Martin Luther King Farm Workers Fund, effective immediately."[42]

Eli's resignation concluded a withdrawal from Chavez and the union that had been in the making for more than a year. The union's failure to reform the hiring halls immediately after the renegotiation of contracts in 1972 compromised its value to Eli as he faced growing pressure to improve United Brands' performance from shareholders, and increasing anxieties among the executives in his Boston and New York City offices. Inter Harvest had never turned a profit and remained peripheral to the company's wider operations, despite Eli's best efforts. Eli found that his association with a just cause and a famous civil rights leader had its limits, especially when it began to distract him from the business of running a successful multinational conglomerate. He knew that if the company failed to match its words about social responsibility with action and impact, the public's faith would be lost. At the same time, pursuing an image of social responsibility with a partner who could not deliver on business imperatives would compromise the viability of the entire enterprise.[43]

Eli wasted little time lamenting the loss of his friends and the failure of his partnership with the UFW. After 1972, his communications with both Cesar and Anna shrank to a handful of cordial but matter-of-fact letters devoid of the personality he had injected into earlier missives, especially at the height of negotiations. Perhaps some awkwardness with Anna after Eli's attempt to bestow a personal gift contributed to the decline of what had been a rewarding relationship. Perhaps the outcome was purely a result of the very different miscalculation he had made regarding Chavez. Chavez's inability to stay focused on the task of building a successful labor management system to benefit both company and field workers had been disappointing. The experience, however, did not fundamentally change Eli's willingness to work with unions, or dampen his commitment to leading a socially responsible company. At Morrell, he saw the AMCBW as an outdated vestige of the New Deal era whose leadership was too focused on defending divisions of employment and labor contracts that reduced the company's ability to prosper and create more good jobs. Chavez's vision had been an inspiring departure from such antiquated unionism, but his organization had lacked the capacity to follow through.

SITRATERCO offered a completely different opportunity to form a mutually beneficial partnership. Oscar Gale Varela, one of the oldest and most capable labor leaders in the hemisphere, had risen through the ranks of the banana workers' union in Honduras. Although unknown to the American public, Gale was a source of insight into economic developments in his country trusted by the US State Department, and a labor leader whose record of winning improvements for members of his union was the envy of his Latin American peers.

The slippage in banana production had not lessened Eli's ambition to maximize his potential for profit and for doing good in Honduras, nor had it put a damper on his passion for changing the narrative of one of the most notorious US companies in Latin America, in partnership with a labor leader he could trust.

Celebratory stories of United Fruit's transformation under Eli's direction overshadowed discouraging news about Inter Harvest in the public eye and maintained the aura around his wizardry as a corporate leader who could do no wrong. If the financial statements in his annual reports were ever to match the growth potential and social good that he claimed for United Brands in his shareholder letters, Eli would have to show real results in Honduras, where in 1973 the lion's share of the company's vast operations still lay.

6

HALF A PICTURE

Oscar Gale Varela arrived to work at La Lima with newfound optimism in the spring of 1972. After a bruising experience with United Fruit negotiators in 1969, Gale's attempts to reset management-labor relations in 1971 had finally produced results. With the start of a new year, field workers began to enjoy the wage increases and improved benefits Gale had promised were coming. Beyond the material gains, Gale felt welcome at La Lima as a partner to Eli's campaign to remake United Fruit as a source of pride and support for a nation struggling to recover from years of Yankee imperialism and political dysfunction.

The transformation had taken some time, but the implementation of new contracts had caught the attention of prominent US newspapers, who sent correspondents to Honduras to verify Eli's claims. Gale willingly played his role as advocate rather than adversary, bearing witness to the substantive changes that had taken place on the North Coast in the years after Eli took control of United Fruit. "The company respects us and we respect the company," he told the *New York Times*, speaking for SITRATERCO's members. "In reality we are better off than other Honduran workers."[1]

Gale's change of heart about United Fruit had been as profound as the policies that precipitated it. During the early 1950s, he and his compadre Céleo González had fought against a company that, among other things, had grown accustomed to charging employees for the cost of any mule that died as they used it in their labor. The common complaint that "a mule is worth more than a worker" compelled Gale and González to lead a labor movement in 1954 that drew the attention of the US State Department and the American AFL-CIO.[2] US diplomats and labor representatives sought the attention of "Don Oscar" if only because they worried about his allegiance to democracy and capitalism during the Cold War. Both invested heavily in his training and worked behind the scenes in the service of his projects and their own anti-communist goals. United Fruit, on the other hand, saw Gale as a threat to its interests, often appealing to the US embassy in Tegucigalpa, the nation's capital, to stop inviting him to political briefings and seminars with other labor leaders in Washington, DC. Company executives so distrusted Gale that they took the unorthodox step of encouraging communists within the labor movement to organize against him.[3] A politically savvy Gale survived these attacks by maintaining important friends inside the United States government and labor movement while holding United Fruit executives at arm's length—at least until Eli welcomed his proposals for change.

Being able to add Gale as an international labor ally complemented Eli's work with Cesar Chavez stateside. By endorsing Eli's new narrative for United Fruit, Gale gave credence to the notion that the company now wanted to be a force for good in society. His testimony served as a response to the company's sordid history, helping to transform its negative image during a time when consumers had become more aware of the social consequences of a company's business practices. Eli knew that changing the public's opinion about United Fruit would have to begin with convincing his employees, so he deeply appreciated

Gale's praise in America's leading newspapers. Eli hoped that such coverage would heal the wounds of the past and open the possibility for a fresh narrative for the company based on a set of new priorities. The coming years would determine whether he could distinguish United Fruit's legacy from US foreign policy aims in Honduras, and build on the relationship he started with Gale and SITRATERCO.

Eli began by trumpeting the new beginning in his annual report. "The year 1972," he wrote, "brought United Brands Company a good deal closer to achieving the goals which the Company has set for itself, and which management believes it can attain." United Fruit more than doubled its profits from 1971, making it the world's leading producer of bananas that year. The combined revenue of all United Brands' subsidiaries yielded a modest net income of nearly $18 million, the first time the company recorded a positive balance sheet for the decade. The improved conditions permitted Eli to move forward on modernization plans at Morrell while cancelling a portion of the company's outstanding debt accrued during the merger. Equally important, Eli celebrated the "dramatic change in the image of our Company," which he attributed to "many years of effort to improve the working and social conditions of our employees, especially in Latin America."[4]

Eli often drew on the testimonies of journalists who bore witness to this transformation as evidence of his success. He made special use of Georgie Ann Geyer's quote that United Fruit "may well be the most socially conscious American company in the hemisphere," by incorporating it into an open letter to the public and the company's 1972 annual report. In the latter, he assured shareholders of his commitment to increasing the value of the company, but warned that neglecting the happiness of host countries and workers threatened to compromise the entire enterprise. "All of this," he concluded, "must be conducted in an atmosphere of social consciousness which takes into account the basic social and health requirements of our employees and the most sophisticated concern for the personal fulfillment of our people in their chosen areas of occupation."[5]

Eli appreciated North American newspapers' coverage of his exploits in Honduras, but his travels to the region taught him a deeper reality than the accounts journalists gave. Correspondents often condescended to Hondurans, perpetuating the perception that a helpless and oft-exploited people lay waiting to be aided by a company only now realizing its capacity to do good. Geyer, for example, contrasted an orderly and well-provisioned La Lima with the boomtown culture of nearby San Pedro Sula on the northeastern side of the Atlantic coast. "To see the United Fruit 'town' at La Lima and the surrounding area," she wrote, "is to see half a picture of the future." The other half, in her estimation, involved "Wild West bars" filled with "Latinos with big bellies, low-slung belts, and Texas-style hats." She attributed San Pedro Sula's "booming" economy to "the company's policy of buying locally." While United Fruit undoubtedly contributed to the health of the city's business sector, Geyer's view discounted the long-standing entrepreneurialism of the city's merchants led by an Arab immigrant community known locally as *Los Turcos* that had thrived since the second decade of the twentieth century. Hailing from Palestine, these shopkeepers and manufacturers endured discrimination and resisted a desire to return to the Middle East to create the first Chamber of Commerce in the city and a thriving export-import business. Second- and third-generation Lebanese and Syrian Hondurans reinforced this community while fully adopting their place among a new class of wealthy entrepreneurs and politicians in Honduras's second-largest city. San Pedro Sula residents maintained a spirit of independence from Tegucigalpa. Free of the responsibility of governing the country, San Pedro Sula evolved into a major commercial center for both Honduras and Latin America.[6]

Eli had spent the first few years as United Brands' CEO acquainting himself with the rich history of Central America and Honduras's place within it. His trip with Leon to Panama, Costa Rica, and especially Colombia in November 1972 convinced him of the superiority of the Honduran North Coast as a site for further investment, given the vitality of its economy, its surplus of experienced labor, and its proven plantations. Colombia had the greatest potential for future development with its "vast lush jungle"—but, sitting in a remote part of the country, it lacked the advantages of the North Coast's ports, which had served as a conduit to US and world markets for more than a century. Eli had been charmed by United Fruit's holdings in Colombia, calling them "the most primitive and perhaps most beautiful and exotic" of the operations, but Honduras remained the most important location among the nodes of production controlled by the company.[7]

Eli fully recognized that a sophisticated labor movement came with the benefits of a developed economy on the North Coast. If anything, the other "half of the picture" to La Lima was not the past and current struggle between chaos and commercialism in the streets of San Pedro Sula but the presence of well-organized unions and their influence on Honduran and Latin American society. Having entertained a collaboration with Cesar Chavez to tackle the problems of the lettuce industry, with real impact on United Brands' reputation for social responsibility, Eli was not fazed by the presence of SITRATERCO or the strength of its leader, Oscar Gale Varela. He saw the situation as an opportunity to build a partnership in Honduras similar to the one he had worked out in California.

In Gale, Eli dealt with a man who had survived dictators, accommodated United Fruit executives, and managed US government agents interested in stamping out communism in Central America. Gale recounted to Geyer how company officials paid former Honduran president and National Party leader Tiburcio Andino Carías to suppress labor organizing. "In 1923," Gale recalled, "[General Carías] told the company that if they gave him six million lempiras, he'd resolve the strike that year." She added: "It was just after the Russian revolution, and sure enough, when he became president, he took Honduras out of the international labor organizations."[8] The United States accepted the undemocratic tendencies of Carías as a necessary counterweight to the threat of what they saw as a Communist revolution.

The North Coast became a primary site of struggle during the Cold War. On May 1, 1954, Tela *finca* and railroad workers celebrated international Workers' Day by walking off their jobs. Within days, a strike that began in and around the North Coast quickly spread throughout the nation. Contrary to popular lore, the general strike came about through careful organizing rather than a spontaneous combustion of worker frustrations. Led by a coalition of the Left, including communists, the action amplified Tela worker challenges of management already underway on *fincas*.[9] By May 3, labor organizing at five Tela Divisions in and around San Pedro Sula coalesced into the most important labor action in Honduran history. Oscar Gale Varela belonged to what he and allies referred to as "the democratic wing" of this coalition, as opposed to the more radical communist members. As Gale told it, the communists wanted to continue the strike and hold out for more concessions, but he and González pushed for a negotiated settlement with United Fruit and the government to settle the conflict and create SITRATERCO.[10]

Gale claimed that it had been his experience working for United Fruit Company that gave him the influence to resolve the conflict, but his familiarity with the US State Department also helped. In Guatemala, Cuba, the Dominican Republic, and Chile, the United States relied on covert military intervention and diplomatic pressure to pursue a change in regimes that officials argued encouraged communism in the region. In each of these cases, national leaders enjoyed significant public support for policies that augured a redistribution of national resources at the expense of US interests. In Honduras, the remnants of Carías's dictatorship carried on in his Nationalist Party, though conflicts among its leaders and an emboldened labor movement and Liberal Party made US officials more cautious in tipping the balance of power through military action. Adolph Berle, for example, assessed President Ramón Villeda Morales's commitment to fighting communism in Honduras during the early 1960s and found him up to the challenge.[11] Meanwhile, less visible US officials cultivated labor leaders like Oscar Gale Varela and Céleo González who had the respect of the people and the ear of politicians.

Gale's more moderate sensibilities fit the priorities of a US State Department and US labor movement hell-bent on preventing communism from taking root in Latin America. The United States' representative, Andrew McLellan, an avowed anti-communist hired by Serafino Romualdi—the official AFL Inter-American representative and a CIA operative—identified Gale as the best person to execute American anti-communist policy in Honduras. He maintained constant communication with Gale through the early years of SITRATERCO's formation.[12] McLellan introduced Gale to the AFL-CIO, which served as a key ally in the US strategy to neutralize the Communist Party by supporting more moderate leaders. George Meany, the president of the AFL in 1954 and the first president of the merged AFL-CIO from 1955 to 1979, played an increasingly important role in directing Latin American labor leaders toward more moderate goals as a member of the International Confederation of Free Trade Unions. Meany waged war against radical unionists in the confederation, especially in its Latin American division, Organización Regional Interamericana de Trabajadores (ORIT). McLellan served as the point person for the AFL-CIO in ORIT and the main advocate for its style of unionism in Honduras.[13] According to Meany, by 1963, the AFL-CIO had spent approximately 25 percent of its income on "international activities," which included the training of González and Gale. The union's American Institute for Free Labor Development (AIFLD), founded in 1962, maintained fourteen field offices throughout Latin America, which educated more than thirty thousand students on union policies, tactics, and organizational procedures used by the AFL-CIO. AIFLD placed five hundred of the most promising students on their payroll, including Gale, and hosted the group in Washington, DC for nine months where students learned about the virtues of American labor unionism and the evils of communism. Paul K. Reed, a former international representative of the United Mine Workers who ran the AIFLD education programs in Bogotá,

Colombia, said, "we feel strongly that through education of the workers it will be possible to halt the wave of communism sweeping through Latin America." AIFLD backed the education of individuals with investments in "social projects" such as housing developments, medical clinics, schools, and financial services in Latin American countries. The Institute often worked hand in glove with the United States Agency for International Development (USAID) to implement these projects, blurring the line between the actions originating from the AFL-CIO and US State Department.[14] The United States government contributed to the merging of the two by investing heavily in personnel at embassies throughout the world specializing in international labor relations. By 1965, sixty-five labor attachés worked in US embassies supported by 125 part-time labor specialists. In Washington, DC, twenty-one labor officers served the State Department and USAID. The AFL-CIO signed off on the employment of all these individuals, making sure that each one shared a militant anti-communist philosophy.[15]

By the time Oscar Gale Varela negotiated the 1971 contracts with Eli Black's United Brands, he enjoyed a deep familiarity with North Americans. Along with Céleo González, the director of the National Honduran Workers Trade Union Federation, Gale emerged as a trusted leader of the Honduran labor movement, groomed by McLellan who maintained a residency in Honduras after the 1954 General Strike. The US State Department found both González and Gale to be "the steadiest, bravest, and most capable" among Honduran leaders, though they showed a preference for Gale. Whereas González could be "emotional, mercurial, even impulsive," Gale was "blunt, straightforward and direct"—the latter being qualities the US government preferred when assessing the possibilities of labor unrest and political revolution.[16] Gale, who served as the president of SITRATERCO from 1954 until his death in 1978, also participated in the National Economic Planning Council with principal government officials and members of the business community in Honduras. According to the US State Department, Gale was "a deliberate and tactful man by nature" who "argued strongly for improvement of official administration and increased public investment to promote general economic development." The inclusion of Gale in economic planning matched the strategy of the United States to cultivate improved conditions for working people within the confines of a pro-business agenda. To that end, Gale faithfully attended meetings and took "a far more active part than the other private sector representative."[17] Gale's faith in bureaucracy and the free market to remedy problems confronting the Honduran working class matched the opinions of those who knew him best. Richard Oulahan, who served as an AIFLD regional director in Central America, appreciated Gale's "civilizing influence in the wild north coast" and counted him as an important ally in achieving the federation's anti-communist goals. "Don Oscar's philosophy," Oulahan remembered, "was that the best offensive weapons were those that inspired respect for the other side and therefore did not have to be used often."[18]

Oscar Gale Varela and Céleo González discussing plans for worker housing at Colonia Sitraterco, La Lima, Honduras, June 1965. *National Archives and Records Administration (NARA).*

Eli knew only the broad outlines of this history, but certainly recognized Gale as a valuable partner who could help him promote his new image of United Fruit with workers and navigate acts of corruption by Honduran politicians. In his dealings with Latin American heads of state, Honduras's president, Oswaldo López Arellano, a former general, conformed to Eli's preconceived notions of Latin American politics as a treacherous and undemocratic game. López Arellano had come to power in a violent military coup in 1963 and tried to impose his policies over the will of the unions. He enjoyed only moderate success, thanks to the strong leadership of Gale and González. When González led Honduran workers in an ill-fated general strike in September 1968 to protest a consumer tax, López Arellano easily crushed the uprising with military repression and refused González reentry to the country after he had traveled to Mexico to consult with fellow labor leaders. Gale brokered the return of González and an end to the conflict by adopting a nonpartisan position with López Arellano.[19] Gale's promise to keep SITRATERCO independent of political parties agreed with Eli's inclination to avoid conflict with foreign governments in places where he did business.[20]

Gale's approach to campesino empowerment and land redistribution also complemented Eli's expansion of the associate growers program. Prior to Eli's arrival, United Fruit angered US officials by resisting peasant wishes to farm and founding the Federación Nacional de Agricultores y Ganaderos de Honduras, a corporate-driven organization meant to blunt redistribution of property. Working with the company and the government, Gale convinced both sides that the failure to resolve this issue increased the communist organizers' influence over Honduran peasants and workers. United Fruit's embrace of the associate growers program earned it credibility with potential converts to a radical peasant uprising. In his dealings with the government, Gale convinced López Arellano of the virtues of a land reform law that would allocate land to Honduran-born peasants. The act satisfied the Honduran working class and peasantry but the exclusion of Salvadoran

immigrants who made up 20 percent of the population laid bare
border disputes with El Salvador and discrimination in the countryside.
In 1969, Honduran-Salvadoran tension had erupted into the "Football
War," named for a series of instigating riots at World Cup qualifying
matches between the national soccer teams. The war disrupted harmony on the Central America isthmus but offered Gale yet another
chance to demonstrate his sway over SITRATERCO members, López
Arellano and the Honduran military.[21] By the time Eli took ownership
of United Fruit, Gale had become a trusted broker for Honduran
peasants and workers in the halls of power from Tegucigalpa to
Washington, DC.

In every way, Eli regarded Gale as an advocate for his gospel of social responsibility. In the wake of his new agreement with Gale and
SITRATERCO, Eli offered his most forthright statement on doing good
through doing business in his 1972 annual report. In a concluding sec-
tion entitled "Our Social Responsibility," Eli acknowledged multiple
constituencies across the globe that demanded "more than words." He
asserted, "We must concern ourselves with causes and United Brands
does." He took pride in the new contracts with Gale and SITRATERCO.
Citing Geyer's article about the agreement in his statement, he heralded
her contention that United Brands had become a company that "anticipated the changes that have swept Latin America and has quietly
set about adjusting to them."[22] In the final analysis, Eli claimed, United
Brands had employed "creative vigilance to unexpected needs which
the Company is equipped to answer."[23]

The dependence on leaders like Oscar Gale Varela went unsaid but
had been assumed. He, along with Céleo González, led a respected
labor movement that the US State Department estimated was "five
times the size of the armed forces and 10 times more than the total
number of university students" in the country at the time of Eli's
acquisition of United Fruit.[24] As US officials in Honduras reported
to Washington, the Honduran labor movement "in recent years has
served as the conscience of the nation and one of [the] principal

restraining factors on excesses on [the] part of [the] government/ military."[25] Gale's role in checking the influence of communism and the brutish militarism of López Arellano also agreed with Eli, who saw both as a threat to his business model. Eli's support of causes and practice of nonpartisan politics had their limits if either jeopardized United Brands, ability to create opportunity for his employees and the nations. For now, his message of social responsibility played well to the average consumer at home and abroad.

Eli could afford to take a hands-off approach to Honduran domestic affairs largely because the US State Department and Oscar Gale Varela engaged in the day-to-day struggle to create an economic environment conducive to United Fruit's success and US foreign policy aims. Gale trusted few in his leadership and even fewer in elected office. Within the union, he constantly shuffled his officers to ferret out radical leftists whom he saw as a challenge to his authority, a practice he adopted during the early years of the union when the company encouraged communists to disrupt his agenda. In a memo to Washington, the ambassador to Honduras, Joseph Jova, reported that "Gale's new efforts to counter infiltration of SITRATERCO by Communists and Zuñiga (Minister of the Presidency) 'agents' are wise, and we hope he will keep them up." The United States rewarded Gale's fidelity to an anti-communist agenda by defending him whenever López Arellano threatened to imprison him for questioning his policies. In 1969, for example, the United States flew Gale to Washington, DC, to shelter him from retribution for his role in the general strike started by González, and to receive counsel on how to resolve the crisis. Throughout his years as president of SITRATERCO, Gale also availed himself of Andrew McLellan's counsel, receiving advice on how to manage threats to his leaderships from within the union.[26]

Together and separately, Gale and Eli served as willing accomplices to a US plan to sideline communist influences in Honduras. Both men shared a sincere faith in the power of the market to remedy social problems. Gale's rise would not have been possible without the support of

AIFLD and the US government, especially Andrew McLellan, who served as his mentor and worked with the Central Intelligence Agency to achieve American foreign policy goals throughout Latin America. Yet, Gale also exercised a level of autonomy and influence that kept the State Department on guard, monitoring his every move, including Gale's challenge of López Arellano in 1970 when López Arellano threatened to continue as president for a third term in violation of the Honduran Constitution. Gale, Céleo González and Andres Victor Artilles, the Secretary General of the Honduran Workers Confederation, successfully ended the crisis by appealing for national unity among political and business leaders. Such clout required more than the approval of the United States. Indeed, all three men enjoyed genuine respect from a broad swath of the Honduran public that turned to them in times of national conflict.

Eli dealt with this complex of labor leaders, US diplomats, and the company executives in Latin America by attempting to please everyone. He expanded the company's community development programs throughout Central America and invested in another film to draw attention to their humanitarian efforts. The documentary film, "To Save a City That Was," described the devastation of a massive earthquake in Managua, Nicaragua, and United Fruit's contributions to rebuild the nation's once-beautiful capital. Aired on network television in December 1972, the film was designed to extend United Fruit's image as a supportive ally to Central American nations in a time of need. In his description of United Brands' philanthropy, Eli framed the company's social work as evidence that it remained "committed to its philosophy of social responsibility."[27]

By the end of 1973, the overall health of United Brands allowed Eli to move forward in building a company with a new purpose and identity. The conglomerate continued to show progress as sales rose from $1,586,747,000 in 1972 to $1,982,312,000, increasing United Brands' earnings per share from $1.42 to $2.11.[28] Eli proudly reported that every division operated profitably, although the Agrimark Group, formerly known as the Banana Group, continued to underperform largely due to a severe storm along the Atlantic Coast that blew down several acres near La Ceiba, Honduras. He anticipated weaker returns from his banana division given United Fruit's forced divestment from Guatemala and increased competition in the industry. Eli agreed to the sale of land—sold to Del Monte, the third-largest producer, rather than to Standard, United Fruit's main competition—knowing that the company could no longer expand its profit rates on bananas in a saturated market. He would have to find new ways of diversifying United Brands products, including palm oil, live animals, and prepared foods from its farms in Latin America. To that end, Eli invested in a program to help local farmers raise eight to ten thousand head of cattle on 19,000 acres of rehabilitated land in Honduras. Through this program, he hoped to capitalize on the potential synergy between two entities in the United Brands family by creating a source for Morrell's beef in Honduras.

Eli also developed new markets in Mexico and Japan while seeking to expand sales of United Brands products to fifteen million potential customers in El Salvador, Guatemala, Honduras, Nicaragua, and Costa Rica. From 1958 to 1967, Central American countries took halting steps toward economic integration and the formation of a common market. These efforts built on a 1951 United Nations Economic Commission for Latin America to study the possibility of lowering tariffs and integrating industries across the region. Early on, Costa Rica, the wealthiest of the five nations, had signed a 1959 accord to adopt a common market, but then failed to ratify the treaty. In 1963, Costa Rica reversed its position, igniting a new free-trade agreement, the Central American Common Market, that resulted in an upsurge in intraregional business. Trade among the Central American countries jumped from $32.7 million in 1960 to $213.6 million in 1967. Economic growth, although uneven, occurred at an average rate of 5.8 percent per year from the mid-1960s to the early 1970s, briefly disrupted by the "Football War" between Honduras and El Salvador. The Central American

Common Market primarily benefited industrial development over agriculture, which inspired Eli's predecessors at United Fruit to acquire
the Costa Rican company Numar S.A., the largest producer of processed
foods in Central America. He also inherited Clemente Jacques, a large
Mexican food-processing company that supplied canned products to
Latin American consumers. Under Eli, Clemente Jacques reversed a
five-year trend of losses to achieve modest profits and new potential
for expansion. Both Numar and Clemente Jacques offered a glimmer
of United Brands' potential in Latin America as an industrial producer
of foods consumed throughout the hemisphere. Although much improved, Central American and Mexican economies had a long way to
go before the newer ventures could make up for losses in banana sales
in North America.

Eli turned to investments in John Morrell and Inter Harvest to overcome sagging banana sales and the yet-to-develop Latin American
market. Inter Harvest continued to be a disappointment through 1973

Eli Black observing banana peelers at work in Honduras, 1972. *Walter P. Reuther*
Library, Archives of Labor and Urban Affairs, Wayne State University.

and beyond. Morrell, on the other hand, had been a proven winner for Eli, providing him the clout to acquire United Fruit and form United Brands. In his 1973 annual report, Eli shared that Morrell "more than compensated" for the losses in Honduras, continuing a string of commercial success that he hoped to perpetuate with upgrades to its processing centers. His report that the company intended to pursue modernization and expansion at its Sioux Falls and Cincinnati plants signaled progress to shareholders.

The report concealed much of the tumult in Ottumwa and the different approaches Eli took to managing organized labor. By 1973, it had become clear that he held Gale and Chavez in higher regard than Merrill and Bankson at Morrell. To be sure, Gale and Chavez faithfully worked on behalf of their rank-and-file members. Both men created unions, whole cloth, from popular uprisings they had a hand in creating and directing. Eli appreciated how both men demonstrated a propensity to think beyond the models of leadership handed to them by a previous generation. Gale navigated despots and diplomats to arrive at a stable place in Honduras, while Chavez blended the tactics of a social movement with labor organizing to create a new reality for farm workers in California. Although they presented challenges, Eli trusted that both had the well-being of the company and its employees in mind as they negotiated conditions for their shared future. In contrast, he regarded union leaders like Merrill and Bankson as relics of Morrell's past and defenders of labor contracts that prevented the company from competing with new companies like IBP. Perhaps Eli arrived at the meat business predisposed to doubt the priorities of union leaders based on the corruption his father encountered in the shohet's union, AFL Local No. 440 in Manhattan. In any case, it's clear that Eli saw Merrill and Bankson as impediments to United Brands' progress that had to be dealt with. Given the challenges he faced elsewhere, he trusted executives on the ground in Iowa—Harry Hansel and Morton Broffman—to handle the final phase of breaking AMCBW's contracts and decommissioning the Morrell-Ottumwa plant, while he built a modern multinational conglomerate in Honduras and California.

Eli's hands-off approach with Morrell proved to be a mistake. The subsidiary showed signs of success on the balance sheet, but attempts to modernize Morrell-Ottumwa had not gone well. In 1970, Hansel and Broffman had been asked to oversee a $6.5 million investment to upgrade the Ottumwa plant and appealed to union leaders to participate in the creation of a blueprint for change. Jesse Merrill and Virgil Bankson demonstrated unusual cooperation by accepting the invitation, partly to strengthen their position in negotiations for a new labor contract in 1971. After months of collaboration, the two leaders arrived at the Amalgamated Meat Cutters and Butcher Workmen union building, at 2800 N. Sheridan Road on the North Shore of Lake Michigan in Chicago, with the expectations that their cooperation would earn them some say over wages and benefits. To their surprise, Hansel instead offered them an ultimatum: the company would invest in the improvement of the plant only if the union agreed to freeze severance pay and accept the modernization plans as written by management. He informed Merrill and Bankson that, if the union chose to reject the offer, the company would have no choice but to shutter Ottumwa and consolidate operations at Morrell's other sites. Hansel backed up these threats with official notifications to managers at the St. Louis and Sioux Falls plants, where workers had been more amenable to time studies.

Merrill and Bankson took a defiant message back to Ottumwa, angered by Hansel's betrayal and committed to fighting the unliteral changes the new management imposed on them. In a report to the rank and file in 1970, the union leaders informed fellow workers, "If they think for one d—minute, we are going back for thirty years to get along with them they can close their d—plant." Morton Broffman refused to back down, issuing an official statement of intent to close the plant within six months.[29] Union president Jesse Merrill had no choice but to accept the demands, even as union leaders vowed not to bend to the "dictatorship" imposed by a company now nested within United Brands.[30] Dave Swanson, who worked at Morrell-Ottumwa in the sales office from 1967 to 1973 and whose father and grandparents worked at the plant and in T. Henry Foster's home, witnessed the conflict first-hand. Management, he recalled, "really got in the plant with time studies, and they wanted more production out of the worker by the hour." According to Swanson, the fact that Morrell executives "constantly" raised the possibility of closing created an "uneasy feeling" for employees and cast a pall over a whole community dependent on the plant as its largest employer.[31]

Eli took no part in the back-and-forth discussions and never came to Ottumwa during the implementation of the plan. He worried little about the union leaders' complaints and insults, largely because he dismissed them as protectors of an order that did not match the reality of the new, consumer-driven market for meat. He left the hard work of managing the anger of Ottumwa employees to Hansel, who relished the opportunity to finish what he had begun under McCallum. As *Fortune* and *Forbes* gushed over Eli's financial acumen and celebrated the deal for United Fruit, Hansel carried out orders to gut departments presumed to be unprofitable at Morrell and to reduce the overall size of the workforce at Ottumwa. Within the first two years of operation under AMK, Hansel cut the workforce in half, employing waves of layoffs that reduced the number of employees to approximately two thousand people by the end of 1969. After the merger, Hansel went one by one through all of Morrell's product lines, eliminating nearly two thousand items. "Everything we do is being re-examined," Hansel told the *Ottumwa Courier*. "Every operation has to stand on its own."[32]

Hansel vowed to "weed out" unprofitable lines but argued that the number of eliminated products amounted to only three to four percent of Ottumwa's total output.[33] Some items had become a particular source of pride for Ottumwa workers, such as the meat products they produced for Hy-Vee grocery stores and the highly regarded Red Heart dog food. Hy-Vee had been one of the largest independent retailers in the country and its Morrell-produced store brands of bacon, sausages, and cured meats placed it among the elite markets. When Hansel moved production for Hy-Vee to Sioux Falls, quality sagged. "AMK senior management didn't understand," Dave Swanson recalled, that "the quality of raw materials that were produced in the Ottumwa plant's geographic area . . . was much higher than the product that you could buy out of the Dakotas." As a consequence, Hy-Vee broke its exclusive relationship with Morrell and began to market the products of Morrell's competitors, including Hormel's Spam and Little Sizzlers pork-link sausages. Morrell's reputation for its dog food also suffered, falling from the ranks of the very best in the United States after Hansel moved production out of Ottumwa.[34]

Shifts in the production site of high-value brands intensified Otttumwa employee suspicions about the sincerity of managers to upgrade operations at the plant. "They wanted to rid themselves of the Ottumwa unions," Swanson recalled, "because that seemed to be where most of the trouble was." Swanson's father kept the machines running at Morrell-Ottumwa in the millwright department. As a part of a union family, Dave Swanson witnessed the relevance of Local P-1 to Ottumwans' lives and the overall security of the community. "It was hard work, injury-prone," he recalled, "and the company kept trying to squeeze these guys out and get more hogs through the line with less hours spent." Although Swanson's position in the sales office was non-union, his loyalties were with his father and family. "All the guys were doing was defending their rights." He credited P-1 with making Morrell a "happy place to work" and Ottumwa "a great place to live," noting that, at its height and for much of his lifetime, Morrell employed a steady workforce of between 3,500 and 5,000 unionized employees, whose families participated in bowling leagues, golf leagues, and Babe Ruth and Little League Baseball cosponsored by the company and the union. "When the Morrell family sold it and AMK bought it," Swanson observed, "that all changed."[35]

In anticipation of a new round of labor negotiations, Hansel chiseled away at the union's strength by reducing or eliminating departments and laying off workers. He pursued full automation of the sliced bacon and canning operations, further eroding the security of women employees who dominated both divisions.[36] In 1971, Morrell had begun to alter beef production at Ottumwa without explanation to the union. In *The Bulletin,* mystified union leaders asked: "Does John Morrell & Company want to continue killing beef in Ottumwa?" The company laid off twenty workers in the Beef Kill department and seven in the Beef By-Products department, while slightly reducing the number of head of cattle but expecting the same rate of production. The new conditions—offered as an ultimatum—strained relations within the division and created uncertainty across the plant. "The company wants out of the beef slaughtering," union leaders told the rank and file, "and would like to leave the impression with the public that it is labor's fault."[37] By 1972, it had become apparent that the company wanted to move beef production from Ottumwa to Sioux Falls, where workers were, management believed, much more efficient.

Amid the layoffs and division closures, management offered glimmers of hope by renaming the plant "Iowa Pride Packing Co." in late 1972 and adjusting the method of delivering meat to market. Morrell shifted from "route cars" catering to small markets to car lots selling to large-scale buyers. These changes promised to cut down on handling costs and increase the profitability at the Ottumwa plant. Jesse Merrill also agreed to promote a "Buy Morrell" campaign with Ottumwa residents to strengthen local sales. The company's continued slashing of positions undermined whatever goodwill existed among workers and undercut the advantages created by the new method of shipment. In late 1972, John Morrell & Company's new president, Elias Paul, informed the union of its intentions to cut the number of hourly paid employees by half at Ottumwa starting on January 1, 1973. True to their word, Morrell laid off eight hundred hourly employees between November 1972 and January 1, 1973. When Morrell workers showed solidarity with striking IBP workers by endorsing a boycott of meat, the company cut another 350 positions the following March and renewed its threat to close Ottumwa altogether. By April, management reduced the total number of employees to seven hundred.[38] Morale at the plant sank to the lowest point since the AMK merger. Shop stewards struggled to maintain workers' pride in their jobs as quality slipped. "If supervision in this plant continues with the attitude 'we don't care what goes out,'" the *Bulletin* intoned, "we don't think we have a future for very long."[39]

Union leaders' concerns about the demise of Morrell-Ottumwa were warranted. Jesse Merrill issued a statement to the rank and file preparing them for the worst. "There are some facts," Merrill wrote employees, "which suggest that what is happening now in Ottumwa may be only a step in a plan to phase out the Ottumwa operation entirely." In an admission that they had miscalculated the intent of management during the 1970s negotiations, Merrill added: "The Company has always pretended that each cutback is an end-point, a final answer to its problems, but each step leads to more, and there is every indication that this layoff may be simply a beginning of the total program of destruction of the union contract at Ottumwa." Merrill took umbrage at the company's refusal to extend benefits to laid-off employees, a consequence of the union's agreement to freeze severance pay in exchange for the company investing in the modernization of the plant in 1970. Morrell's relocation of production to facilities staffed with non-union members or low-wage employees permanently undermined the clout of Local P-1 to fight for its members.[40]

Morrell managers had such little regard for Local P-1 by 1973 that it directed its communication to the international office of the Amalgamated Meat Cutters and Butcher Workmen of North America, in Chicago. As a representative of all AMCBW members, including Ottumwa and Sioux Falls, the office considered what was best for all unionized workers across many locations. In April 1973, Elias Paul met with Eli in New York where "the matter of the death of the Ottumwa plant was sealed."[41] Paul chose to share the news with AMCBW's International Secretary-Treasurer Patrick Gorman in Chicago rather than meet with Local P-1 officials in Ottumwa. He claimed that Ottumwa's mismanagement had made all of Morrell's divisions more vulnerable to elimination. Citing McCallum's attempts to make Ottumwa more efficient in 1947, Paul told Gorman, "John Morrell & Co. has been taking money from other locations for most of these past twenty-five years and putting it into Ottumwa in an attempt to turn the situation around."[42]

When Jesse Merrill and Harold Trimble, the new P-1 chief steward, learned of the meeting, they wrote Gorman to denounce Paul and ask the international office to include them in any future meetings. They claimed that "Morrell's intentions weren't honorable" at any time since the merger and suggested that the international had sold them out. "God knows," they told Gorman, "we tried, and we find [Paul] crying on your shoulder for more concessions."[43] The accusation stung Gorman, judging from his response: "Don't you think we should be intensely interested in the closing?" Their suspicions about his motives, he complained, "indicate that you two good brothers don't care a hoot whether the plant closes or not."[44] Merrill and Trimble's challenge of Gorman underscored the long-standing divisions between AMCBW's international office in Chicago and the local union in Ottumwa. Ottumwa's tradition of militancy contrasted with Sioux Falls, where AMCBW members had been more accommodating of management's desire to implement time-study. The 1956 merger under one international AFL-CIO union, AMCBW, had papered over differences that persisted just below the surface. The company's decision to move more of its production to Sioux Falls exacerbated conflict within the union and made Local P-1 distrustful of its international officials. If United Brands had intended to shutter the plant and dismantle Local P-1 all along, as Merrill and Trimble alleged, the exploitation of divisions between Sioux Falls and Ottumwa helped achieve that goal.

On April 14, 1973, the *Ottumwa Courier* announced that the company would permanently close Morrell-Ottumwa on July 14, more than a month before the master agreement with Local P-1 was due to expire on August 31, 1973. Even at this late date, some employees doubted the resolve of the company to close given past threats and subsequent solutions. "There were guys in the plant," Swanson recalled, still saying, "well, they're never going to do that." Paul's message to the community attempted to clarify the company's intentions. "In spite of all the efforts by management and by the employes," he told the *Ottumwa Courier,* "substantial losses continued through 1971 and 1972." He cited a deficit of more than $5 million in 1972 as a contributor to United Brands' decision. "Morrell regrets deeply the loss of jobs to its employes and its impact on their families and the Ottumwa community." For many who made Ottumwa their home, such words rang hollow given the acrimony endured by employees over the last three years and the devastation Morrell's departure was sure to trigger.[45]

Dave Swanson accepted a transfer to Sioux Falls. "My life was turned upside-down at that point," he said, "and I ended up leaving Morrell and went to work for Rath Packing Company." Swanson's father and uncle were old enough to retire, while other employees also considered a transfer to Sioux Falls. Those who moved did not retain their seniority in the union ranks, since it had been earned within a division rather than the entire plant. Such indignities paled in comparison to the suffering of those who stayed behind in Ottumwa. Swanson noted the near-complete collapse of all associate businesses that depended on Morrell for their existence, from trucking to utilities to local schools. "They went bye-bye," he remembered. Nothing was spared from the destruction, he recalled, including small things like sports leagues and high school athletic programs that had given the city's youth a sense of pride.[46]

If Eli cared about these changes, the people of Ottumwa never knew it. After Eli's purchase of Morrell under AMK and his initial visit to the plant in 1967, he had not made his presence felt, assigning others to carry out the dismantling of Ottumwa and the total transformation of Morrell. From 1968 until 1970, he used the glowing balance sheet of AMK—made possible by the purchase of Morrell—to acquire United Fruit and form United Brands. From 1970 until Ottumwa's closure in 1973, he remained true to the men he chose to run it, no matter the pain they caused. His celebration of record profits at Morrell in the annual reports disguised a company that had been torn apart by a "system" that Eli told himself had been working.

Few in Ottumwa recognized their role in the larger conglomerate that aimed not only to grab a greater share of the meat industry but also to dominate banana and lettuce sales in North America. Much of the business world accepted at face value Eli's assertions that he would achieve these goals while honoring worker rights. The employees of Morrell-Ottumwa knew better. Like his use of Morrell assets to create a bigger, more glamorous company, Eli leveraged the security of Local P-1 members to achieve high-profile labor agreements with the United Farm Workers in California and the banana workers union, Sindicato de Trabajadores de la Tela Railroad Co., in Honduras. These agreements hid the tumult in Iowa and preserved his stellar reputation on Wall Street.

Amid a mostly rosy picture Eli painted in his 1973 annual report, signs of trouble appeared on the horizon. Far from home and close to his heart, Eli watched the evolving conflict in the Middle East, where the state of Israel fought off challenges to its existence from hostile neighbors. On October 6, 1973, Egypt led a coalition of Arab states in an attack on Israel during Yom Kippur, the holy day of rest, fasting, and prayer. The Israeli army absorbed the initial blow and split the Arab forces with a massive counterattack on Damascus and Suez that divided the Egyptian front. The United States' support for Israel and the Soviet Union's backing of the Arab states made the conflict a proxy war for the two superpowers. In retaliation, the Organization of Arab Petroleum Exporting Countries (OPEC) imposed an embargo of crude oil on the United States. The abrupt loss of oil "shocked" the American system by raising the cost for most US producers, including United Brands, to transport goods domestically and around the world. By the time the 1973 annual report went off to the printer in March 1974, the price of oil had risen 300 percent, from $3.00 per barrel to $11.65 globally. In the United States, the prices rose higher, causing panic at the gas pump. For Eli, who shipped bananas from Honduras, lettuce from

California, and meat from Iowa and South Dakota, concern mounted about how to maintain profit margins in the face of rising transportation costs.[47]

And OPEC was not even the cartel causing Eli the biggest worry. Feeling the effects of the oil shock and inflationary pressures on food and the cost of living, banana-producing nations in Latin America— Costa Rica, Honduras, Panama, Guatemala, El Salvador, and Colombia— began meeting as the Unión de Países Exportadores de Banano. The new cartel took stock of its importance to agricultural businesses like United Fruit and Standard Fruit and the value of its primary contribution, bananas, in the global economy. "It is a primary duty of the governments to take whatever measures are necessary in order to achieve an adequate remuneration," Eli conceded to shareholders. The cartel proposed an increase of the "f.o.b." (free on board) export price of between 1 and 2.5 cents per pound. Eli promised to "do everything in our power to cooperate in finding the means for achieving more stable and profitable solutions for all," but without providing elaboration.[48] With multiple storm clouds gathering, he would have to dig deeper into his bag of tricks to maintain the momentum he had managed to establish at United Brands.

7

UNITED, WE FALL

THE ELI BLACK who stepped to the podium on January 21, 1973, to deliver a major address at the Harvard Business School Agribusiness Seminar was poised and confident, bolstered by recent accomplishments. United Brands had just turned a profit for the first time in its three-year existence, but the moment was also a major milestone in Eli's personal journey. He had overcome a lot to arrive on campus that day. He had built his way up from poverty on the Lower East Side, and had risked disappointing his father in 1945 when he turned his back on the rabbinate for a career in business. Now, the most elite educational institution in his adopted country wanted to hear from him about a business that he billed as a beacon of social responsibility. Employing approximately fifty-three thousand employees across the western hemisphere, Eli had earned high praise from journalists, who heralded a reversal of United Fruit's notorious history.[1] The man at the podium counted Cesar Chavez as a friend and enjoyed the support of Honduras's most influential union leader, Oscar Gale Varela. In his annual reports and public appearances, he extolled the virtues of free enterprise and the opportunities it extended to all who participated in it. Although his mission was far from complete, Eli embraced the opportunity to address the leading minds of his profession, and at an institution that would soon provide his son the training to follow in his footsteps.

Eli began his address with a challenge. He asked his audience: "How does one reach the thousands of business leaders whose enlightened self-interest must now be identified with the public good?" The failure to end war and remedy social division had taken its toll on public confidence in government. Richard Nixon, who had come into office promising a reduction in the size of government, had embarked on more radical reform after his landslide reelection victory in 1972. He sought to roll back many of the Great Society programs established by his predecessor, Lyndon B. Johnson. Eli agreed with this impulse. "Many of us who cherish freedom and the free enterprise system," he said, "view with grave concern the size and power of the federal government, the increased centralization of authority, and the growing tendency of all segments of society to look to government for solutions." Rather than eliminate useful services that had become part of the social safety net, however, Eli urged business leaders, in cooperation with labor organizations, to take on more responsibility for providing them. "Socially conscious, responsible corporate executives," he advised, "should view the Nixon exhortation to self-help as an opportunity to regain the loyalty of employees and the esteem of the public." According to Eli, the time had come for business leaders to apply their skills to managing "socially conscious programs" at home and abroad. The speech, and its later adaptation into a short *Harvard Business Review* article, enjoyed a receptive audience intrigued by what appeared to be a successful marriage of business and social benefit in United Brands.[2] They wondered: Could the modern multinational corporation equally serve the interests of its owners, its workers, and the public, as Eli argued it must? And what if United Brands' high-minded efforts failed?

Eli's advice offered a variation on a message that others had been advocating since the early 1950s. By 1973, US corporations had accumulated a mixed record, having prioritized the enrichment of their owners and management over the well-being of even their employees, let alone customers and other "stakeholders." Mergers had become the order of the day, promising higher profitability through scale efficiencies and more professional management by executives focused on modernization. Often, corporate management cast labor unions as impediments to progress, and did all they could to prevent workers from gaining more collective power.

Eli had been sympathetic to that view among managers at John Morrell, where he believed the AMCBW clung to outdated contracts and divisions of labor that kept the company from reaching its full potential. Finally closing the Ottumwa plant had been an unfortunate but necessary move, he told himself, and did not mean United Brands was unwilling to work with union leaders to care for the needs of its employees. Likewise, Eli's attempt at labor-management collaboration at Inter Harvest had stalled out because of an intractable internecine labor war and Chavez's inability to rectify the hiring system he proposed. He believed he had found more willing and able partners at SITRATERCO in Honduras, where Oscar Gale Varela shared his faith in private enterprise to solve the problems of working people. "Governments generally tend to make bad administrators," Gale had told a *New York Times* reporter, explaining why he opposed government expropriation of unused United Fruit land, and endorsing collaboration between the company and SITRATERCO to supply housing, electricity, and, most importantly, jobs to the Honduran people. "The banana business is a good business," he told the reporter, "if you have economic recourse—the production techniques, the transportation facilities, the store outlets, the experience."[3]

The main impediment to this coalition was not any rival union but the government, led as it was by a military leader who had grown accustomed to bullying those who stood in the way of his using political power to accumulate personal wealth. The autocracy of Oswaldo López Arellano and the instability of Honduran politics informed Gale's preference for working with Eli and his associates. From 1963 to 1971, Gale had walked a fine line with López Arellano. In 1970, Gale had opposed López Arellano's threat to cancel elections and defused tension by negotiating a commitment from him to abide by the Honduran constitution and not remain in office past his tenure. It helped that Gale worked with the director of the United States Agency for International Development (USAID) to secure an $8 million National Development Bank loan to extend crop credit to small farmers, an act that López Arellano claimed as his own to secure support from the countryside.[4] When López Arellano threatened to go back on his promise to hold free and fair elections in 1970, Gale resisted the "continuismo" of his regime and consulted the AFL-CIO's Andrew McLellan on how to manage the situation. López Arellano eventually allowed elections to happen, but engineered a coup d'état in 1972 against the democratically elected Ramón Ernesto Cruz. Gale ultimately supported López Arellano in exchange for an agrarian reform law that provided farmland to peasants and unionized workers. He had been content to accommodate López Arellano's occasional transgression against democracy in Tegucigalpa as long as he continued to hold sway over the country's north coast, where most of its economic vitality lay. From Gale's vantage point, the unwavering support of United Fruit and the US State Department served as a bulwark against the seemingly never-ending political corruption of Oswaldo López Arellano.

Eli managed to remain above the fray of Honduran politics by relying on Gale and the State Department to dictate the terms of US involvement in Honduras. Both pursued an aggressive anti-communist agenda, to which López Arellano did not object as long as his material interests were served and his political leadership went unchallenged. United Fruit's investment in housing, education, and health in Honduras complemented US-sponsored programs funded by USAID, the American Institute for Free Labor Development, the Organization of American States, and the Inter-American Development Bank. All these organizations assisted in the creation of El Banco de Los Trabajadores (Honduran Worker's Bank) in 1967. In 1971, the bank contributed

$400,000 in loans to members of SITRATERCO and the Federation of National Workers of Honduras (Federación Sindical Nacional de Trabajadores de Honduras) to purchase homes, including housing developments constructed with United Fruit funds.[5]

Eli's comfortable distance from the politics of Honduras changed dramatically in 1973 as disasters of multiple origins and magnitude rolled across the Central American isthmus. In January, Gale suffered a massive stroke and, in his diminished state, the Honduran labor leader was less able to serve as an advocate for Eli and his company. He recovered sufficiently to retain the presidency of SITRATERCO at the biannual national labor convention, but would remain vulnerable to opposing forces within the union. Gale spent a good portion of his time battling what he characterized as a communist takeover of SITRATERCO led by younger members of the union. The embassy confirmed such challenges but reported to Washington that Gale successfully marshalled "democratic forces" to "smash it."[6] Despite his victory, Gale remained on the defensive and committed to identifying a worthy successor within two years.

Gale's illness and internal union struggles occurred at the time Eli needed him most. The oil crisis in 1973 had dramatically increased the cost of transportation of bananas and undermined United Brands' momentum. In part, Eli had set up a multinational conglomerate to create a diversified portfolio of revenue streams that could withstand the uncertainty of changing economic conditions. The effects of the conflict in the Middle East, however, were pervasive, disrupting all commercial sectors and increasing the cost of every product United Brands marketed. They also threw the entire Western Hemisphere into recession, prompting Latin American leaders, including Oswaldo López Arellano, to seek revenue from their region's main source of income—bananas—by organizing the Union of Banana-Exporting Countries (Unión de Países Exportadores de Banano, or UPEB). The cartel's proposal to impose new tariffs forced Eli to reconsider his hands-off approach to Latin American politics, especially with Gale still recovering and battling rivals within the union.

Eli could not look to other subsidiaries in the United Brands network to make up losses associated with the high cost of moving bananas. The luster of being the maverick grower who agreed to contracts with Cesar Chavez and the United Farm Workers in 1970 had worn off by 1973 as the union's conflict with the Teamsters and its failure to shield Inter Harvest from the boycott consumed public opinion. Chavez remained a darling of the Left, but his unpredictable actions made it difficult for Eli to capitalize on their relationship. Morrell continued to be a stabilizing force within the company, although a tumultuous year in hog production and the imposition of price controls by the federal government limited its performance. United Brands' shift in beef production to its southwestern plants allowed the company to profit from continued expansion of a growing Sunbelt market. Morrell emulated IBP with the production of boxed beef, under the brand name E-Z Redi, that increased efficient handling and cutting of steaks and roasts at the point of sale in retail stores across the country. The company's investment in cattle feedlot operations in 1972 allowed it to stabilize its supply of beef and make pricing more predictable regardless of season. As a primary site for pork production, Ottumwa saw none of these benefits and suffered through a shortage of hogs due to a lack of feed grains. Although the relative scarcity of livestock resulted in record-high prices, the Nixon administration pressured retailers to hold down food prices and implemented price controls that hurt profits.[7] These developments deepened the despair among Morrell's Ottumwa workers whose relationship with the parent company had become adversarial.

United Brands had failed to live up to its expectations since its genesis in 1970. After losing more than two million dollars in its first year, the company bounced back enough in 1972 to register modest gains, which Eli quickly sank into technological improvements at

Morrell, United Fruit, and Inter Harvest. Eli projected a positive future in his annual report and corporate prospectus in 1973, but the underlying numbers told a different story. Members of the business press began to expose these discrepancies. *Forbes*, for example, observed that United Brands sold "about $1.7 billion worth of meat, bananas, and ice cream, and yet, in the past five years, has only managed to average about $6.6 million in earnings." The annual profit margin amounted to .4 percent, or three times less than that of the average supermarket.[8]

The failure to generate internal growth within a merged company had been the greatest threat to the new conglomerates of the multimarket corporation era. Like many companies of its time, United Brands came together because Eli was able to convince United Fruit shareholders and short-term traders to invest in debt securities commonly referred to as "paper" because its value, unlike cash, fluctuated according to what it could be traded for at any given moment. These securities—debentures and warrants—increased their value based on the assumption that Eli would boost the overall profits of the merged company through his management wizardry. For those holding United Fruit stock, Eli sold them on the idea that he knew how to expand the value of their assets beyond what the company's managers had achieved at the time. Given that he had to compete with larger, more profitable companies than AMK for the right to own United Fruit, he promised higher returns on investment to persuade United Fruit shareholders to convert their existing stock to securities, or what amounted to IOUs that would be paid in the future when Eli's vision for a more profitable company came to fruition. According to Robert Barbanell, managing director of Bankers Trust, "the typical shareholder considers only what he bought the stock for, what it is selling for, and what is being offered." He added, "if he is convinced he can cash in on the deal, he is for it."[9] Eli's genius lay in his ability to make a persuasive pitch—but by 1973, stockholders and members of his management team had begun to wonder if the company he had built could cover the initial cost of its creation. Tension had been mounting with each passing year of losses, and the meager gains of 1973 did not placate savvy investors or deter critical journalists from taking a deeper dive into United Brands' finances.

Eli responded to lagging profits by taking advantage of an accounting maneuver that created an illusion of growth. His approach had its origins in the new way that the government regulated how companies reported their assets. The Accounting Principles Board (APB)—predecessor to today's Financial Accounting Standards Board—had determined the accepted practices for companies when calculating and reporting their financial health to the public from 1959 to 1973. Composed of between eighteen and twenty-one accountants from reputable accounting firms, the APB established new rules, or "opinions," based on a two-thirds majority vote of its members. It issued thirty-one opinions in its time, many of which came at the end of the 1960s and early 1970s, when CEOs had incentives to conceal losses to hold on to critical investors and stave off takeover bids by rival suitors.[10] Contrary to its purpose, APB's opinions often initiated new rules for reporting and retiring debt that benefited management teams in conglomerates.

On November 21, 1972, APB announced Opinion 26, which stipulated that any difference in principle arising from an early extinguishment of debt must be reported as earnings for the upcoming year. In layman's terms, this meant that Eli could use the existing cash reserves at United Fruit and the savings he produced from layoffs and decommissioned facilities to refinance the debt created by his purchase of the company just three years into the ownership of United Brands. This was a betrayal of his promise to invest the money in opportunities that would lead to greater production and a wider profile of goods. United Fruit stockholders were counting on this when they pressured William Donaldson to find an alternative to John Fox, who they saw as too timid for the merger era. Eli now inherited this pressure, which he began to feel from his own employees and fellow executives. In Boston and La Lima, United Fruit managers had suspended their judgment of a man who had turned a small bottle-cap producer into the fourth-largest meat producer in the United States, giving him time to adapt to the international scale of production at United Fruit. By 1973, they began to question whether Eli was up to the challenge. La Lima manager Houston Lacombe spoke for many when he questioned the logic of paying for social programs to SITRATERCO members while the banana business showed signs of decline and the company had just sold United Fruit's stake in Guatemalan production to a rival, Del Monte. Meanwhile, in Iowa, Morrell shuttered the flagship plant in Ottumwa, destroying the livelihoods of thousands of residents.

Eli had disappointed many employees, but he believed he could buy himself some time by satisfying shareholders. He offered $10 in cash and $60 in higher interest bonds per stock to United Brands shareholders to replace up to $125 million of securities that originally cost $100. By and large, shareholders agreed to trade $100 for $70 largely because the actual market value of the bonds had slipped to about $61. The reduced value of $70 gave shareholders a reason to be optimistic and Eli an opportunity to buy back $125 million worth of United Brands stock at $75 million. APB Opinion 26 required him to claim the $50 million difference as pretax earnings in 1973. To defer the cost of the deal, Eli renegotiated the interest rate on the bond upward by nearly four percent and extended the due date by four years so that bondholders would not lose any interest in the swap and United Brands could defer spending $75 million to acquire its own stocks. The deal allowed Eli to push the sizable debt incurred in the purchase of United Fruit into the future and move the converted amount to the profit side of his balance sheet, even though he did not dramatically increase production at any of the subsidiaries held by United Brands. *Forbes* speculated that Eli had eluded federal taxes on approximately $12.5 million by showing a net operating loss on its domestic operations and claiming that amount against prior years' tax returns. His exploitation of APB rules and the federal tax code created the appearance of a net gain of between $20 million and $33 million without selling a single additional banana.[11]

Eli's actions remained within the boundaries of the law, but they may have violated ethical standards he had set for himself. They also attracted attention to the company's financial troubles. Journalists passed harsh judgment on him and began to look critically at his original deal to secure United Fruit. Calling his renegotiation of debt a "fiscal fairy tale," *Forbes* consulted accountants and professors to get their opinion. Philip Defliese, head of the APB, disapproved of Eli's actions: "This is precisely the type of thing I was concerned about when I dissented from Opinion 26." Abraham Briloff, a noted professor of accounting at the City University of New York offered a more profane assessment, calling "the deal . . . so much fiscal masturbation." *Forbes,* which had mostly celebrated Eli's managerial acumen, now chided him for running a "magic show," one that cast doubts on the soundness of his decision to acquire United Fruit in the first place. In revisiting the terms of the merger, the authors observed that goodwill accounted for one-fourth, or $281 million, of United Brands' total assets. Since goodwill amounted to a promise to make up the difference with future growth, the anemic state of the company three years into United Brands' existence was cause for concern. As *Forbes* observed, "most of the intangible good will, or $252.9 million to be precise, resulted from AMK's 1970 merger with United Fruit." This amount, they opined, was "an incredibly high value to attach to the reputation, trademarks and patents of a company that even in a good year when there were no hurricanes had difficulty earning a decent return on its assets."[12]

John Morrell, on the other hand, had been undervalued when AMK purchased it in 1966. The savings and sustained growth of the subsidiary meant that Morrell's surplus value, or negative goodwill, contributed to United Brands' overall financial health and allowed Eli to write off the expense of owning United Fruit.[13] Competition from IBP and other competitors in the meat industry required United Brands to invest in major improvements to save jobs and return Ottumwa to its glory days. Eli's decision to use the money, instead, to eliminate debt accrued during the purchase of United Fruit angered employees and community members in Ottumwa. His deals with municipal officials in other Midwestern cities to improve existing facilities or build new ones revealed his true intention: to relieve the company of its onerous labor agreements and ownership arrangements. Eli found his excuse to move on from Ottumwa when elected officials in Estherville, Iowa, Sioux Falls, South Dakota and Cincinnati, Ohio convinced residents to support industrial bonds that covered the construction or redesign of factories for the benefit of Morrell.[14]

Eli's deals to lower overhead costs and convert debt to profit on a short-term basis played well to investors but drew scrutiny from outside observers. *Forbes* recalled that the acquisition of Morrell had produced a net gain of $6.4 million and the ability to claim earnings of $641,000 per year from 1966 to 1976. *Forbes* asked why the company would "charge earnings in order to write off positive goodwill on United Fruit if he didn't absolutely have to?"[15] Eli's decision to restructure debt suggested the depths of the problems facing United Brands and hid the devastating effects on communities like Ottumwa, which became a casualty of what now looked like an elaborate pyramid scheme.

Eli characterized "the cash impact" of Morrell-Ottumwa's closure as "minimal." In his announcement to shareholders, he claimed that the debt-exchange program generated an estimated $38 million that would make up for the shortfall of $32 million caused by shuttering the plant. Black boasted that the dismantling of Morrell-Ottumwa combined with the restructuring of debt produced "a gain of approximately $6 million, before taxes." He promised that the plant's closure would "end a long-time and major drain on Morrell and United Brands earnings, resources, and management time." None of these developments, he claimed, came as a surprise to Ottumwans. "Ottumwa un-

A cartoonist's version of United Fruit's financial restructuring plan in 1973. *Reproduced from "The Numbers Game," Forbes, April 15, 1973, 42.*

derstands," Eli reported, "that Morrell management fought to the very end to save the plant." In recounting Morrell-Ottumwa's recent history, he placed the burden entirely on its employees and conveyed the belief that he had done all that he could do for them. "Management was optimistic about the chance for a 'turnaround' in 1971," he concluded, "but subsequent events did not justify that optimism."[16]

Ottumwans largely rejected Eli's interpretation of the past. In the *Ottumwa Courier*, editor Lewis Debo laid out the recent history of a situation that had been brewing for a decade, explaining how, first, AMK, then United Brands had decided to close Morrell-Ottumwa as early as 1970. He blamed in part the "somewhat callous indifference of conglomerate moguls" and criticized management for failing to pay laid-off workers a severance equivalent to six months of their current salaries. In 1972, Local P-1 had agreed to adjust any possible payouts to 1970 levels in exchange for a commitment to extend the life of Ottumwa-Morrell by shifting production to car-lot quantities for large-scale purchasers.[17] When United Brands closed the plant in April 1973, less than a year after the agreement, the newspaper and union accused management of bargaining in bad faith. "If a company is going to close," Debo told his readers, "it should pay off the workers with dignity." The company further upset the community by restricting these payments to full-time employees only.[18]

Former Morrell employees and Ottumwa residents shared alternating messages of anger and hope in the pages of the local newspaper. Debo noted that Eli's statement had been "written for investors rather than for their impact on the affected people in Ottumwa."[19] In a letter to the editor, a local citizen, Mrs. Kenneth Sands, expressed her disgust in seeing Morrell meats in Ottumwa grocery stores and urged fellow residents to boycott the company. "After all," she wrote, "they walked out on the people of Ottumwa, why should we buy their products?" Such a position ran counter to union members' pledges to buy only Morrell meats when Local P-1 negotiated a stay of execution for the plant in 1971. William Williams, a retired employee of Morrell, expressed the common hope that "a restart in our old plant could mean a fabulous profit to United Brands."[20] Neither organized protest nor Eli's reinvestment occurred.

John Morrell posted a $6 million loss in 1974, its worst year in living memory for current and former employees. United Brands blamed Morrell's poor performance on significant increases in feed costs for cattle and Nixon's price controls on meat to offset inflation, but that did not fully explain its struggles.[21] Dave Swanson noted a series of decisions that knocked Morrell off its perch. United Brands, he observed, "didn't understand the meat business and they didn't really care to learn it." Eli's belief that he could move all production from Ottumwa proved to be a fatal mistake for some of its leading brands, including its canned meats division. Swanson recalled that Morrell had been number one in wet dog food with its Red Heart brand, while its version of Hormel's Spam, called "Snack," had been competitive. According to Swanson, "That went bye-bye when Ottumwa closed, because that's where that product was produced."[22] Embarrassed by its decline, Swanson left the company to work for its competitor, Rath. Meanwhile, in Ottumwa, the former headquarters of Morrell played host to a series of companies that preyed upon the community's desperation, paying workers a fraction of their old wages before moving on to other locations.[23]

Eli's less public moves also drew attention to the precarious state of the company. When AMK purchased United Fruit, it had also assumed controlling interest of Baskin-Robbins and A&W Root Beer, two companies that now gave United Brands a stake in the prepared foods and restaurant business. Both had grown out of the "drive-up" culture in California, where customers had become accustomed to eating in their cars. From its first root beer stand in Lodi, California, opened in 1919, A&W had quickly grown into the number one producer of the beverage as it opened more local hangouts for young people looking for a quick meal on a hot summer night. In the mid-1960s, the company boasted the second largest number of fast-food restaurants in the world next to McDonald's, with six hundred locations across North America, including Canada. Baskin-Robbins, born nearly three decades later in 1945 and further south in Glendale, also took advantage of California's warm weather to sell its original thirty-one flavors. By the early 1970s United Brands controlled franchises across North America, Japan, Saudi Arabia, South Korea, and Australia.

Eli saw the restaurant chains as investments that he could relinquish to save money. Their purchase had not been his idea and clearly a product of the previous management's anxiety over losing control of the company. Having contemplated investing in food processing versus retail, Eli favored the former and sought to make a name for himself as the leading producer and distributor of agricultural products through its Agrimark Group that included United Fruit bananas and Inter Harvest vegetables. "At this moment," he told his investors, "the countries of the world may be entering the first phase of a food 'revolution.'" He took pride in owning a company known for "nutritious, value-oriented foods" that promised "to meet the potential shortfall in the world food supply."[24] Neither Baskin-Robbins nor A&W fit the "nutritious" profile he sought. The "fast" unhealthy food these subsidiaries represented made it easy for Eli to sell, although his obligation to shore up losses and eliminate debt drove his desire to dispense with all or a portion of both franchises. Eli parted with 83 percent of Baskin-Robbins on the last day of 1973. He also imposed a 2 percent royalty fee on distributors of A&W root beer and sold the Canadian division of A&W Food Services, which had lost nearly $400,000 the previous year.[25] Eli had little feel for the growing appeal of the American fast-food industry, which flourished in the years ahead as US families sought less expensive and mobile options to feed themselves during the recession. In 1973, Eli also sold a relic of United Fruit's past, Revere Sugar Refinery, another subsidiary that did not conform to the healthy image of United Brands.

Eli made few exceptions to his preference for the food industry—the notable one being his purchase of a controlling interest in the sunglasses maker Foster Grant. Known for its celebrity ads and catchy slogan ("who's that behind those Foster Grants?"), the company sold its product through department stores and in pharmacies, but also represented untapped value in its capability to manufacture and mold polystyrene and styrene monomer, critical elements of its eyewear that also lent themselves to untold other applications. Foster Grant's plastics and chemicals business gave the company significant market share in industrial-grade piping such as Acrylonitrile Butadiene Styrene (ABS) pipe and a range of other products. The investment made sense for United Brands given its use of plastics in its food divisions as packaging. Foster Grant expanded the company's ability to meet its own supply needs while developing more revenue streams elsewhere. Eli's purchase of Polymer United, a manufacturing subsidiary located primarily in Costa Rica, and a network of chemical and plastics producers throughout the Midwest and Northeast created a potentially profitable wing of the company.

Record sales of Foster Grant sunglasses in 1973 hid more than they revealed. The OPEC oil embargo created a scarcity of raw materials, especially benzene, a major ingredient in styrene monomer. When United Brands could get its hands on it, limited supply and exorbitant costs made production prohibitively expensive. Nixon's imposition of price controls to regulate inflation on consumer goods further cut into the company's profit margins. Making matters worse, in May of 1973, devastating floods hit the Mississippi and Illinois River Valleys, disrupting the transportation of goods from one of United Brands' major production sites in Peru, Illinois. The three-week interruption curtailed the flow of polystyrene and crimped the potential of Foster Grant's plastics business. To overcome these challenges, Eli invested precious resources in new facilities in Chesapeake, Virginia, and upgraded existing plants in Louisiana, New Hampshire, Massachusetts, and Ohio—the last site producing dairy containers that harked back to AMK's origins as a milk cap producer.[26] The demand for these products remained high, but the uncertain political situation, the limited availability of raw materials, and less-than-ideal earnings made these ventures risky.

Eli shifted investments by predicting winners and losers among his subsidiaries in an attempt to survive the ill-effects of the oil embargo. Most Central American nations did not have this luxury. The struggle of Central American governments to create a Central American Common Market delayed hopes of industrial development and forced the five republics back to their historic dependence on the sale of commodities. The creation of tax exemptions as incentives for industrialization remained despite the Common Market's failure, producing a serious deficit in public revenues even before the oil embargo struck in 1973. Honduras, for example, relied heavily on income tax rather than export tax to cover the cost of key public expenditures like education, health, and transportation: 26.3 percent of the government's revenue came from income taxes while export taxes accounted for only 3.6 percent.[27] The demise of the Common Market and the acceleration of global inflation during the early 1970s encouraged Central American nations to lean more heavily on export commodities as a source of revenue. This included a 32 percent increase in banana production from 1970 to 1973, which glutted the market and forced prices downward.[28] The oversupply of bananas continued to suppress prices in the United States through the first half of 1974.[29]

In March 1974, six months into the oil crisis, outgoing Costa Rican president Jose Figueres and Panamanian dictator General Omar Torrijos hosted the first meeting of what would become the UPEB in Panama. Modeled after OPEC, the UPEB gathered representatives from Colombia, Ecuador, Guatemala, Costa Rica, Honduras, Nicaragua, and Panama. These seven countries accounted for 80 percent of the world's banana sales, somewhere between 250 million and 350 million crates of the fruit shipped to the United States, Canada, and Europe each year. Figueres and Torrijos knew that this dominance gave them leverage to demand higher export taxes if they acted collectively. By 1973, Ecuador claimed the top spot among producers of bananas, a consequence of United Fruit's increased dependence on Ecuadorian producers abandoning the disease-ridden coasts for the relatively uncultivated lands near the mountains. As with the associate grower program in Honduras, United Fruit bought bananas produced by local landowners who hired their own workers, freeing the company of overhead costs and union contracts.[30] When the rest of the cartel members agreed to increase export taxes by a dollar per crate, Ecuador balked, siding with the three multinational fruit companies and refusing to participate in any further UPEB meetings.[31]

The defection of Ecuador diminished the UPEB's clout, but raising revenues by increasing export taxes remained one of the only avenues for Central and South American nations to cover petroleum payments amid the deepening oil crisis. The absence of taxes on bananas from Guatemala, Colombia, and Nicaragua further diminished the cartels' leverage. The remaining core group—Costa Rica, Honduras, and Panama—held export agreements up for renegotiation on a country-by-country basis. The Honduran economic minister Abraham Bennaton Ramos handled the negotiations for President López Arellano. In April 1974, Bennaton announced Honduras's plan to impose an export tax of fifty cents per forty-pound box of bananas, amounting to an annual $15 million increase that would begin in June. Panama drove the hardest bargain, sticking to its proposed increase of a dollar per box, while Costa Rica promised to increase its tax to twenty-five cents per box. The total of the new banana export taxes in Central America, combined with the new labor agreements, promised to raise United Brands' annual costs by $18.8 million.[32] Eli addressed the "banana wars" with the United Brands board in August, stating that the increases "violated and breached the provisions of existing agreements with these countries." Nevertheless, he acknowledged the predicament these nations found themselves in, facing a global financial crisis, and promised to work towards a reasonable settlement that would serve all parties.[33]

The crisis forced Eli to lean heavily on United Fruit veteran executives for solutions at a time when they had become skeptical of his abilities. The Boston-based management team had initially resisted AMK's acquisition of their company and the fact that Eli continued their employment and maintained operations in Boston had not been enough to win them over. In the years that followed the merger, Eli had shifted the balance of power to New York, spending only Tuesday through Thursday at the office in Boston, and working Fridays and Mondays in his Park Avenue office, closer to his home in Connecticut. Still, he stuck to a management style that the *Wall Street Journal* called "authoritarian direction." He frequently overruled his vice presidents during contentious meetings that left some feeling bruised and battered. One holdover from pre-merger days, T. K. Warner, later complained to the press that Eli had played managers off against each other—leading him, for one, to quit his position as a vice president in the finance department over what he described as "a difference in management and philosophy." Eli's shuttling between the two offices left little time for building trusting relationships with his New England-based colleagues and emboldened some to question their boss.

In July 1974, Eli proudly brought in Edward Gelsthorpe, a former president of Ocean Spray Cranberries, Hunt-Wesson Foods, and Gillette, as his executive vice president and chief operating officer, a hire that signaled Eli's doubt that the current team was equal to the challenges and opportunities now facing United Brands. Eli regarded his recruitment of Gelsthorpe as "a major coup," and expected the well regarded business executive to pull the Boston team in line with his vision.[34] Among his first assignments was to handle the evolving conflict over export taxes in Central America. Gelsthorpe's deep roots in New England and direct manner quickly won over the office, including Harvey Johnson, the vice president of banana operations who had first received the news from the Honduran minister of the economy, Bennaton, that his country planned to impose a fifty-cent tax on each forty-pound box of United Fruit bananas. Gelsthorpe also consulted vice presidents John Taylor and Donald Meltzer about how to handle the situations in Honduras, Panama, and Costa Rica.

The fast friendship that developed among Gelsthorpe, Taylor, and Meltzer alarmed some associates close to Eli, who saw the triumvirate as a rival force in the organization rather than a group of loyal staff. Gelsthorpe denied there was anything conspiratorial going on, but perhaps the rumors of a Boston mutiny made Eli increasingly anxious.[35] The multiple losses across virtually all subsidiaries of United Brands and growing attention to his failures as a manager contributed to insomnia, which became debilitating by the summer of 1974. His personal physician in New York, Isadore Gerber, treated him with the sedative Seconal, a sleep aid known to have side effects including paranoia, suicidal ideation, and the impairment of memory, judgment, and coordination. In public, Eli maintained his usual stoic demeanor, but some colleagues saw he was shaky. Gelsthorpe and Meltzer recalled his being "disoriented" during visits in September, noting some slurring of his speech. After one meeting, Meltzer watched him "stagger from the room." During a meeting in August, Eli seemed to lose track of why he and Gelsthorpe had scheduled a meeting, asking, "Did I call you or did you call me?" At other moments, he displayed a quick temper that alienated members of his team and created the perception that he "was afraid to go into the Boston office." Even among friends, he appeared not to be himself. His longtime confidant and legal adviser Robert Gallop noted that Eli "seemed awfully tired and depressed." His family also noticed his weakened state. Leon, who was now attending Harvard Business School and saw his father whenever he was in town, knew that Eli often woke up in the night and took another Seconal capsule to go back to sleep. "Sometimes the effects didn't wear off," Leon later told the *Wall Street Journal*, "and he'd be exhausted in the morning."[36]

The palace intrigue in Boston took a back seat to the primacy of the deteriorating situation in Central America. United Fruit, once again, traded places for the top spot among banana producers with its rival Standard Fruit. Although Standard and Del Monte both suffered from the same taxes, the absence of significant revenue from Inter Harvest and Morrell made Eli more eager to resolve the conflict with Panama, Honduras, and Costa Rica. Given United Fruit's history of collaboration with the Honduran government on housing, education, and healthcare, Eli and his associates focused most of their attention on negotiations with Honduras. It was reportedly during a meeting in Miami in August 1974 that Bennaton met with United Fruit vice president Harvey Johnson to convey an offer from President Oswaldo López Arellano to reduce the Honduran banana tax in exchange for $5 million. The payoff would not be part of the official negotiations on the matter, and the money would have to be delivered to a private Swiss bank account. The promise in return was to lower taxes on 35 percent of United Fruit's banana harvest, giving it a clear edge vis-à-vis its competitors and helping the company weather what had become a brutal year of losses. Johnson reported the offer to Eli, who rejected López Arellano's attempted extortion and directed Johnson to inform his immediate superior, John Taylor.

The details of what happened next are in dispute, but the actions of the company and its consequences are not. Friends of Eli say that Taylor assured his boss that he would "take care of it." Others in the Boston office assert that Eli entertained López Arellano's offer and even met with the dictator. Whether under orders from Eli or not, Taylor wired $1.25 million from United Brands' coffers to López Arellano's bank account in Switzerland in August 1974. Taylor covered the transfer up in the company's ledger by listing it as a "cost of European sales," an entry later flagged as suspicious by its auditor, Price Waterhouse. In the words of one unnamed party at the company, the recording of the expense "was very clumsily handled. The entry stuck out like a sore thumb." The payment was meant to be the first of two, with the second one due to drop in the spring of 1975. The initial transfer of funds produced the desired result. In late August, United Brands announced it had reached an "understanding" with Honduras to reduce the per-box tax from fifty to twenty-five cents beginning in 1975. According to subsequent accounts offered to the *Wall Street Journal,* only Eli, Taylor, and Johnson had known the intimate details of the bribe—but colleagues sympathetic to Eli alleged that Donald Meltzer had also been privy to the broad outlines of the agreement. Eli was said to have disclosed the deal to him, in part, because he feared that Taylor would arrange further such transfers. Meltzer never confirmed this. Such secrecy and distrust speak to the depths of division among Eli and the executives in Boston.

A believer in fate might say that what escaped the attention of the mortal world did not slip by the divine. On September 18, 1974, Hurricane Fifí lashed Honduras, triggering massive landslides and severe flooding that killed 8,210 people in the Sula Valley. Tropical storms had always posed a threat to doing business in Central America. During the time of Eli's courtship of United Fruit, he watched with disapproval how company management chose to lay off workers and cut wages in the wake of Hurricane Francelia in 1969. In contrast, Eli had followed through on a new union contract with SITRATERCO despite the devastating effects of Hurricane Edith in September 1971. Oscar Gale Varela had hailed his decision as a turning point in the company's history. In truth, neither storm hit Honduras directly. Banana production remained close to its usual production levels before and after Francelia;

production levels rose slightly during and after Edith. Nonetheless, Eli used the difference in how he met the challenge versus his predecessors to accentuate the social consciousness of the new company he had created.

Fifí was a disaster of an entirely different magnitude. A category-two hurricane, the storm had not been the strongest of the 1974 season, yet its path made it especially destructive. Beginning as a tropical depression just beyond the western coast of Jamaica on September 16, the storm quickly intensified to a hurricane that brushed the northern coast of Honduras, then made landfall in Belize, before heading across the isthmus into the Pacific Ocean where it later became Hurricane Orlene. The storm touched nine countries in its path and produced $1.8 billion ($10.32 billion in 2022 dollars) in damage. Fifí destroyed 85 percent of the acres cultivated by the company and associate-producers and washed away 35 percent of United Fruit's most fertile land in Honduras.[37] The overall cost in crops and facilities amounted to $19.5 million.[38] After previous hurricanes hit La Lima, production had bounced back quickly, but that wasn't the case this time. By 1975, banana production in Honduras had dipped to 783,426 tons, the lowest annual peak during Eli's tenure as CEO of United Brands.[39] Hurricane Fifí remains the third deadliest storm on record, surpassed only by Hurricane Mitch in 1998 and an unnamed storm in 1780 that killed between 22,000 to 27,501 people throughout the Caribbean and North America.[40]

The unfolding tragedy in Honduras could only have intensified the turmoil brewing inside of Eli. Until Fifí struck, he might have told himself that his failures could be chalked up to excessive ambition. The deal to acquire United Fruit placed a burden on the company to perform at a level it had not seen since the 1950s, but his experience of squeezing greater efficiency from AMK and Morrell made the idea that he would succeed plausible. When union officials in Ottumwa raged that Eli's elaborate pyramid scheme had cost them their jobs, he could point to years of unprofitable performance at the plant as the real source of their pain. Secretly preventing revenue from reaching the public treasury of a struggling nation could not be explained away so easily. The act contradicted his public statements about the social consciousness of United Brands and ran counter to his philosophy of doing good by doing business. In the aftermath of Fifí, Eli pledged United Brands' resources to rescue efforts, but these commitments paled in comparison to the value of the banana trade to both company and country. His agreement with López Arellano had violated the trust of his employees as well as the communities and nations that had believed him when he claimed United Fruit's dishonesty and manipulations of governments were a thing of the past.

Eli may have struggled with his conscience, but certainly he feared the disclosure of the deal by enemies seeking to bring him down. Friends had raised suspicions about Gelsthorpe, Taylor, and Meltzer in particular. The imperative to end the banana wars remained his top priority, however, and he needed an experienced team to do that. In November, Eli disclosed to Gelsthorpe and Meltzer what he assumed they already knew—that the taxes in Honduras had been reduced by way of a secret deal with López Arellano. He asked that they turn their attention to Panama and dispatched Gelsthorpe to pursue a reduction in taxes on commodities and property owned by United Brands in the country. Once again, the Panamanians refused. Acknowledging the hemorrhaging of money from the company, Gelsthorpe suggested cutting expenses by selling off all of its Panamanian holdings rather than continuing to negotiate.

Eli saw Gelsthorpe's recommendation as a failure to do his job and a betrayal of him and the company. Although speculations of a coup against Eli continued to swirl, his former financial assistant Tony Tegnelia saw it differently. According to Tegnelia, Eli's long spells of despondency mixed with angry outbursts made it impossible for Gelsthorpe and his vice presidents to work for him. "You just couldn't communicate with him," Tegnelia later told the *Wall Street Journal*, adding, "what do you do if you're a senior vice president and your chief isn't communicating?" He claimed that Gelsthorpe, along with Taylor and Meltzer, had been trying to save the man and the company for months, to no avail. Troubled by Eli's unpredictability, Gelsthorpe reached out to George P. Gardner, Jr., the only holdover from the United Fruit board still serving as a United Brands director, to seek his support and advice. When word got out about their conversation, Eli saw it as confirmation of Gelsthorpe's infidelity. Tegnelia disagreed. "You have to talk with a peer," he said, "which is insubordination or mutiny." He added, "What can you do that isn't interpreted as a power play?"[41]

Eli moved to quash what he saw as a rebellion among his top executives. Although he threatened to fire Gelsthorpe, he kept him on, perhaps to avoid making the discord within the Boston office public. Instead, he privately asked Gardner for his resignation from the board. Gardner refused, in part because Gelsthorpe had conveyed Eli's unstable behavior and indicated to him that he would be "a useful and necessary board member" if matters further deteriorated. Gardner's rejection of Eli's request to quit revealed the degree to which Eli had lost control of his own company.

December brought matters to a head on several fronts. Eli hated the thought of selling off any more subsidiaries but the company's dismal performance during the past twelve months required him to take Gelsthorpe's suggestion seriously. United Fruit reported a staggering loss of $40.2 million in the third quarter alone on its way to incurring $71.3 million in losses for 1974.[42] By December, it was already apparent to Eli that his investors would see no dividend for the year. This promised to upset shareholders while making the company's financial statements only a little less bloody when the annual report came out in March 1975. Whether he liked it or not, the financial condition of United Brands made the decision for him. Once again, as the year came to a close, he looked across the company for a new candidate to sell. Embracing Gelsthorpe's recommendation to sell Panamanian holdings would do only so much to stave the bleeding.

Eli grudgingly looked to his best performer, United Brands' stake in Foster Grant, as the likeliest candidate to be sacrificed. The company had become one of his prized possessions soon after he purchased a majority interest on January 1, 1973. By May of 1974, he had increased his equity to 70 percent on the faith that it could claim a greater share of United Brands' productive capacity. Despite challenges due to the oil crisis and bad weather, Foster Grant remained resilient largely because its main product, plastics, had been excluded from Nixon's price controls on essential goods. The company possessed undeniable upside that confirmed Eli's fleeting image as a visionary businessman. One executive regarded Foster Grant as Eli's "last, very brilliant coup."[43] Robert Gallop, United Brands senior vice president and general counsel, saw the subsidiary as the bridge to the company's future. Eli understood its value but his bank, Morgan Guaranty, had been pressuring him since October to sell the subsidiary to meet his debt obligations. He privately met with J. G. Brookhuis, president of the American Hoechst Corporation, to explore a possible deal with his parent company in Germany, Hoechst AG. Eli, recalled Brookhuis, "made it clear that, if he parted with Foster Grant, he would do it reluctantly." By December, conditions had deteriorated so much that Eli had no choice. On December 20, he had agreed to sell 62 percent of his interest to Hoechst AG for $69 million, pending approval from United Brands' board.[44]

The deal may have satisfied the bank and brought the company back from total collapse, but it did little to lighten Eli's mood. According to Bernard Fischman, his personal lawyer, Eli "took it all personally" as business problems erupted on multiple fronts. "He identified with the company as though he was it."[45] Friends and family noted signs of his depression around the time that negotiations began with Hoechst. He started seeing a psychiatrist but his feelings of despair over the future of his company, the security of Israel, and the state of the economy continued to dominate his thoughts. By December, Leon, Judy, and Judy's husband, Allen Nadler, regularly visited Eli and Shirley in Westport to try to take his mind off his troubles. Leon later told the *Wall Street Journal* that his father "never had so many pressures accumulated from so many angles before." As a result, "he never had time to rest."[46] Eli spent the better portion of Saturdays at home observing the Jewish sabbath with his friend and rabbi, Jonathan Levine. In spite of these many interventions, nothing seemed to cheer him as long as the future of United Brands remained uncertain.

On December 27, the company board met to review the past year and approve the sale of assets. There was pushback on the proposed divestment of Foster Grant from some of United Fruit's executives, especially Robert Gallop. Eli's friend of over twenty years, the lawyer had served as general counsel and board director to AMK from the beginning and simply saw the growing company as too good an investment to part with. Eli took no joy from the sale but saw the value of trading the promise of one subsidiary for the good of the entire company. At a time when some doubted his leadership, the decision had the added benefit of reminding Eli's colleagues of his ability to set emotion aside and make tough calls. He accepted the fate of the deal when the board voted to approve it. To his surprise, however, the board also invited Edward Gelsthorpe to present a plan to sell the company's Panamanian assets—the very plan Eli had rejected the previous month. Gelsthorpe later claimed that he had run the decision to present it to the board by Meltzer, and that Meltzer had informed Eli. Eli denied that Gelsthorpe had shared his intentions in advance and angrily rejected the proposal.

The meeting devolved into a round of recriminations for the state of United Brands that laid bare the degree to which Eli had lost control of the company. "Mr. Black expressed his disapproval of the agreement," Gelsthorpe later told *Wall Street Journal*, adding, "I was dumbfounded." The conflict ignited a tense exchange between Eli and Gelsthorpe that forced those who had avoided getting involved in their tug-of-war to take a side. Robert Gallop had been someone Eli trusted amidst the chaos of the past months. Now, Gallop spoke up in support of Gelsthorpe's proposal, urging his friend to accept the agreement. Eli coolly demanded Gallop's resignation. Gallop responded, "Why should I? I haven't done anything wrong. You should resign!" Only a handful of people in the room knew what "wrong" Eli had committed, leaving others to wonder what Gallop meant. On this day, the argument did not go beyond innuendo, but the damage was done. Friends who spoke to Eli after the meeting later claimed that Gallop's outburst "broke his heart."[47]

The entire affair confirmed Eli's failure to unite the company and emboldened his critics. At the next board meeting on January 10, 1975, George Gardner surprised the board by inviting John Taylor to address the Honduran situation. A brief discussion of the company's payments to Honduran officials ensued before a director close to Eli demanded an end to it because it had not been on the agenda. Eli took it as a clear warning from men who, he believed, had been planning a coup. Gallop tried to convince his old friend that no one sought to unseat him, but Eli refused to listen. Eli "felt vulnerable," Allen Nadler told the *Wall Street Journal,* adding, "he felt the Honduras payment could possibly be used against him if there were a power struggle."[48]

The nightmare of 1974 had followed Eli into the new year as he sat down to write his annual letter to shareholders. The occasion typically had been an opportunity for him to recommit to his philosophy of social responsibility through profitability, but the accumulated losses of United Brands made the task too unbearable to contemplate. His failures had done nothing to prove that society could reduce its dependence on government-administered social services and be well served by a managerial class of men of good will and virtuous ethics. In the 1940s, when he first began to imagine a career beyond the rabbinate, he saw an abundance of such men in the schools and synagogues he attended. He asked why their insights and talent had not done more to mitigate the violence and injustice in the world, most notably the near annihilation of his own people. To him, the wisdom of the Talmud and the practice of its teachings had nurtured a strong but insular community of love and support that had potential to intervene in the pernicious forces of evil around it. Raised in a city that put its faith in the free market to resolve most differences, Eli may have dared to believe that taking the wisdom he gained from men like Rabbi Lookstein and Rabbi Belkin into the financial system would result in a more hopeful, equitable existence for everyone. In what amounted to his theory of social change, he may have miscalculated the selfish motivations of the marketplace while overestimating the power of men of unquestionable character to change it. Perhaps as he sat in front of a blank pad of paper, unable to write a report he had crafted many times before, he came face to face with the devastating realization that the world had not become what he thought it would when he left Woodmere for Wall Street in 1945. The man who had promised to save others through business now couldn't even save himself.

Monday, February 3, 1975, began like any other morning in New York City, with cars shuttling titans of capitalism to their headquarters in preparation for a new week. Eli joined the stream, climbing into his 1973 Cadillac Fleetwood to travel the thirty-five blocks to his office in midtown. His chauffeur, Jim Thomas, sensed nothing out of the ordinary, receiving the usual "big 'Hello'" from his boss and instructions to keep the car in the garage since this would be an "in day." While Thomas parked, Eli rode the elevator of the Pan American Building to the forty-fourth floor where he disembarked for the offices of United Brands. Carrying an oversized steel attaché case, Eli entered the suite, turned, and bolted the large double wooden doors to the reception area. He did the same to another metal door on his way to his own office, which he closed and locked behind him in similar fashion. Then, the man who arrived in New York as Eliasz Menasze Blachowicz smashed a hole through the quarter-inch-thick window with his briefcase, looked with despair toward the raised parkway next to Grand Central Station below, and launched himself from the sill.

EPILOGUE

Reporters descended on New York and Boston on Monday, February 3, 1975, to learn more about Eli and why he had taken his own life. Eventually information surfaced about the first clandestine payment to Oswaldo López Arellano and plans for another one that spring. SEC investigators also found evidence of a payoff to Italian officials in the amount of $750,000, the purpose of which has never been divulged, except that it related to the cost of transporting bananas to Europe.[1] In the weeks and months that followed, news of bananas, bribes, and a Latin American dictator reinforced the public's impression of United Fruit, a company infamous for sordid doings that added to human suffering. Any distinct memory of Eli would soon be absorbed into the general awareness of corrupt activity by one of the most notorious US companies doing business in Latin America.

Eli's choice of death fits a pattern many Americans think they understand. We have been trained by popular culture and real-life drama to see someone's decision to jump from a tall building as a response to material loss, revelation of bad behavior, or both. The sensational image of business investors doing so dates back to October 24, 1929, when newspapers reported scenes of distraught Wall Street speculators choosing to leap to their deaths rather than face ruin after the stock market crash. Although economist John Kenneth Galbraith later exposed the rash of stories as fraudulent, Americans continued to believe them to be true.[2] Fictional accounts of the jump have contributed to the legend. In the television drama *Mad Men,* the show opens with a silhouette of a businessman descending against the backdrop of a Madison Avenue tower while images of excess and debauchery flash against the facade. Similarly, the dramatic satire *Succession,* about cutthroat sibling rivals vying to become the heir to a fictional media and entertainment conglomerate, plays on the threat of the oldest son, Kendall Roy, leaping from the top of his father's building. Eli's jump, indeed, inspired filmmakers Joel and Ethan Coen to insert a recurring scene of businessmen throwing themselves from a New York City skyscraper in their 1994 comedy *The Hudsucker Proxy.* These scenes provide wonderful plot devices but offer little in the way of explanation as to why someone would be compelled to leap.

Eli's death and life invites an additional perspective on this phenomenon. As an observant Jew, and indeed an ordained rabbi, Eli knowingly violated Judaism's clear prohibitions against taking one's own life. Historically, temples refused to bury victims of suicide in Jewish cemeteries. The ancient collection of laws known as "Ethics of the Fathers," a text commonly studied since 200 CE, instructs that one should "give a judgment and accounting" before God rather than settle matters by one's own hand, a rule familiar to most Jews.[3] In *Stay: A History of Suicide and the Philosophies Against It,* Jennifer Michael Hecht emphasizes that religions' admonitions against suicide often make people think twice before doing the unspeakable. Why did Eli's faith not keep him from doing it?

Eli left little physical evidence of his motivation for jumping except a brief note with "early retirement—55" scribbled across a loose leaf of paper found at the scene.[4] Initial reporting by the *New York Times* and *Wall Street Journal* hinted that Eli's despair probably came from trying—and failing—to improve the world for humanity from within a system that many warned only valued capital accumulation and individual success. As a young man, he had forfeited a life of noble service to his people and the fulfillment of his father's dream by turning his back on the rabbinate for something he felt would be more consequential. Many had sacrificed to give him the life he refused, including his mother and father who braved the long journey from Lublin, Poland, and his sisters who took up jobs from a young age so that he could study the Talmud and become a rabbi. Intellectually, and spiritually, his application of lessons learned from Rabbis Joseph Lookstein and Samuel Belkin to the art of doing business must have felt to Eli like a misappropriation of their wisdom in the wake of his actions, or worse, a betrayal of his faith. In executing his plan to fuse business with social responsibility, he had given hope to the downtrodden and inspired a belief that labor and management could work together to improve the conditions of workers and feed the world. The dismantling of Morrell-Ottumwa and the collapse of United Brands revealed that the imperatives of turning a profit and serving investors outweighed any virtuous impulse. Along the way, he compromised employees and communities in the service of a greater good that never came to pass. During moments of success, Eli exhibited the conceit he had faulted others for, and betrayed Shirley, who had been instrumental in reconciling his faith with his material ambition.

Eli's failures tempt us to see his death as the consequence of a man who strayed from a virtuous path, but the reality is far more complicated. He had his faults, to be sure, but much of what led him to that fateful day in February 1975 could be described as good intentions gone awry. Eli did not so much betray his vision as remain stubbornly loyal to honoring the dignity of every human being—displaying that quality of *derekh eretz* Belkin praised—in a system that did not value such a moral commitment. His trust in Cesar Chavez to resolve the hiring process at Inter Harvest and his expenditures on Honduran workers at United Fruit raised objections from within his executive core, yet he stayed the course in hopes that losses in one subsidiary or one year would be offset by the eventual benefits of building a company based on the principles of corporate social responsibility. In the end, Eli's recognition that business would not serve as the best vehicle for achieving his higher goals led him to his final act. In this regard, Eli's suicide might be seen as a tragic consequence of an unshakable, if overly idealistic, faith in American capitalism.

Echoes of Eli's actions have reverberated through the global food chain in more recent times. When investigators found conditions "close to slavery" on Florida tomato farms in the late 1990s, a farm worker organization, Coalition of Immokalee Workers (CIW), began to speak of social responsibility, though this time from the perspective of workers. Their analysis, corroborated by Oxfam America, found that the purchase of tomatoes in large volumes by companies like Taco Bell and Walmart empowered these big produce buyers to drive down prices. Growers passed on the costs and risks imposed on them from above by lowering wages and hiring contractors to coerce immigrant, often undocumented, farm workers into service. CIW brought attention to these conditions and changed the fortunes of farm workers by initiating a boycott against Taco Bell in 2001 that asked consumers not to eat at the fast-food restaurant until it agreed to pay one penny more per pound of tomatoes to raise farm worker wages, to adopt a human rights-based code of conduct, and to buy Florida tomatoes only from farms that complied with the code. The success of CIW's campaign resulted in the Fair Food Program that includes an oversight board funded by the company's contribution to ensure compliance with the code of conduct the two sides agreed upon.[5] To distinguish it from the kind of corporate-driven social responsibility that Eli experimented with in the 1970s, CIW called their approach "worker-driven social responsibility" and built a network of farm worker programs working in coalition with food producers to bring justice to the global food system.[6]

Although workers have become the drivers of this version of social responsibility, their model relies on the participation of corporate partners. These companies range in their motivations, but at least in one case, Ben & Jerry's, the company's values align with the agreement. Ben & Jerry's founders, Ben Cohen and Jerry Greenfield, Jewish men who have been friends since childhood, attracted a loyal following with a message of social justice and their purchase of fair-trade ingredients. These commitments continued even after the Dutch global conglomerate Unilever purchased the Vermont-based ice cream company in 2000. Jostein Solheim, Ben and Jerry's next CEO, promised to continue the founders' vision by building a "values-led company" based on empathy.[7] In 2015, a member organization of the Worker-Driven Social Responsibility Network, Migrant Justice, put the company's words to the test when they challenged Ben & Jerry's to sign an agreement that insured safety and fair pay for dairy workers in Vermont. On October 3, 2017, Solheim and members of Migrant Justice publicly signed the "Milk with Dignity" agreement that, among other things, created a third-party standards council to coordinate regular audits of labor conditions in dairies supplying milk for Ben & Jerry's ice cream.[8] While the meaning and substance of these programs continues to evolve, it is clear that some companies have learned what Eli believed to be possible in his own time: social responsibility sells.

In the immediate aftermath of his death, these lessons remained obscure. In 1978, United Brands pled guilty to conspiring to pay a bribe to a former official of the Honduras government in a suit brought by the US Department of Justice in the Southern District of New York. The case had been one of forty questionable foreign payments by US corporations investigated by the US Securities and Exchange Commission. The executives who took the helm next at United Brands believed it served their interests simply to pay the maximum penalty of $15,000 and put the matter behind them. That year, the company achieved sales of $2.4 billion, largely from its banana division. Seemingly untarnished by the scandal, the Chiquita brand lives on today as a separate entity with headquarters in Cincinnati, Ohio.[9]

Eli's death brought unwanted attention to the Black family, but that, too, passed as the family retained some of its private wealth and all the benefits that come with being connected to the rich. Shirley moved to Paradise Valley, Arizona, in the wake of the controversy to pursue her love of painting and cultivate her new passion of gardening. She married William Kash in 1982 and escaped whatever scrutiny followed the ignominious end of her former husband. Judy remained in Connecticut but stayed out of the spotlight as she had done for most of her life. Eli's death had its greatest influence on Leon, who revered his father and spent a significant amount of time with him up until the day before he died. "My father was a God to me," he later told one reporter. He added, "Suicides, you know, aren't usually committed by gods."[10] Leon still managed to complete his degree at Harvard Business School but the loss of his father sent him into therapy and initially drove him to hunker down in his aunt's Park Avenue apartment where he reflected on the lessons of Eli's life and career.

The tragedy did not limit Leon's access to the material benefits afforded to a millionaire's son. Searching for "where [Eli] ended and [he] began," he interviewed with Lehman Brothers but the company that gave his father his start passed on Leon because "he didn't have the brains or personality to succeed on Wall Street."[11] In 1977, Leon asked a friend of the family to introduce him to Fred Joseph, a rising star at an obscure investment bank, Drexel Burnham Lambert Inc. Drexel had begun to distinguish itself through the questionable investment strategies of its Beverly Hills–based partner, Michael Milken, who worked tirelessly to cobble together leveraged buyouts of companies he argued had underperformed. Milken convinced his clients that they could acquire a company by using only a small portion of their equity combined with a secured loan from a bank and about 30 percent of unsecured debt. Like Eli, Milken and his clients painted a rosy picture of the company under new ownership. Unlike Eli, once the company had been acquired, Milken helped the clients sell off the unsecured debt, now known as junk bonds, to mostly savings and loans while the new owners laid off workers, downsized production, and sold valuable subsidiaries. This work had been vaguely familiar to Leon through his father, who had successfully convinced executives and shareholders of Morrell and United Fruit that they could do better with him as CEO. Leon's knowledge of this business competed with his tendency to stay out until dawn and arrive late to work the next day. After a stern talking-to, Joseph welcomed Leon to his corporate finance department at Drexel, where they quickly discovered that Leon "had more contacts than all the rest of us put together."[12] By 1981, Leon had endeared himself to Milken, while Joseph named him co-head of the mergers and acquisitions department in Drexel's Manhattan office.

Perhaps unmoored by the absence of his father's virtue, Leon embarked on a career in high finance that redefined the notion of the cold and calculated entrepreneur. Drexel's cynical scheme to help corporate raiders take over formerly rock-solid companies relied on a big lie invented and perpetrated by Leon—the "highly confident" letter. Such a letter took the place of the usual commitment letter supplied by banks, confirming buyer's creditworthiness. In its place, Leon recommended that the firm communicate that it was "highly confident" it could raise the financing to cover the ultimate cost of the deal. When Leon first submitted such a letter on behalf of businessman Carl Icahn in 1985, in an attempt to buy Phillips Petroleum, the stunt failed—but it forced Phillips executives to radically restructure the company in a way that included layoffs and improved stock prices for shareholders, including Icahn.[13] In 1986, Leon's strategy produced the hostile takeover of Beatrice, an American food processing company, by Drexel client Henry Kravis of Kohlberg Kravis Roberts & Co (KKR). The deal was, at the time, the largest leveraged buyout in history. Over the next four years, KKR sold off the company, division by division, to cover the unsecured debt. These sales produced handsome short-term profits for investors, but all the while, the new management team shuttered plants and laid off hundreds of employees. Leon's innovation at Drexel triggered panic among CEOs throughout corporate America who now looked over their shoulder at any would-be robber baron armed with a piece of paper that enough stockholders believed made him a more worthy manager than the one they had. Such deals came with signifi-cant arm-twisting of Drexel clients and a significant amount of insider information that gave them the confidence to invest. When one of Drexel's clients, Ivan Boesky, pled guilty in 1986 to SEC charges of insider-trading violations and turned state's evidence against Milken, Drexel came under federal investigation, the result of which was the arrest of Milken in 1988. In 1989, at the age of thirty-eight, Leon has-tened the end of Drexel with riskier deals before managing to extract a $12 million bonus from Joseph prior to the firm's declaring bank-ruptcy in 1990.[14]

The junk bond scandal that Leon helped create set up his next act in the 1990s. As Congress sought to clean up the financial mess, it passed the Financial Institutions Reform, Recovery, and Enforcement Act in 1989, which ordered the country's savings and loans to sell all assets created by the junk bond crisis of the 1980s. Leon's participation in the creation of these troubled assets meant that he had intimate knowl-edge of the value hiding in these Frankenstein conglomerates. When French bank Crédit Lyonnais called Leon in 1990 to pick his brain about where to find investment opportunities, he struck a deal with them to underwrite a majority share of his private equity firm, Apollo Advisors, later to be renamed Apollo Global Management. From 1990 to 1994, the two bought distressed securities that few other businesses would touch, because Leon could distinguish the good deals from the bad.

If Drexel had been the primogenitor of the 1960s merger moment Eli participated in, Apollo was the Death Star of the next phase of capitalism—the era in which we now live. Leon often paid pennies on the dollar for companies that he would later restructure and make prof-itable through forcing managers to consolidate expenses and cut ben-efits to employees. In perhaps the most notorious case, California's first insurance commissioner, John Garamendi, seized the assets of trou-bled insurance company Executive Life for having $3 billion of losses due to junk bonds. At the time of the deal in 1991, the recovery of the market had already begun, and the number of policyholders who had cashed out in the wake of the recession had subsided. Garamendi ignored a deal worked out by Executive Life CEO Fred Carr to sell some of the distressed assets to Hartford Insurance and Leon's Apollo, while allowing the bond market to continue to improve. Garamendi opted, instead, to sell the entire package to Apollo, handing Leon a portfolio that included 424 companies, some of which he knew could be rehabilitated. Leon ended up paying $3.25 billion for junk bonds that had a face value of $6.1 billion. In the time between negotiating the deal and writing a check to pay for it, the value of the securities increased $800 million. By becoming the new manager of the debt, Leon also extracted another half-billion dollars in management fees, a formula that would later become a cornerstone of Apollo's capital accumulation strategy. Meanwhile, because of restructuring plans imposed by Apollo, Executive Life policyholders saw their benefits slashed by up to 50 percent.[15]

From the Executive Life deal, Leon went on to define American business practices in the twenty-first century. By 2013, this included the purchase and restructuring of Hostess, the company best known for its Twinkies brand. After Hostess filed for bankruptcy in 2012, Leon worked with Metropoulos & Co. to purchase the iconic snack maker for a mere $186 million in cash. Four years later, he sold the company for $2.3 billion, thirteen times his original investment. How did he improve it? Apollo slashed the payroll of the company by shuttering unionized bakeries in Illinois and consolidating operations in the right-to-work state of Georgia. The company laid off nearly eight thousand people in the wake of the buyout, reducing the overall workforce at Hostess to twelve hundred. The new and supposedly improved Hostess also launched a campaign to reintroduce the Twinkie to the public, landing spots on NBC's *Good Morning America*. The slick media blitz played on the nostalgia of many consumers to buy a treat whose ingredients label flew in the face of public health efforts to combat unhealthy food choices. Placing profit over jobs and health,

Apollo came to symbolize the ills born of an economy significantly influenced by private equity companies.[16]

Today we remain in a world where corporate leaders speak of social responsibility but place profit over the good of the public and the planet. Many live for the moment and themselves, and seek attention for their good deeds only to throw critics off the scent of their bad ones. When plutocrats do turn their attention to larger concerns, it is often well after they have made their fortunes. When their small efforts to improve workers' lives, reduce their carbon footprints, or support the arts and humanities are overshadowed by their abuses of power, most do not have the decency to admit they were wrong and remove themselves.

While Eli removed himself in the most extreme of ways, his son has taken a different path. Leon did not go quietly when allegations of sexual abuse and trafficking of his girlfriend, Guzel Ganieva, emerged, ending his run as chair and chief executive officer of the company he founded. Despite submitting his resignation on March 21, 2021, he surprised his cofounders, Marc Rowan and Joshua Harris, who had planned to convene the executive committee that morning to discuss how to move forward. When Leon insisted on staying at a meeting reserved only for management, Rowan and Harris capitulated, later explaining that they permitted Leon's presence only because he remained the largest shareholder of the company. They redesignated the gathering as an "informational meeting" after the fact, and assured the public that "Mr. Black did not, and will not, attend executive committee meetings following such date." For his part, Leon confirmed his role as "Apollo's largest shareholder and its biggest supporter," and expressed his "hope to return at some point."[17] Some people just don't know when to leave.

NOTES

PREFACE

1. Marshall Ganz, interview by author, March 26, 2008, Cambridge, MA, Matt Garcia Papers, box 14, folder 43, Special Collections, Claremont Colleges Library, Claremont, CA.

2. Abraham Cahan, *The Rise of David Levinsky* (New York: Harper and Bros., 1917).

3. Matt Garcia, "'A Just and Righteous Man': Eli Black and the Transformation of United Fruit," in *The Jewish Role in American Life: An Annual Review* 16 (2018), ed. Hasia Diner, series editor Steven J. Ross.

4. More than fifty biographies have been published so far in the Jewish Lives Series by Yale University Press: https://yalebooks.yale.edu/series/jewish-lives.

5. Caleb Melby and Heather Perlberg, "Nobody Makes Money Like Apollo's Ruthless Founder Leon Black," *Bloomberg Businessweek,* January 16, 2020.

6. William D. Cohan, "'What a Sad Tale of Sycophants': Wall Street Isn't Buying Leon Black's Epstein Story," *Vanity Fair,* January 29, 2021.

7. Matthew Goldstein, "Leon Black Leaves Apollo Sooner Than Expected," *New York Times,* March 22, 2021; Sabrina Willmer, "Black's Apollo Exit Follows 'Deeply Trying' Fallout over Epstein," *Bloomberg,* March 22, 2021; Gabriel Sherman, "'You Have to Let Them Do Whatever They Want': Billionaire Leon Black Flew a Russian Model to Meet Jeffrey Epstein, New Filing Claims," *Vanity Fair,* August 9, 2021.

8. Rich Cohen, *The Fish That Ate the Whale: The Life and Times of America's Banana King* (New York: Farrar, Straus and Giroux, 2012); Watt Stewart,

Keith and Costa Rica: The Biography of Minor Cooper Keith, American Entrepreneur (Albuquerque: University of New Mexico Press, 1964). Mark Baldwin, *Tropical Iron: The Saga of Minor Keith,* Baldwin Film Works, Inc. 2018. As Rich Cohen shows, Boston Fruit, owned by Andrew Preston, "had money but needed bananas; Minor Keith had bananas but needed money." The merging of the two interests in 1899 created United Fruit Company, with Preston serving as the first president of United Fruit and Minor Keith the first Vice President. Cohen, *The Fish That Ate the Whale,* 45–46. Samuel Zemurray seized control of United Fruit in 1932 after selling his banana business, Cuyamel, to the company in 1929. Cohen, *The Fish That Ate the Whale,* 119, 143–144.

PROLOGUE

1. Beacon Journal Wire Services, "Pulled between 2 Worlds, Then He Came Apart," *Akron Beacon Journal,* February 21, 1975, A1. The poetic line is from Robert Browning's "Andrea del Sarto," in *Men and Women,* 1855.

2. Beacon Journal Wire Services, "Pulled between 2 Worlds," A11.

3. Leonard Sloane, "A.M.K.'s Chief Prepares for an Encore," *New York Times,* October 20, 1968, F3.

4. Stanley H. Brown, "United Fruit's Shotgun Marriage," *Fortune,* April 1969: 132–134, 133.

5. "United Fruit Co. Says It Is Not for Sale, Is Open to Right Bid," *Wall Street Journal,* October 4, 1968, 7.

6. Chris Welles, "Battle for United Fruit," *Investment Banking and Corporate Financing,* 1969, 30. Also see Ernest Holsendolph, "Textron: Father of the Conglomerates," *New York Times,* June 1, 1974.

7. Welles, "Battle for United Fruit," 32.

8. Quote from anonymous investment banker, in Peter T. Kilborn, "Suicide of Big Executive: Stress of Corporate Life," *New York Times,* February 14, 1975, 1.

9. Welles, "The Battle for United Fruit," 26–33, 84–88, quotes on 86, 87.

10. Welles, "Battle for United Fruit," 88.

1. TALMID

1. Names of immigrants to the United States frequently vary in their spellings and evolve in degrees of Anglicization. The Polish spelling of Eli's first name would have been Eliasz Menasze. On his Atlantic crossing, Eli is listed at "Menasie Blachowitz." Because his mother and sisters are listed with the

surname of "Blachowicz," I use that spelling here, while noting that in later references in American sources the original family name is most often rendered as Blackowitz. US Department of Labor, Immigration Service, List or Manifest of Alien Passengers for the United States, Affidavit of Surgeon. S.S. *Republic*, from Bremen, Germany, February 19, 1925.

2. For just two of many references to Lublin as the "Jewish Oxford" see Rebecca Weiner, "Virtual Jewish World: Lublin, Poland," Jewish Virtual Library, n.d., https://www.jewishvirtuallibrary.org/lublin-virtual-jewish-history -tour; and "Heritage Trail of the Lublin Jews," Lublin City Office, Tourist Trails, n.d., https://lublin.eu/en/what-to-see-do/attractions-sights/tourist-trails /heritage-trail-of-the-lublin-jews/.

3. Hasia Diner, *The Jews of the United States, 1654 to 2000* (Berkeley: University of California Press, 2004), 77, 88.

4. Abraham Cahan, *The Rise of David Levinsky: A Novel* (New York: Harper and Row, 1917), 330. See also Phillip Barrish, "'The Genuine Article': Ethnicity, Capital, and the Rise of David Levinsky," *American Literary History* 5, no. 4 (1993): 643–662.

5. Maddalena Marinari, *Unwanted: Italian and Jewish Mobilization against Restrictive Immigration Laws, 1882–1965* (Chapel Hill: University of North Carolina Press, 2020), 2.

6. Department of State, Consular Service, "Reports Concerning Prospective Immigration," December 4, 1920, transmitted by Wilbur J. Carr and entered into Congressional Record by Rep. Albert Johnson in US Senate Committee on Immigration Hearing on Emergency Immigration Legislation, January 3, 1921 (Washington: Government Printing Office, 1921), 11.

7. Harold Gastwirt, *Fraud, Corruption, and Holiness: The Controversy over the Supervision of Jewish Dietary Practices in New York City, 1881–1940* (Port Washington, NY: Kennikat Press, 1974), 7.

8. Marinari, *Unwanted: Italian and Jewish Mobilization,* 60.

9. Annie Polland and Daniel Soyer, "Conclusion: The Jewish Metropolis at the End of the Immigrant Era," in *City of Promises: A History of the Jews of New York,* vol. 2: *Emerging Metropolis: New York Jews in the Age of Immigration, 1840–1920,* gen. ed. Deborah Dash Moore, 245–254 (New York: New York University Press, 2012), 248; Libby Garland, "Not-Quite-Closed Gates: Jewish Alien Smuggling in the Post-Quota Years," *American Jewish History* 94, no. 3 (September 2008): 197–224, 199. The legislation succeeded in crimping the flow of immigrants from 800,000 in 1920 to 295,000 by the time Eli passed through Ellis Island in 1925. In the same period, the number of Jewish immigrants shrank from 120,000 to 10,000.

10. Diner, *Jews of the United States,* 138–139.

11. Harold Gastwirt claims that by 1892, 136 religious societies existed on the Lower East Side, and by 1903, 307 *Heder,* or religious elementary schools, served Jewish families in the borough. Gastwirt, *Fraud, Corruption, and Holiness,* 5.

12. US Department of Labor, Immigration Service, List or Manifest of Alien Passengers for the United States, Affidavit of Surgeon. S.S. *Paris,* from Le Havre, France, January 27, 1924.

13. Diner, *Jews of the United States,* 105–107.

14. Gastwirt, *Fraud, Corruption, and Holiness,* 28, 44. Benzion Blachowitz, US Social Security Act Application for Account Number, XXX-XX-1064, December 3, 1926.

15. Gastwirt, *Fraud, Corruption, and Holiness,* 48–50.

16. "Blachowitz, Bennie," Year: 1925, Census Place: New York, New York, Page: 16; "Blachowitz, Benj," Year: 1930 Census Place: New York, New York, Enumeration District: 3–524, Supervisor's District: 26.

17. Cahan, *The Rise of David Levinsky,* 324.

18. Diner, *Jews of the United States,* 211–212.

19. Gastwirt, *Fraud, Corruption, and Holiness,* 50–52.

20. Diner, *Jews of the United States,* 247.

21. Diner, *Jews of the United States,* 249–253.

22. Rabbi Joseph Lookstein to Shirley Black, February 5, 1975, Kehilath Jeshurun, Yeshiva University Archives.

23. "Our History," Ramaz, n.d., https://www.ramaz.org/page.cfm?p=512.

24. Rabbi Joseph Lookstein to Shirley Black, February 5, 1975.

25. Jeffrey S. Gurock, *The Men and Women of Yeshiva* (New York: Columbia University Press, 1988), 32–33.

26. Samuel Belkin, "Eulogy for Eli M. Black," February 5, 1975, 2, Yeshiva College Archive, Yeshiva University.

27. Belkin, "Eulogy for Eli M. Black," 2.

28. "Debaters Will Vote for New Officers," *The Commentator* [Yeshiva College newspaper], May 9, 1940, 1.

29. "Yeshiva Seniors," *Masmid* [Yeshiva University Yearbook], 1940, 38.

30. Belkin, "Eulogy for Eli M. Black," 3.

31. Mary Bralove, "Giving Up: Was Eli Black's Suicide Caused by the Tensions of Conflicting Worlds?" *Wall Street Journal,* February 14, 1975, 1.

32. Belkin, "Eulogy for Eli M. Black," 3.

33. Draft Registration Cards for New York City, 10 / 16 / 1940–03 / 31 / 1947. . NAI: 7644743. Records of the Selective Service System, 1926–1975, Record

Group 147, box 1,376. National Archives and Records Administration, St. Louis, Missouri.

34. Grzegorz Berendt, "Violence against Jews in Poland, 1944–1947: The State of Research and Its Presentation," in *New Directions in the History of Jews in the Polish Lands,* ed. Antony Polonsky, Hanna Węgrzynek, and Andrzej Żbikowski, 442–451 (Boston: Academic Studies Press, 2018), 443; "'Final Solution': Overview," The Holocaust Encyclopedia, United States Holocaust Museum, https://encyclopedia.ushmm.org/content/en/article/final-solution-overview?series=97.

35. Diner, *Jews of the United States,* 251.

36. Adolph Berle quoted in "New Deal Is Held Aid to Individual," *New York Times,* March 4, 1934, N1, cited in Jordan Schwarz, *Liberal: Adolph A. Berle and the Vision of an American Era* (New York: Free Press, 1987), 69.

37. Diner, *Jews of the United States,* 253–255; Jeffrey Gurock and Jacob Schacter, *A Modern Heretic and a Traditional Community: Mordecai M. Kaplan, Orthodoxy, and American Judaism* (New York: Columbia University Press, 1997), 140–141.

38. Ivan G. Marcus, *The Jewish Life Cycle: Rites of Passage from Biblical to Modern Times* (Seattle: University of Washington Press, 2004), 109.

39. Robert E. Kessler, "Eli Black's Depression Transcended Business," *Newsday,* February 5, 1975, 44.

40. Kessler, "Eli Black's Depression," 44.

41. "Called as Rabbi," *The Nassau Daily Review-Star,* April 30, 1942, 13; "Heads Congregation," *Daily News* (New York), May 3, 1942, B36; "Rabbi Blackowitz Called to Branch," *Newsday* (Nassau edition), April 24, 1942, 14.

42. "Postwar Job Surety Seen as Basis for Firm Peace," *Newsday* (Nassau edition), November 17, 1944, 6.

43. "Youth Groups Gather $1,000 for United Jewish Appeal," *Newsday* (Nassau edition), May 17, 1944, 8; "Co-ops Give $1,500 as European Fund," *Newsday* (Nassau edition), November 14, 1944, 9.

44. Bralove, "Giving Up."

45. Belkin, "Eulogy for Eli M. Black," 4–5.

46. Petition, City Court: New York County, In the Matter of Application of Max Elias Blackowitz for leave to assume the name of Elias Max Black, filed October 26, 1944; resolved December 9, 1944.

47. David Farber, *Everybody Ought to Be Rich: The Life and Times of John J. Raskob, Capitalist* (New York: Oxford University Press, 2013).

48. John Chamberlain, "Robert R. Young," *Life,* February 24, 1947, 102, 104.

49. "Lind, Bluhdorn, Look Sharp!" *Forbes,* November 1, 1968, 60; Schine quoted in Kessler, "Eli Black's Depression," 44.

50. "The Littlest Texan," *Forbes,* February 1, 1958, 18; "Pulled Between 2 Worlds, Then He Came Apart," A-11.

51. "Robert Young, Financier, Ends Life in Palm Beach," *New York Times,* January 26, 1958, 1, 78.

52. "The Littlest Texan," 18.

53. "The Littlest Texan," 18.

2. AN HONEST BUSINESS

1. "William Rosenwald Dies; Benefactor to Many Was 93," *New York Times,* November 1, 1996, B14; Hasia Diner, *Julius Rosenwald: Repairing the World* (New Haven: Yale University Press, 2017).

2. Brendan M. Jones, "Still Pays to Stick to Thy Last, or Lids," *New York Times,* February 16, 1957, 31.

3. "Announcement," *Creamery and Milk Plant Monthly,* January 1926, 11; "Machinery Markets and News of the Works: New England," *The Iron Age* 108, no. 7 (August 18, 1921), 444; Official Gazette of the United States Patent Office, May 2, 1939, 194; Federal Trade Commission Decisions, vol. 83: July 1, 1973, to June 30, 1974, 1616.

4. "The Fabulous Market for Food," *Fortune,* October 1953, 135; "The 'Ordinary' $125-Billion Market," *Fortune,* September 1959, 132–135; Leonard Sloane, "A.M.K.'s Chief Prepares for an Encore," *New York Times,* October 20, 1968.

5. Sloane, "A.M.K.'s Chief Prepares for an Encore."

6. Robert Kessler, "Eli Black's Depression Transcended Business," *Newsday,* February 5, 1975, 9, 44; Samuel Belkin, "Eulogy for Eli M. Black," February 5, 1975, Yeshiva College Archive, Yeshiva University.

7. "Seal-Kap Expansion Approved," *New York Times,* December 21, 1954, 44.

8. "American Seal-Kap," *New York Times,* December 30, 1955, 5; "American Seal-Kap Corp.: 47% Stock Interest Acquired in Rubber Machinery Co.," *New York Times,* January 16, 1957, 45; "American Seal-Kap Acquires," *New York Times,* July 30, 1957.

9. Jones, "Still Pays to Stick to Thy Last."

10. "American Seal-Kap," *New York Times,* August 19, 1960, 29.

11. "Concern Formed to Promote Plastic Drink Containers," *New York Times,* April 12, 1964, F24.

12. "American Seal-Kap Corp.: 47% Stock Interest Acquired in Rubber Machinery Co."

13. "Plastic Is New Entry in Battle of the Milk Bottles," *New York Times*, August 2, 1964, 101.

14. Lizabeth Cohen, *A Consumer's Republic: The Politics of Mass Consumption in Postwar America* (New York: Knopf, 2003).

15. "The Fabulous Market for Food," 139.

16. Shane Hamilton, *Supermarket USA: Food and Power in the Cold War Farms Race* (New Haven: Yale University Press, 2018), 6–8; Marc Levinson, *The Great A&P and the Struggle for Small Business in America* (New York: Hill and Wang, 2011), 258.

17. "The Fabulous Market for Food," 139. Shane Hamilton, "The Economies and Conveniences of Modern-Day Living: Frozen Foods and Mass Marketing, 1945–1965," *Business History Review* 77, no. 1 (Spring 2003): 33–60, 40.

18. "The Fabulous Market for Food," 271. "The 'Ordinary' $125-Billion Market"; "The Great A&P," *Fortune*, November 1, 1947, 103. In its heyday in 1946, A&P cleared $30 million on $1.9 billion in sales, a relatively thin profit margin of just 1.6 percent.

19. Levinson, *The Great A&P*, 251.

20. Levinson, *The Great A&P*, 209, 250–252.

21. Levinson, *The Great A&P*, 258.

22. "The Sardine That Became a Whale," *Fortune*, June 15, 1968, 262.

23. Levinson, *The Great A&P*, 258–259.

24. Duncan Norton-Taylor, "What the U.S. Can Do about World Hunger," *Fortune*, June 1966, 111.

25. Levinson, *The Great A&P*, 28–30, 91–93.

26. "The Great A&P," 103.

27. Harold B. Meyers, "For the Old Meatpackers, Things Are Tough All Over," *Fortune*, February 1969, 136; "The Fabulous Market for Food"; "The 'Ordinary' $125-Billion Market." Oscar Mayer, for example, led the way for packers as the first to brand its hot dogs in 1929 by wrapping them in a yellow band and trademarking its name, a trend that grew among all packers in the years after the war.

28. AMK Corporation, 1966 Annual Report, New York, 2018, 3, 9; "The Sardine That Became a Whale," 260.

29. Steven Fraser, *Labor Will Rule* (New York: Free Press, 1991), 508; Jason Scott Smith, *Building New Deal Liberalism: The Political Economy of Public Works, 1933–1956* (New York: Cambridge University Press, 2006), 259.

30. Kim Phillips-Fein, "'If Business and the Country Will Be Run Right': The Business Challenge to the Liberal Consensus," *International Labor and*

Working-Class History 72, no. 1 (2007): 192–215, 195–197; Howell John Harris, *The Right to Manage: Industrial Relations Policies of American Business in the 1940s* (Madison: University of Wisconsin Press, 1982), 118–120.

31. Samuel Rosenberg, *American Economic Development since 1945* (London: Palgrave, 2003), 107. Although a temporary target, policymakers accepted 4 percent as an indication that "full employment" had been achieved in the United States.

32. Phillips-Fein, "If Business and the Country," 193, 198; Nancy MacLean, *Democracy in Chains: The Deep History of the Radical Right's Stealth Plan for America* (New York: Viking, 2017), 37–40.

33. Rosenberg, *American Economic Development*, 108–109; Phillips-Fein, "If Business and the Country," 194.

34. Gilbert Burck, "The Merger Movement Rides High," *Fortune*, February 1969, 82.

35. Burck, "The Merger Movement Rides High," 82; "The Numbers Game," *Forbes*, April 15, 1973, 42–44.

36. "The Multi-Market Corporation," *Fortune*, February 1967, 131.

37. Burck, "The Merger Movement Rides High," 79, 81, 161. Even General Motors and telecommunications giant ATT became vulnerable to this movement.

38. "Ling, Bluhdorn, Look Sharp!" *Forbes*, November 1, 1968; Burck, "The Merger Movement Rides High," 80–81.

39. "Gulf & Western's Rambunctious 'Conservatism,'" *Fortune*, March 1968, 123–124.

40. "Gulf & Western's Rambunctious 'Conservatism,'" 122–125; Robert Sam Anson, "Hurricane Charlie," *Vanity Fair*, April 2001.

41. Wilson J. Warren, *Struggling with "Iowa's Pride": Labor Relations, Unionism, and Politics in the Rural Midwest since 1877* (Iowa City: University of Iowa Press, 2000), 21–25.

42. "Meat Workers Win Fight for More Pay," *New York Times*, March 31, 1918, 14; Warren, *Struggling with "Iowa's Pride,"* 26.

43. Warren, *Struggling with "Iowa's Pride,"* 33.

44. "C.I.O. Group in Ottumwa," *Des Moines Tribune*, May 20, 1937, 5.

45. Warren, *Struggling with "Iowa's Pride,"* 56.

46. Warren, *Struggling with "Iowa's Pride,"* 61.

47. Warren, *Struggling with "Iowa's Pride,"* 70–71, 76; G. M. Foster, "Latest Offer Is Absolute Limit," *Ottumwa Daily Courier*, April 15, 1948, 1.

48. "Morrell's McCallum," *Fortune*, March 1955, 108; Warren, *Struggling with "Iowa's Pride,"* 76–77.

49. William Clark, "McCallum: C.P.A. Turned Meat Packer," *Chicago Tribune,* October 3, 1960, 7; "Companies Shift High Executives," *New York Times,* April 6, 1967

50. "Companies Shift High Executives"; "The Sardine That Became a Whale," 260.

51. "The Sardine That Became a Whale," 262.

52. Meyers, "For the Old Meatpackers," 90.

53. "AMK Executives See Morrell in Operation," *Ottumwa Courier,* February 7, 1967, 1.

54. "The Sardine That Became a Whale," 264.

55. "The Sardine That Became a Whale," 260.

56. "The Sardine That Became a Whale," 264.

57. "The Sardine That Became a Whale," 264.

58. "The Sardine That Became a Whale," 260.

59. E. M. Black to All John Morrell Employees, December 11, 1967, Iowa Labor Collection, Amalgamated Meat Cutters and Butcher Workmen of North America, Local P-1, Records, 1939–1986, Z23, Bulletins, 1958–1976, Iowa Historical Society, Iowa City, Iowa.

3. PYRAMIDS

1. "Morrell in Ottumwa," *Morrell Magazine,* July–August 1965, 14, Iowa Labor Collection, Amalgamated Meat Cutters and Butcher Workmen of North America, Local P-1, Records, 1939–1986, Z23, Bulletins, 1958–1976, Iowa Historical Society, Iowa City, Iowa (hereafter Iowa Labor Collection, Amalgamated Meat Cutters, Iowa Historical Society).

2. Wilson J. Warren, *Struggling with "Iowa's Pride": Labor Relations, Unionism, and Politics in the Rural Midwest since 1877* (Iowa City: University of Iowa Press, 2000), 81.

3. Lewis Debo, "Past Efforts to Save Morrell Plant," *Ottumwa Courier,* April 14, 1973.

4. Warren, *Struggling with "Iowa's Pride,"* 116. Jesse Merrill quoted in Shelton Stromquist, *Solidarity and Survival: An Oral History of Iowa Labor in the Twentieth Century* (Iowa City: University of Iowa Press, 1993), 233.

5. Ethel Jerred Oral History Interview, October 5, 1981, Iowa Historical Society, Iowa City, Iowa, audio files at https://islandora.lib.uiowa.edu /islandora/object/ui%3Ailhop_1678, quoted in Warren, *Struggling with "Iowa's Pride,"* 116.

6. Harold B. Meyers, "For the Old Meatpackers, Things Are Tough All Over," *Fortune*, February 1969, 134.

7. "The Sardine That Became a Whale," *Fortune*, June 15, 1968, 264.

8. Leonard Sloane, "A.M.K.'s Chief Prepares for an Encore," *New York Times*, October 20, 1968.

9. Stanley H. Brown, "United Fruit's Shotgun Marriage," *Fortune*, April 1969, 133.

10. "Nat'l General Corp. Controls 75% of Great American Holding's Stock; Moves to Block GAH-AMK Merger," *Variety* 252, no. 8 (October 9, 1968): 5, 15; William D. Smith, "Acquisition Bid Called Success: National General Says It Has 75% of Great American," *New York Times*, October 7, 1968, 69. For details of the equity financing behind National General's takeover, see A. D. Murphy, "Natl. Generals Why-Not-Take-All Move Re Great American Holding," *Variety* 251, no. 7 (July 3, 1968): 5.

11. Gilbert Burck, "The Merger Movement Rides High," *Fortune*, February 1969, 79–83.

12. The long list of publications and media covering United Fruit's exploits includes: Stacy May and Galo Plaza Lasso, *The United Fruit Company in Latin America* (Washington: National Planning Association, 1958); Thomas McCann, *An American Company: The Tragedy of United Fruit* (New York: Crown, 1976); Stephen Schlesinger and Stephen Kinzer, *Bitter Fruit: The Untold Story of the American Coup in Guatemala* (New York: Doubleday, 1982); Paul J. Dosal, *Doing Business with the Dictators: A Political History of United Fruit in Guatemala, 1899–1944* (Lanham, MD: SR Books, 1993); Steve Striffler, *In the Shadows of State and Capital* (Durham: Duke University Press, 2002) John Soluri, *Banana Cultures: Agriculture, Consumption, and Environmental Change in Honduras and the United States* (Austin: University of Texas Press, 2005); Peter Chapman, *Bananas: How the United Fruit Company Shaped the World* (Edinburgh: Cannongate, 2007); Dan Koeppel, *Banana: The Fate of the Fruit That Changed the World* (New York: Penguin, 2008); Jason M. Colby, *The Business of Empire: United Fruit, Race, and U.S. Expansion in Central America* (Ithaca, NY: Cornell University Press, 2011); Rich Cohen, *The Fish That Ate the Whale: The Life and Times of America's Banana King* (New York: Farrar, Straus, and Giroux, 2012); Suyapa Portillo Villeda, *Roots of Resistance: A Story of Gender, Race, and Labor on the North Coast of Honduras* (Austin: University of Texas Press, 2021). For a podcast on how United Fruit transformed Latin America, see "Reframing History: Bananas," *Throughline*, National Public Radio, August 27, 2020. For a documentary film on Minor C. Keith, see *Tropical Iron: The Saga of Minor Keith*, dir. Mark C. Baldwin, Baldwin Inc. Productions, 2018.

NOTES TO PAGES 76–83

13. Brown, "United Fruit's Shotgun Marriage."

14. David Lilienthal, *TVA: Democracy on the March* (New York: Harper and Brothers, 1944), 34–35.

15. The boast was part of a speech Lilienthal gave at a convention at the University of Minnesota, January 16, 1941, printed in full as "TVA Proves Powerful Factor in U.S. National Defense," Sheboygan (Wis.) Press, January 16, 1941, 2. The quote was memorable enough to be included in his *New York Times* obituary, January 16, 1981. For more on Lilienthal's TVA career, see Jordan A. Schwarz, *The New Dealers: Power Politics in the Age of Roosevelt* (New York: Alfred A. Knopf, 1993), 195–244.

16. David E. Lilienthal, testimony before Senate Joint Committee on Atomic Energy, February, 1947. Reprinted in full in "An American Speaks Out," *Brownsville Herald,* February 20, 1947.

17. The phrase was Iowa Senator Bourke Hickenlooper's. "Investigations: The Accuser," *Time,* June 13, 1949.

18. "The Goal of Management Is to 'Get Things Done': An Interview with David E. Lilienthal," *Columbia Journal of World Business,* November–December 1968, 56.

19. David E. Lilienthal, *Management: A Humanist Art* (New York: Carnegie Institute of Technology, distributed by Columbia University Press, 1967), 11.

20. "The Goal of Management Is to 'Get Things Done,'" 57.

21. Jordan Schwarz, *Liberal: Adolph A. Berle and the Vision of an American Era* (New York: Free Press, 1987), 318.

22. "The Goal of Management Is to 'Get Things Done,'" 57.

23. James Scott, *Seeing Like a State: How Certain Schemes to Improve the Human Condition Have Failed* (New Haven: Yale University Press, 1999), 88. For more on Lilienthal during the 1960s, see Amy Offner, *Sorting Out the Mixed Economy: The Rise and Fall of Welfare and Developmental States in the Americas* (Princeton: Princeton University Press, 2019), 179–183; Jason Scott Smith, *Building New Deal Liberalism: The Political Economy of Public Works, 1933–1956* (New York: Cambridge University Press, 2006), 254–255.

24. E. M. Black, "Social Welfare Challenge for Business and Labor," *Harvard Business Review,* July–August 1973, 6–7.

25. Brown, "United Fruit's Shotgun Marriage," 133.

26. "Don't Crowd Morrell Workers," May 7, 1969, Bulletins, 1958–1972, Z023, box 4, folder 11, Iowa Labor Collection, Amalgamated Meat Cutters, Iowa Historical Society.

27. "Don't Crowd Morrell Workers."

28. Meyers, "For the Old Meatpackers," 134.

29. Eli Black quoted in Meyers, "For the Old Meatpackers," 134.

30. Meyers, "For the Old Meatpackers," 91.

31. Meyers, "For the Old Meatpackers," 136.

32. Meyers, "For the Old Meatpackers," 92–93.

33. Shane Hamilton, "The Economies and Conveniences of Modern-Day Living: Frozen Foods and Mass Marketing, 1945–1965," *Business History Review* 77, no. 1 (Spring 2003): 33–60, 45.

34. Meyers, "For the Old Meatpackers," 90, 134.

35. Warren, *Struggling with "Iowa's Pride,"* 118.

36. Eli M. Black, United Brands Company Annual Report 1970, April 20, 1971, 4.

37. Department of State, "Annual Labor Report: Honduras. Confidential," National Archives, A-109 Documents, Declassified NND96908, November 2, 1973, 21–22.

38. Georgie Ann Geyer, "It's a New United Fruit," *Chicago Daily News,* May 6, 1972, 25, 27.

39. Department of State, "Annual Labor Report: Honduras."

40. Georgie Ann Geyer, "United Fruit—A Malefactor Turned Benefactor," *Boston Evening Globe,* May 10, 1972.

41. Herbert Cornuelle, United Fruit Annual Report 1968, 4. Quoted in Marcelo Bucheli, "Multinational Corporations, Totalitarian Regimes and Economic Nationalism: United Fruit Company in Central America, 1899–1975," *Business History* 50, no. 4 (2008): 433–454.

42. Georgie Ann Geyer, quoted in United Brands Company Annual Report 1972, 5.

4. SHADOWS

1. Leon Black, Ethical Culture Fieldston School Yearbook, 1969, 131.

2. Eli M. Black, "To the Shareholders of United Brands," United Brands Company Annual Report 1970, 1. R. H. Simpson and Arnold L. Sugg, "The Atlantic Hurricane Season of 1969," *Monthly Weather Review* 98, no. 4 (1970): 293–306, 303.

3. Chris Welles, "The Battle for United Fruit," *Investment Banking and Corporate Financing,* Spring 1969, 26–33, 84–88, 28; "United Fruit Is Not Chiquita," source and date unknown, p. 122, Interfaith Center on Corporate Responsibility records, 1966–2011, Series V: Company Files, United Brands,

1978–1986, box 60, folder 10, Columbia University Archives. See also David Tobis, "United Fruit Is Not Chiquita," *NACLA Newsletter* 5, no. 6 (1971): 7–15; Jacques Levy, *Cesar Chavez: Autobiography of La Causa* (Minneapolis: University of Minnesota Press, 2007), 331.

4. "United Fruit Is Not Chiquita," 123. Welles, "The Battle for United Fruit," 28. Eli Black to Honorable Seybourne Lynne, November 27, 1972, "Re: Civil Action No. 4562," Anna Andreini-Brophy Papers, box 1, folder 16, Walter P. Reuther Library, Archive of Labor and Urban Affairs, Wayne State University (hereafter Andreini-Brophy Papers, Reuther Library).

5. Eli Black to Honorable Seybourne Lynne, November 27, 1972.

6. F. Robert Nunes, *Foxy: The Creation of a Brand* (F. Robert Nunes, 2005), 30; Carol Lynn McKibben, *Salinas: A History of Race and Resilience in an Agricultural City* (Stanford: Stanford University Press, 2022), 106–114.

7. Wendy Cheng, "Landscapes of Beauty and Plunder: Japanese American Flower Growers and an Elite Public Garden in Los Angeles," paper presented at Dartmouth College, May 9, 2019. See also Cecilia Tsu, *Garden of the World: Asian Immigrants and the Making of Agriculture in California's Santa Clara Valley* (Oxford: Oxford University Press, 2013); and David Mas Masumoto, *Epitaph for a Peach: Four Seasons on My Family Farm* (San Francisco: Harper Collins, 1995), 106–110.

8. Duncan Norton-Taylor, "World Hunger," *Fortune*, June 1966, 112.

9. The same population-explosion projections were used by government officials to justify sterilization campaigns of women in Puerto Rico and Mexican immigrant communities in California. Alexandra Minna Stern, "Sterilized in the Name of Public Health: Race, Immigration, and Reproductive Control in Modern California," *American Journal of Public Health* 95, no. 7 (2005): 1128–1138; Renee Tajima-Pena, *No Más Bebés*, season 17, episode 7 of *Independent Lens*, 2016.

10. Dan Cordtz, "Corporate Farming: A Tough Row to Hoe," *Fortune*, August, 1972, 139.

11. Cordtz, "Corporate Farming," 136, 137, 139; Nunes, *Foxy*, 42.

12. Nunes, *Foxy*, 42.

13. Harold B. Meyers, "For the Old Meatpackers, Things Are Tough All Over," *Fortune*, February 1969, 134.

14. Cordtz, "Corporate Farming," 137.

15. Cordtz, "Corporate Farming," 139.

16. Nunes, *Foxy*, 42–43.

17. Nunes, *Foxy*, 44.

18. Nunes, *Foxy*, 45.

19. Cordtz, "Corporate Farming," 139, 172.

20. Miriam Pawel, *The Crusades of Cesar Chavez: A Biography* (New York: Bloomsbury Press, 2014), 214, 221; "Farm Union Halts 'Salad Bowl' Work," *New York Times*, August 25, 1970, 41.

21. "Editorial: Teamster Invasion in the Fields: Another Back Door Deal," *El Malcriado*, August 1, 1970. *El Malcriado* was the newspaper founded by Chavez in 1964 to communicate to supporters of the movement, in later years published by the United Farm Workers Organizing Committee.

22. Declaration of Mann Packing Workers, n.d., in *Mann Packing Co. v. Cesar Chavez*, S.F. No. 22941, Superior Court of California, Monterey County; Pawel, *The Crusades of Cesar Chavez*, 216.

23. Nunes, *Foxy*, 45.

24. Marshall Ganz, *Why David Sometimes Wins: Leadership, Organization, and Strategy in the California Farm Workers Movement* (New York: Oxford University Press, 2009), 158–159; Matt Garcia, *From the Jaws of Victory: The Triumph and Tragedy of Cesar Chavez and the Farm Worker Movement* (Berkeley: University of California Press, 2012), 49–50, 56.

25. "Information on United Brands Corp," August 3, 1970, Ana Puharich Papers, 1–16, Correspondence, Eli Black & United Brands Co, 1970–1974, Walter P. Reuther Library, Archives of Labor and Urban Affairs, Wayne State University.

26. Levy, *Cesar Chavez*, 333; Michael T. Kaufman, "Coast Farm Strikers Picket Here," *New York Times*, April 21, 1973, 31.

27. "Anna Andreini-Brophy Played Historic Roles with Cesar Chavez, UFW since '60s," *UFW Newsletter*, November 18, 2020.

28. Levy, *Cesar Chavez*, 332–334.

29. Cousins quoted in Peter Kihss, "44-Story Plunge Kills Head of United Brands," *New York Times*, February 4, 1975, 10.

30. Levy, *Cesar Chavez*, 332–334.

31. Eli Black to Cesar Chavez, December 13, 1972, box 1, folder 16, Correspondence, Eli Black & United Brands, 1970–1974, Andreini-Brophy Papers, Reuther Library.

32. Levy, *Cesar Chavez*, 370.

33. Levy, *Cesar Chavez*, 372.

34. Levy, *Cesar Chavez*, 372–373.

35. "Msgr. George Higgins 1993," n.d., 16, Jacques E. Levy Research Collection on Cesar Chavez, box 37, folder 743, file 52, Beinecke Rare Books Library, Yale University.

36. Levy, *Cesar Chavez*, 387–388.

37. Levy, *Cesar Chavez*, 398.

38. Levy, *Cesar Chavez*, 402.

39. Nunes, *Foxy*, 45–46.

40. Eli M. Black, United Brands Company 1970 Annual Report issued April 20, 1971, 3–4.

5. ISRAELITE

1. "From an Address by Henry Merritt Wriston, President Emeritus of Brown University and the Council on Foreign Relations," *Seder 1971*, Anna Andreini-Brophy Papers, Walter P. Reuther Library, Archives of Labor and Urban Affairs, Wayne State University (hereafter Andreini-Brophy Papers, Reuther Library).

2. Milton Friedman, "A Friedman Doctrine—The Social Responsibility of Business Is to Increase Its Profits," *New York Times*, September 13, 1970, 379.

3. Eli Black, United Brands Company Annual Report 1970, April 20, 1971, 35. Italics in the original.

4. "How Business Faces a Hostile Climate," *Business Week*, September 16, 1972, 72. McCann offers more detail on the film in his book: Thomas McCann, *An American Company: The Tragedy of United Fruit* (New York: Crown, 1976).

5. "How Business Faces a Hostile Climate," 71.

6. Black, United Brands Company Annual Report 1970, 35.

7. Richard Severo, "United Fruit Lives Down a 'Colonialist' Past," *New York Times*, April 24, 1972.

8. Severo, "United Fruit Lives Down a 'Colonialist' Past."

9. Black, United Brands Company Annual Report 1970, 36.

10. Black, United Brands Company Annual Report, 1970, 35. Italics in the original.

11. Severo, "United Fruit Lives Down a 'Colonialist' Past."

12. Georgie Anne Geyer, "It's a New United Fruit," *Chicago Daily News*, May 6, 1972, 25.

13. Eli M. Black, United Brands Company Annual Report 1971, 29.

14. Eli M. Black, United Brands Company Annual Report 1971, 9, 40.

15. Dan Cordtz, "Corporate Farming: A Tough Row to Hoe," *Fortune*, August 1972, 139. Frank Bardacke, *Trampling Out the Vintage: Cesar Chavez and the Two Souls of the United Farm Workers* (London: Verso, 2011), 399–400; Matt Garcia, *From the Jaws of Victory: The Triumph and Tragedy of Cesar Chavez and the Farm Worker Movement* (Berkeley: University of California

Press, 2012), 123–124; Miriam Pawel, *The Crusades of Cesar Chavez: A Biography* (New York: Bloomsbury Press, 2014), 253–255.

16. Cordtz, "Corporate Farming," 172.

17. Cordtz, "Corporate Farming," 172.

18. Black, United Brands Company Annual Report 1971, 19.

19. James F. Oates Jr., "The Contradictions of Leadership," *Seder 1972*, Andreini-Brophy Papers, Reuther Library. Eli Black would have encountered the speech in a recently published book: James F. Oates, Jr., *The Contradictions of Leadership: A Selection of Speeches* (New York: Meredith, 1970).

20. Meeting notes of July 26, 1972, box 1, folder 17, Eli Black & United Brands Co., Notes, 1972; Richard C. Johnson to Cesar Chavez, August 2, 1972, box 1, folder 16, Correspondence, Eli Black & United Brands Co., 1970–1974, both in Andreini-Brophy Papers, Reuther Library.

21. Johnson to Chavez, August 2, 1972.

22. Meeting notes of July 26, 1972, box 1, folder 17, Notes, Eli Black & United Brands Co., 1972, Andreini-Brophy Papers, Reuther Library.

23. Meeting notes of July 26, 1972.

24. Anna Puharich to Cesar Chavez, October 24, 1972, box 1, folder 16, Correspondence, Eli Black & United Brands Co., 1970–1974, Andreini-Brophy Papers, Reuther Library.

25. Eli Black to Anna Puharich, October 4, 1972, box 1, folder 16, Correspondence, Eli Black & United Brands, 1970–1974, Anna Andreini-Brophy Papers, Reuther Library.

26. Black to Puharich, October 4, 1972.

27. Eli Black to Anna Puharich, "Miercoles," November 1972, box 1, folder 16, Correspondence, Eli Black & United Brands, 1970–1974, Andreini-Brophy Papers, Reuther Library.

28. Eli Black to Anna Puharich, December 18, 1972, box 1, folder 16, Correspondence, Eli Black and United Brands, 1970–1974, Andreini-Brophy Papers, Reuther Library.

29. Eli Black to Anna Puharich, n.d., box 1, folder 16, Correspondence, Eli Black & United Brands Co., 1970–1974, Andreini-Brophy Papers, Reuther Library.

30. Eli Black to Cesar Chavez, December 13, 1972, box 1, folder 16, Correspondence, Eli Black & United Brands, 1970–1974, Andreini-Brophy Papers, Reuther Library; Executive Education, Short Programs, Administration and Program Files, 1960–1984, Agribusiness Seminar, 1973, box 1, folder 8, Baker Library, Harvard Business School.

31. Ronald B. Taylor, *Chavez and the Farm Workers* (Boston: Beacon Press, 1975), 275; Garcia, *From the Jaws of Victory,* 138.

32. Garcia, *From the Jaws of Victory,* 133.

33. Pawel, *The Crusades of Cesar Chavez,* 218.

34. Jerry Cohen, interview by the author, August 18, 2008, Carmel, CA, Matt Garcia Papers, box 14, folder 42, Special Collections, Claremont Colleges Library, Claremont, CA; Garcia, *From the Jaws of Victory,* 139.

35. Pawel, *The Crusades of Cesar Chavez,* 268.

36. Anna Puharich to Cesar Chavez, October 25, 1972, box 1, folder 16, Correspondence, Eli Black & United Brands Co, 1970–1974, Andreini-Brophy Papers, Reuther Library.

37. Cesar Chavez to Eli Black, February 24, 1973, box 1, folder 16, Correspondence, Eli Black & United Brands Co, 1970–1974, Andreini-Brophy Papers, Reuther Library.

38. Harold G. Bradshaw to Cesar Chavez, September 25, 1974, box 1, folder 16, Correspondence, Eli Black & United Brands Co, 1970–1974, Andreini-Brophy Papers, Reuther Library.

39. Black, United Brands Company Annual Report 1972, 16; Black, United Brands Company Annual Report 1973, 19, 21.

40. Black, United Brands Company Annual Report 1973, 19, 21.

41. Eli Black to Bruce Hanson, National Farm Workers Service Center, June 24, 1974, box 1, folder 16, Correspondence, Eli Black & United Brands Co., 1970–1974, Andreini-Brophy Papers, Reuther Library.

42. Eli Black to Cesar Chavez, December 13, 1974, box 1, folder 16, Correspondence, Eli Black & United Brands Co., 1970–1974, Andreini-Brophy Papers, Reuther Library.

43. "How Business Faces a Hostile Climate."

6. HALF A PICTURE

1. Richard Severo, "United Fruit Lives Down a 'Colonialist' Past," *New York Times,* April 24, 1972.

2. Richard V. Oulahan, "Real Leadership: My Mentors in Honduras," October 25, 2017, 5, Richard Oulahan Latin American Labor History Collection, Haverford College.

3. Briefing for George Meany and Serafino Romualdi, "Anti-Union Campaign of United Fruit Company," 2, August 15, 1958, SR 9-5, Dana Frank Collection, National Archives.

4. E. M. Black, United Brands Company Annual Report 1972, March 28, 1973, 5.

5. "Taking Stock: A Message from E. M. Black, Chairman of the Board," source unknown, box 1, folder 16, Correspondence, Eli Black & United Brands Co., 1970–1974, Anna Brophy-Andreini Papers, Walter P. Reuter Library, Archives of Labor and Urban Affairs, Wayne State University (hereafter Brophy-Andreini Papers, Reuther Library); Black, United Brands Company Annual Report 1971, 5.

6. Darío A. Euraque, *Reinterpreting the "Banana Republic": Region and State in Honduras, 1870–1972* (Chapel Hill: University of North Carolina Press, 1996), 34–39; Suyapa G. Portillo Villeda, *Roots of Resistance: A Story of Gender, Race, and Labor on the North Coast of Honduras* (Austin: University of Texas Press, 2021).

7. Eli Black to Anna Puharich, "Miercoles," November 1972, box 1, folder 16, Correspondence, Eli Black & United Brands Co., 1970–1974, Brophy-Andreini Papers, Reuther Library

8. Georgie Anne Geyer, "United Fruit: A Malefactor Turned Benefactor," *Boston Evening Globe*, May 10, 1972.

9. Portillo Villeda, *Roots of Resistance*, 188.

10. Portillo Villeda, *Roots of Resistance*, 189.

11. Euraque, *Reinterpreting the "Banana Republic,"* 108.

12. Charles H. Logan to Serafino Romualdi, December 12, 1958, RG 18-009, box 4, folder 47, "Andrew McLellan, 1958," George Meany Memorial Archives, University of Maryland Libraries, Silver Spring. Andrew McLellan to Oscar Gale Varela, January 19, 1972; and Andrew McLellan to Oscar Gale Varela, April 24, 1972; both in RG 18-010, box 6, folder 10, George Meany Memorial Archives.

13. Dana Frank published two books on Honduras: *Bananeras: Women Transforming the Banana Unions of Latin America* (Cambridge, MA: South End Press, 2005), and *The Long Honduran Night: Resistance, Terror, and the United States in the Aftermath of the Coup* (Chicago: Haymarket Books, 2018). Both books cover more recent histories of labor activism and popular resistance in Honduras, but Frank has also done yeowoman's work on the earlier history, including an archive and unpublished papers that she generously contributed to this project. They include, Dana Frank, "The AFL-CIO's Cold War in Honduras: The Early Years, 1954–59," presentation at the Latin American Studies Association annual conference, Rio de Janeiro, Brazil, June 12, 2009, 5–7, 12; Dana Frank, "Andrew McLellan: From Cross-Border Organ-

izing in Texas to the AFL-CIA in Latin America," unpublished manuscript, n.d., provided by Dana Frank in the author's possession.

14. Paul K. Reed, quoted in Henry W. Berger, "American Labor Overseas," *The Nation*, January 16, 1967, 83.

15. Berger, "American Labor Overseas," 83.

16. Department of State, Airgram, Annual Labor Report: Honduras, Confidential, A-109, November 2, 1973, 5, RG 59, Identifier, 2602882, National Archives and Records Administration (hereafter NARA).

17. Department of State, "Labor Participation in Government Planning," Confidential, A-374, June 25, 1968, RG 59, Identifier 2602882, NARA.

18. Oulahan, "Real Leadership: My Mentors in Honduras."

19. Embassy Tegucigalpa, telegram to Secretary of State, Washington DC, confidential, LAB 43, RG 59, Identifier 2602882, NARA.

20. Department of State, Convention of Confederation of Honduran Workers (CTH), A-74, May 2, 1969, Confidential, 3, RG 59, Identifier 2602882, NARA.

21. Department of State, Convention of Confederation of Honduran Workers (CTH), A-74, May 2, 1969, Confidential, 3, RG 59, Identifier 2602882, NARA.

22. Severo, "United Fruit Lives Down a 'Colonialist' Past."

23. Eli M. Black, "Our Social Responsibility," United Brands Company Annual Report 1972, 38.

24. Airgram A-372, June 21, 1968, RG 59, Identifier 2602882, NARA.

25. Telegram Teguci O 242215Z Sep 68 (Lab 3-2 Hond), RG 59, Identifier 2602882, NARA.

26. Frank, "The AFL-CIO's Cold War in Honduras," 18; Frank, "Andrew McLellan."

27. Black, United Brands Company Annual Report 1973, 5.

28. Black, United Brands Company Annual Report 1973, 25.

29. "Morrell Plant Will Close," *Ottumwa Courier*, February 25, 1970. 1.

30. "Vicious Rumors," *The Bulletin*, February 24, 1970, Bulletins, 1958–1972, box 4, folder 11, Iowa Labor Collection, Amalgamated Meat Cutters and Butcher Workmen of North America, Local P-1, Records, 1939–1986, Z 023, Iowa Historical Society (hereafter Iowa Labor Collection, Amalgamated Meat Cutters, Iowa Historical Society).

31. Dave Swanson, phone interview by the author, January 28, 2020. "This Is It! Morrell Plant Hope Is Gone," *Ottumwa Courier*, March 9, 1970, 1.

32. "200 Laid Off at Morrell," *Ottumwa Courier*, March 21, 1969, 1; "Morrell Layoff Top Ottumwa Story of 1972," *Ottumwa Courier*, January 1, 1973.

33. "200 Laid Off at Morrell," *Ottumwa Courier*, March 21, 1969, 1.

34. Swanson interview.

35. Swanson interview, 10–12.

36. "Modernization," *The Bulletin*, November 23, 1970, Z 023, box 4, folder 11, Iowa Labor Collection, Amalgamated Meat Cutters, Iowa Historical Society.

37. "Something You Should Know!" *The Bulletin*, April 9, 1971, Z 023, box 4, folder 12, Iowa Labor Collection, Amalgamated Meat Cutters, Iowa Historical Society.

38. "Past Efforts to Save Morrell Plant," *The Bulletin*, April 14, 1973, Z 023, box 4, folder 12, Iowa Labor Collection, Amalgamated Meat Cutters, Iowa Historical Society.

39. "Have We a Future," *The Bulletin*, December 7, 1970, Z 023, box 4, folder 11, Iowa Labor Collection, Amalgamated Meat Cutters, Iowa Historical Society.

40. "Statement on Morrell-Ottumwa Plant," n.d., Z 023, box 38, folder 11, Iowa Labor Collection, Amalgamated Meat Cutters, Iowa Historical Society.

41. Patrick Gorman to Jesse Merrill and Harold Trimble, May 11, 1973, Z 023, box 38, folder 11, Iowa Labor Collection, Amalgamated Meat Cutters, Iowa Historical Society.

42. Elias Paul to Patrick Gorman, April 24, 1973, Z 023, box 38, folder 11, Iowa Labor Collection, Amalgamated Meat Cutters, Iowa Historical Society.

43. Jesse Merrill and Harold Trimble to Patrick Gorman, Secretary-Treasurer, AMCBW, May 6, 1973, Z 023, box 38, folder 11, Iowa Labor Collection, Amalgamated Meat Cutters, Iowa Historical Society.

44. Patrick Gorman, Secretary-Treasurer, AMCBW, to Jesse Merrill and Harold Trimble, May 11, 1973, Z 023, box 38, folder 11, Iowa Labor Collection, Amalgamated Meat Cutters, Iowa Historical Society.

45. "Iowa Pride to Close July 14," *Ottumwa Courier*, April 14, 1973.

46. Swanson interview, 18–19.

47. Meg Jacobs, *Panic at the Pump: The Energy Crisis and the Transformation of American Politics in the 1970s* (New York: Hill and Wang, 2016), 80–85.

48. United Brands Company 1973 Annual Report, March 25, 1974, 5.

7. UNITED, WE FALL

1. Peter T. Kilborn, "Suicide of Big Executive: Stress of Corporate Life," *New York Times*, February 14, 1975, 1.

2. E. M. Black, "Social Welfare Challenge for Business and Labor," *Harvard Business Review*, July–August 1973, 1–2.

3. Richard Severo, "United Fruit Lives Down a 'Colonialist' Past," *New York Times,* April 24, 1972, 20.

4. US State Department, "Top Labor Leader's Observations re: U.S. Companies, National Economic Planning Council, Political Situation, Agrarian Reform," A-14, January 30, 1970, 4; US State Department, Annual Labor Report: Honduras, May 2, 1971, A-49, 7, RG 59, National Archives and Records Administration (NARA), College Park, MD

5. State Department, A-49, 26–27, NARA. The Honduran government supplied second-stage loans to complete the projects but the initial investment came from United Fruit and USAID.

6. State Department, A-49, 26–27, NARA.

7. Eli Black, United Brands Company Annual Report 1973, March 25, 1974, 21–22.

8. "The Numbers Game," *Forbes,* April 15, 1973, 42.

9. Gilbert Burck, "The Merger Movement Rides High," *Fortune,* February 1969, 158.

10. Will Kenton, "Accounting Principles Board," Investopedia, April 3, 2019, updated July 17, 2021, https://www.investopedia.com/terms/a/accounting -priciples-board.asp.

11. "The Numbers Game," 42.

12. "The Numbers Game," 44.

13. "The Numbers Game," 44. *Forbes* also speculated that Black closed the deal in advance of APB Opinion 17, which would have required him to account for the $252.9 million each year, for the next forty years, as a $6 million deficit on earnings rather than the $20 million gain that it became in 1973 as result of Opinion 26.

14. Black, United Brands Company Annual Report 1973, 24.

15. "The Numbers Game," 44.

16. Lewis Debo, "United Brands Expects 'Minimal Cash Impact' from Morrell Closing," *Ottumwa Courier,* April 25,1973.

17. "Grievances," *Ottumwa Courier,* April 19, 1973.

18. "Phew! Decision Has Odor," editorial, *Ottumwa Courier,* April 16, 1973.

19. Debo, "United Brands Expects 'Minimal Cash Impact.'"

20. Mrs. Kenneth Sands, "Boycott?" *Ottumwa Courier,* April 24, 1973; William I. Williams, "Now That We Are Dead," *Ottumwa Courier,* May 7, 1973.

21. Black, United Brands Company Annual Report 1974, 6.

22. Dave Swanson, interview by author, January 28, 2020, transcript, 5.

23. Hormel briefly leased the plant after Morrell departed. Today, Brazilian conglomerate JBS operates out of Ottumwa. During the pandemic, JBS

petitioned the federal government to designate its employees as "essential workers" and JBS employees suffered some of the highest rates of infection and death in the nation. "Dread Persists on Slaughterhouse Floor," *New York Times,* December 30, 2021.

24. Black, United Brands Company Annual Report 1973, 24, 30, 33.

25. Peter Romeo, "At Age 100, A&W Considers the Next Century," *Restaurant Business,* July 11, 2019, https://www.restaurantbusinessonline.com /leadership/age-100-aw-considers-next-century.

26. Black, United Brands Company Annual Report 1973, 21, 23.

27. Victor Bulmer-Thomas, *The Political Economy of Central America since 1920* (New York: Cambridge University Press, 1987), 182.

28. Bulmer-Thomas, *Political Economy of Central America,* 203.

29. Peter Nehemkis, "Business Payoffs Abroad: Rhetoric and Reality," *California Management Review* 18, no. 2 (1975): 5–20, 10.

30. Steve Striffler, *In the Shadows of State and Capital: The United Fruit Company, Popular Struggle, and Agrarian Restructuring in Ecuador, 1900–1995* (Durham, NC: Duke University Press, 2002), 152.

31. Nehemkis, "Business Payoffs Abroad," 9.

32. Black, United Brands Company Annual Report 1974, 4.

33. Nehemkis, "Business Payoffs Abroad," 10.

34. Mary Bralove, "Power Struggle: At United Brands Co., Fight for Control Came after Honduras Payoff," *Wall Street Journal,* May 7, 1975, 1.

35. Bralove, "Power Struggle."

36. Bralove, "Power Struggle."

37. Black, United Brands Company Annual Report 1974, 4.

38. Black, United Brands Company Annual Report 1974, 10.

39. Our World in Data, "Banana Production, 1970–1975," University of Oxford, 2018, https://ourworldindata.org/grapher/banana-production?tab =chart&time=1970..1975&country=COL~CRI~ECU~GTM~HND ~NIC~PAN.

40. David Longshore, *Encyclopedia of Hurricanes, Typhoons, and Cyclones* (New York: Facts on File, 2008).

41. Bralove, "Power Struggle."

42. Black, United Brands Company Annual Report 1974, 26.

43. Mary Bralove, "Giving Up: Was Eli Black's Suicide Caused by the Tensions of Conflicting Worlds?" *Wall Street Journal,* February 14, 1975, 1.

44. Bralove, "Giving Up"; Kilborn, "Suicide of Big Executive."

45. Kilborn, "Suicide of Big Executive."

46. Bralove, "Giving Up."

47. Bralove, "Power Struggle."

48. Bralove, "Power Struggle."

EPILOGUE

1. Kenneth H. Bacon and Mary Bralove, "United Brands Accused by SEC of Second Payoff: Agency's Civil Suit Alleges Firm Also Paid $750,000 to Officials in Europe," *Wall Street Journal,* April 10, 1975, 2.

2. John Kenneth Galbraith, *The Great Crash 1929* (Boston: Houghton Mifflin, 1955), 133–136.

3. Jennifer Michael Hecht, *Stay: A History of Suicide and the Philosophies against It* (New Haven: Yale University Press, 2013), 58–59.

4. Beacon Journal Wire Services, "Businessman with Social Conscience: Pulled Between 2 Worlds, Then He Came Apart," n.d. Yeshiva University Archives.

5. Greg Asbed and Steve Hitov, "Preventing Forced Labor in Corporate Supply Chains: The Fair Food Program and Worker-Driven Social Responsibility," *Wake Forest Law Review* 52, no. 2 (2017): 497–531, 507.

6. Worker-Driven Social Responsibility Network, https://wsr-network.org/.

7. Michael D. Zakaras, "Jostein Solheim of Ben & Jerry's: Empathy Is Not Simply the Flavor of the Month," Ashoka, August 3, 2016, https://www .ashoka.org/id/story/jostein-solheim-ben-jerrys-empathy-not-simply-flavor -month.

8. Teresa M. Mares, *Life on the Other Border: Farmworkers and Food Justice in Vermont* (Berkeley: University of California Press, 2019), 159–163.

9. John F. Berry, "Food Co. Guilty of Conspiracy," *Washington Post,* July 20, 1978.

10. Caleb Melby and Heather Perlberg, "Nobody Makes Money Like Apollo's Ruthless Founder Leon Black," *Bloomberg Businessweek,* January 16, 2020.

11. Melby and Perlberg, "Nobody Makes Money Like Apollo's Ruthless Founder."

12. Connie Bruck, *The Predators' Ball: The Junk-Bond Raiders and the Man Who Staked Them* (New York: Simon and Schuster, 1988), 65.

13. Hilary Rosenberg, *The Vulture Investors: The Winners and Losers of the Great American Bankruptcy Feeding Frenzy* (New York: Wiley, 1992), 327–329.

14. Brett Duval Fromson, "The Last Days of Drexel Burnham," *Fortune,* May 21, 1990, 93.

15. Ellie Winninghoff, "Smart Buyer, Dumb Seller," *Forbes,* March 14, 1994, 71–76.

16. Michael Corkery and Ben Protess, "How the Twinkie Made the Superrich Even Richer," *New York Times,* December 10, 2016. In 2013, companies controlled by private equity firms employed 4.4 million Americans at over 7,500 businesses. For more on the ills of private equity, see Daniel Scott Souleles, *Songs of Profit, Songs of Loss* (Lincoln: University of Nebraska Press, 2019).

17. "Leon Black Attended Apollo Global Meeting Days after Resignation," *Financial Times,* April 13, 2021.

ACKNOWLEDGMENTS

Every book has a story of how it came to be, and the people who made it possible. I am grateful to Marshall Ganz who, during an interview for my last book, planted the seed for this one by wondering aloud why a rabbi who became a CEO of a multinational food corporation would agree to labor contracts with Cesar Chavez and the UFW. I wondered, too. My curiosity launched me into archives across the hemisphere to write this third book in a trilogy on the history of farm work and food production in California and beyond.

Eli Black's extraordinary life introduced me to new historiography and new ways of writing. Hasia Diner and Susannah Heschel gave me advice on navigating Jewish history and religious traditions. They both read early versions of this book in manuscript form, for which I will eternally be grateful. Karl Jacoby read an early version, too, and introduced me to the challenges and rewards of writing biography. Through Harvard University Press, Nelson Lichtenstein and an anonymous reader provided useful suggestions on how Eli fits in the history of business and conservative politics in America. Steven Ross and Julian Zelizer hosted me at the University of Southern California and Princeton University, respectively, in the early stages of this project and contributed to the book's improvement.

Dana Frank has been an extraordinary friend and supporter of this project from its earliest stages. She introduced me to Honduran scholars and shared archival material that became inaccessible to me when the pandemic forced the closure of numerous libraries across the Americas. Her scholarship, both published and unpublished, deeply influenced my perspectives on US foreign policy, the AFL-CIO in Latin America, and the power of unionized banana workers. Historians Marvin Barahona and Darío Euraque answered my questions and shared important perspectives on the history of Honduras. Mario Panchame combed the Honduran and Guatemalan archives for evidence of Eli's influence in Central America. At Dartmouth, two brilliant undergraduates, Teresa Alvarado-Pátlan and Mia Nelson, served as my research assistants, organizing the various physical and digital files I collected, and turned up new leads and information that shaped this book. Juliana DeVaan, a tenacious researcher, and current graduate student in History at Columbia University, found critical sources in New York City and tracked down essential documents and photos. Morgan Hamilton, a graduate student at Dartmouth, read the full manuscript and provided useful feedback. Jill Baron, the subject librarian for Latin American, Latino, and Caribbean Studies at Dartmouth, helped me acquire access to expensive databases, facilitated contact with Latin American archivists, and worked closely with me and her colleagues to reproduce photos and secure permissions. Deborah Heller, Thomas Knight, and Tobias Choyt read early drafts of the manuscript and gave me helpful tips on how to reach a non-academic audience.

Sarah Heller connected me with the business world in my attempt to reach Leon Black and has been a source of inspiration throughout this process. Jim Wright tried to reach Leon Black on my behalf. Charlotte Bacon encouraged me to keep writing, including for the American Council of Learned Societies fellowship, which helped fund this project. She also put me in touch with Sam Douglas who provided essential editorial advice. Genealogist Susan Berlowitz provided helpful information during the early stages of this book before her untimely passing. Michael Moritz provided useful genealogical research towards the end of the project that expanded greatly on Susan's initial work. Alberto Paniagua and Eli Burakian provided photos for the book. Joseph Stoll at Syracuse University created useful maps, which can be found at http://www.mattgarcia.org/. Ryan Shaw of Gift of Fresh Design Studio created and maintains my website. Mary Wallace and Kathy Schmeling at the Walter P. Reuther Library, Archives of Labor and Urban Affairs, Wayne State University in Detroit, gave me access to documents and facilitated the reproduction of photos. Julia Minerva at the National Archives and Records Administration provided helpful citation research during copyediting.

My son, Mauricio, accompanied me on a research trip to Detroit to do research in the Anna Puharich Papers. Andrew Kinney, editor at Harvard University Press, understood what this book could be from the start and helped me make it what it is through many hours of conversation. Julia Kirby, my copyeditor at Harvard University Press, corrected errors and offered last-minute recommendations. Laurie Furch in Latin American, Latino, and Caribbean Studies at Dartmouth helped keep departmental business moving and reduced distractions as I put the final touches on the book.

My deepest gratitude goes to those closest to me: my dear daughters, Edith and Timotea, and the love of my life, Desirée Garcia. Timotea, for always asking me, "Is it done yet?" from her dorm room at Wellesley College or as she came in from the pastures after tending to the animals so that I could write. Edith, for reminding me of what *really* matters. And Desirée, for your patience, love, encouragement, and perspective. You mean everything to me.

INDEX

Organization of American States,
181
Organization of Arab Petroleum
Exporting Countries (OPEC),
176–177
ORIT. *See* Organización Regional
Interamericana de Trabjadores
Oscar Mayer, 43, 76
Ottumwa, Iowa, 52–54; "Buy Morrell" campaign, 56, 172; effects of
plant closure on, 175, 188–191;
Morrell's effects on, 171; relation
with Morrell, 56. *See also* Morrell
Meat Company; Ottumwa plant
Ottumwa Courier (newspaper), 170,
174, 175, 189–190
Ottumwa plant: attempts to modernize, 169, 170; automation at,
171; Black's plans for improving,
88; Black's visit to, 58; closure of,
168–176, 180, 186, 188–191, 199, 208;
elimination of jobs at, 171–173; importance of, 64; management of,
66–69, 83, 92, 168–175 (*see also*
Broffman, Morton; Hansel, Harry
E., Jr.); productivity and, 66; quality
of products, 170–171, 173; renamed
Iowa Pride Packing Co., 172; strike
at, 55; threats to close, 67; union
at (*see* Amalgamated Meat Cutters and Butcher Workmen of
North America; Local P-1; United
Packinghouse Workers of America);
viability of, 64; women workers
at, 68, 171–172. *See also* Bankson,
Virgil; Merrill, Jesse; Morrell Meat
Company
Oulahan, Richard, 161
Oxfam America, 209

packinghouses. *See* meatpacking
companies; Morrell Meat Company
Palestine, 156
palm oil, 132, 166
Panama: banana export tax and, 177,
194, 195, 196, 200; Black's travel to,
144; United Brands holdings in,
201, 203; United Fruit and, 197,
200
paper lids, 37. *See also* American
Seal-Kap
Paper Tube Company, 36
Paramount Pictures, 51
Passover Seder, 125–127, 134–136
paternalism, corporate, 53
Paul, Elias, 95, 172, 173–174, 175
people's dividend, 78
Perlman, Nathan, 12
philanthropy: Black's, 113–114, 116;
foregrounding causes in, 36; Rosenwald's, 34–35, 36; Spectemur
Agendo, 111, 143
Phillips Petroleum, 212
picketing: legal limitations to, 54; of
United Fruit, 121
Pic 'n Pac Foods, 100, 104
S. S. Pierce, 100, 104
plastics, 38, 132, 192
Podhoretz, Norman, 113
Poland, 10, 21–22, 41. *See also* Lublin,
Poland
polyethylene, 38
Polymer United, 192
polystyrene, 192–193
pooling-of-interest method, 46, 48,
50, 59, 60
population bombs, 42, 100
population growth, food production
and, 100

United Farm Workers (UFW)
(*continued*)
workers campaign, 111; Martin Luther King Farm Workers Fund, 137, 150; membership cards, 108; National Farm Worker Service Center, 137, 150; Schenley Industries and, 109; strategies of, 109 (*see also* boycotts); support for, 108; Teamsters and, 140; United Brands' relationship with, 125–127; United Fruit and, 109–124, 127. *See also* boycotts; Chavez, Cesar; Huerta, Dolores; Puharich, Anna

United Farm Workers Organizing Committee, 106

United Fresh Fruit and Vegetable Association, 100

United Fruit, ix, 1, 102, 177, 181, 191; acknowledgement of past behavior, 129; antitrust and, 75, 96–97; associate growers program, 91; banana revenues, 89; Black's controlling interest in, 2; Black's evaluation of, 77; Black's pitch to, 184; Black's plans for, 89; Black's promises to shareholders, 184; Black's purchase of stock, 4, 81–82; Black's takeover of, 7–8; bribery by, x, 197–198, 200, 206, 210; competitors for, 4–7; debt incurred in purchase of, 186, 188; dependence on Ecuadorian producers, 194; diversification of, 96–97; expenditures on Honduran workers, 130, 208; exploitation by, 74, 128, 154; host countries (*see* Central America; Colombia; Costa Rica; Honduras; Latin America); intervention in gov-

ernments by, 74–75, 76–77, 80, 127, 131; jobbers network, 104–105; lack of company archive, xiii; land redistribution resisted by, 162; letter to shareholders (1970), 124; lettuce production and, 100 (*see also* Inter Harvest); Lilienthal's assessment of, 79; management team, 81, 195–196, 198, 200–201, 203–204; origins of, 73–74; performance of, 92, 95, 132, 155, 201; picketing of, 121; public relations efforts, 129, 165; purchase of Morrell and, 175; reputational makeover, 128–131, 178; reputation of, x, 75, 76, 77, 89, 91–92, 97, 113, 120, 127, 128, 154, 155, 206; shares for purchase, 73; subsidiaries of, 132; takeovers by, 96; transformation of, 152; UFW and, 109–124; unions and, 74 (*see also* Sindicato de Trabajadores de la Tela Railroad Co.); workers imported by, 129–130; working conditions, 90. *See also* Chiquita brand; Fox, John; Honduras; La Lima

United Jewish Appeal, 34

United Mine Workers, 159

United Nations Economic Commission for Latin America, 166

United Packinghouse Workers of America (UPWA), 54, 55, 64, 88. *See also* Local 1

United States: anti-Semitism in, 21; expansion of role in world, 2; Jewish migration to, 10–11

United States Agency for International Development (USAID), 160, 181